PORTFOLIO MANAGEMENT
FOR NEW PRODUCTS

Also by Robert G. Cooper

Winning at New Products

PORTFOLIO MANAGEMENT FOR NEW PRODUCTS

ROBERT G. COOPER,
SCOTT J. EDGETT,
and ELKO J. KLEINSCHMIDT

PERSEUS BOOKS

Cambridge, Massachusetts

Library of Congress Cataloging-in-Publication Data
Cooper, Robert G. (Robert Gravlin), 1943–
    Portfolio management for new products / Robert G. Cooper, Scott J.
Edgett and Elko J. Kleinschmidt.
      p. cm.
    Includes bibliographical references and index.
    ISBN 0-201-32814-3 (alk. paper)
     1. Portfolio management—Mathematical models.   I. Edgett, Scott
J. II. Kelinschmidt, Elko J. III. Title
HG4529.5.C67   1998
332.6—dc21   97-49937
                                                  CIP

Perseus Books is a member of the Perseus Books Group

Jacket design by Suzanne Heiser
Text design by David C. denBoer
Set in 10-point Times Roman by Nighthawk Design

6 7 8 9   02 01 00 99

Perseus Books are available at special discounts for bulk purchases in the U.S. by corporations, institutions, and other organizations. For more information, please contact the Special Markets Department at HarperCollins Publishers, 10 East 53rd Street, New York, NY 10022, or call 212-207-7528.

Find us on the World Wide Web at
http://www.perseusbooks.com

Contents

Exhibits

Acknowledgments

No research is possible without financial support. Over the years our research has benefited from two generous benefactors:

- Esso Chemical Canada Ltd. (Exxon in Canada). In particular, Bill Brennan has been a constant source of financial support and encouragement for our research efforts for many years.
- Innovation Research Centre (Chris Bart, Director) at the Michael G. DeGroote School of Business, McMaster University, which has repeatedly supported our research into new products and portfolio management.

A special thanks to Jens Arleth, Managing Director of U3 Consultants, Copenhagen, Denmark, who proofread sections of the manuscript and offered valuable suggestions for Chapters 6 and 7. Jens also provided a major European test setting for the proposed techniques profiled in this book. In addition, we would like to thank Alec Pettit of New Product Consultancy, Rickmansworth, England, who also reviewed the book and made helpful suggestions.

A number of other people and organizations have also kindly helped us in writing this book. Companies and people that provided us with insightful comments and their views on portfolio management included: Martin Brennan and Mike Harley of Reckitt & Colman; Tom Chorman of Procter & Gamble; Patricia Evans of Strategic Decisions Group; Bob Gill and Beebe Nelson of Product Development Partners, Inc.; Ray Kilminster of Hoechst-U.S.; Wolf-Rudiger Lange of Rhode & Schwarz; Dan Panfil of English China Clay; Kathryn Sachse and Marg Kneebone of the Royal Bank of Canada; Barry Siadat of Allied Signal; Erik Lahn Sorensen of Danish Technological Institute; Fred Squires of Specialty Minerals; Gary Tritle of 3M; Per Velde of Telenor Privat (Norwegian Telephone System); and Bob Wood, James Barrett, and Ed Bartkus of Rohm and Haas.

A final and heartfelt thanks to our families for their continued support throughout this time consuming exercise.

PORTFOLIO MANAGEMENT
FOR NEW PRODUCTS

CHAPTER 1

The Quest for the Right Portfolio Management Process

New products are vital to the success and future prosperity of the modern corporation. The period of downsizing that characterized the mid-80s to mid-90s is over: senior executives are beginning to sober up to the reality that no corporation ever shrank itself to greatness. As we move into the next millennium, the growth game is on—and faster than ever. Front and center in this game is the desire for new products—successful, significant, winning new products. Driven by rapidly advancing technologies, globalization of markets, and increasing competition at home and abroad, effective new product development is emerging as the *major corporate strategic initiative* of the decades ahead. Those corporations that succeed at new product development will be the future Mercks, HPs, 3Ms, and Microsofts; those companies that fail to excel at developing new products will invariably disappear or be gobbled up by the winners.

A vital question in this new product battleground is: How should corporations most effectively invest their R&D and new product resources? That's what portfolio management is all about: resource allocation to achieve corporate new product objectives. Much like stock market portfolio managers, those senior executives who manage to optimize their R&D investments—to define the right new product strategy for the firm, select the winning new product projects, and achieve the ideal balance of projects—will win in the long run. This book is about how winners manage their R&D and new product portfolio and the lessons your company can put into practice in order to achieve a higher return from R&D investment.

Before moving ahead, consider the plight of this product developer heading for trouble:

> The Modified Plastics business within a major chemical company was almost blindsided by its new product portfolio problems. The business's strategy centered on the development of many new products, which leveraged its core competencies in modifying polyolefins (the business unit possessed a unique ability to modify low-end polymers and upgrade their performance). Specifically, the strategy was to target the lower end of high-performance engineering resins with very cost-effective modified polymers. The business unit had a formal new product process in place, in which the

new general manager of the business was a key gatekeeper. After several months on the job, he called a portfolio review meeting to provide an overview of the status of projects; to his dismay, five disturbing things were discovered:

- First, projects were taking far too long. Some, in fact, had been in the pipeline for years. When queried, the standard answer was that project teams were working as hard as they could, but they were stretched across too many projects. The result was pipeline gridlock: too many projects in the pipe.
- Second, while some of the projects were fairly good, there were too many substandard ones in the pipeline; clearly, the project reviews were not doing the job of stopping poor projects.
- Of the 34 projects underway, no two were in the same product performance/ market segment areas. Strategically, it was a scattergun effort. Projects were aimed at a multitude of different markets—packaging, construction, automotive, agricultural equipment, and so on. Many of these markets the business unit did not sell to, and some were off-strategy. Further, the proposed products offered a wide variety of benefits in many different performance segments, ranging from fire resistance to stiffness/toughness. There was simply no rhyme or reason to the list of projects—there was no focus at all.
- Virtually all the projects were fairly high-reward but high-risk ones—translating into a reasonable probability of technical or commercial failure. There were no sure bets in this portfolio.
- Almost all projects were long-term. There were no "quick hits" to balance the long-term initiatives.

The point is that while some individual projects were alright, the portfolio as a whole stunk! The portfolio was unfocused; it contained too many projects and hence spread resources too thinly; there were too many marginal-value projects in the portfolio; it was poorly balanced; and it did not support the business unit's strategy very well.

POINTS FOR MANAGEMENT TO PONDER

If you detect elements of your own business in the above example, then you may find solutions here! Take a hard look at your own business's new product portfolio and the way it's managed, and you be the judge. Later in this book, we'll observe what winners do; we'll also see what action this general manager and others took to introduce effective portfolio management into their businesses.

What Is Portfolio Management?

Portfolio management and the prioritization of new product projects is a critical management task. Roussel, Saad, and Erikson in their widely read book claim that "portfolio analysis and planning will grow in the 1990s to become the powerful tool that business portfolio planning became in the 1970s and 1980s."[25]

Portfolio management and project prioritization is about resource allocation in the firm. That is, which new product projects from the many opportunities the corporation faces will it fund? And which ones will receive top priority and be accelerated to market? It is also about business strategy, for today's new product projects decide tomorrow's product/market profile of the firm. Note that an estimated 50% of firms' sales today come from new products introduced within the past five years.[15,24] Finally, it is about balance: about the optimal investment mix between risk versus return, maintenance versus growth, and short-term versus long-term new product projects.

Before charging into the topic of what techniques work best, let's stand back and reflect on what portfolio management is. We define portfolio management formally as follows:

> Portfolio management is a dynamic decision process, whereby a business's list of active new product (and R&D) projects is constantly updated and revised. In this process, new projects are evaluated, selected, and prioritized; existing projects may be accelerated, killed, or deprioritized; and resources are allocated and reallocated to the active projects. The portfolio decision process is characterized by uncertain and changing information, dynamic opportunities, multiple goals and strategic considerations, interdependence among projects, and multiple decision-makers and locations.
>
> The portfolio decision process encompasses or overlaps a number of decision-making processes within the business, including periodic reviews of the total portfolio of all projects (looking at the entire set of projects, and comparing all projects against each other); making Go/Kill decisions on individual projects on an ongoing basis; and developing a new product strategy for the business, complete with strategic resource allocation decisions.

The point is that portfolio management is a pervasive and all-encompassing topic. It is more than project selection, although that is part of it; it's much more than annual budgeting or resource allocation across projects; it goes beyond simply developing a prioritized list of projects; and it certainly is more than strategizing and trying to arrive at the best set of projects to meet strategic needs, although strategy and strategic imperatives are certainly key components. Portfolio management is all of these. One problem is that everyone sees portfolio management a little differently, depending on his or her perspective: the strategist or planner sees portfolio management as developing a *strategically correct portfolio* to support the business's vision and mission; the financial person looks to portfolio management to *allocate financial resources efficiently* and optimally; the technical community looks to portfolio management to *pick the right projects* and foster the right kind of innovation; the marketing person hopes that portfolio management *yields better priorities* and faster times to market; and the CEO prays that portfolio management will deliver big winners with *positive financial impacts*—and soon!

Portfolio management is thus multifaceted and complex. But one cannot duck the issue—refuse to deal with portfolio management—just because it's complex and challenging, since portfolio management is also vital to new product success.

What Happens When You Lack
Effective Portfolio Management

Companies without effective new product portfolio management and project selection face a slippery road downhill (see Exhibit 1.1). Indeed, many of the problems that beset product development initiatives in businesses can be directly
traced to a lack of effective portfolio management. The plastics business unit described earlier in this chapter provides an example of only some of the problems
that arise when portfolio management is lacking. Here are some of the agonies
that firms endure when they don't have proper portfolio management.

First, weak portfolio management translates into a strong *reluctance to kill*
new product projects. There are no or ineffective Go/Kill criteria and no consistent mechanism for evaluating and, if necessary, culling weak projects. Projects
seem to take on a life of their own, running like express trains past review points.
Further, new projects simply get added to the "active list" with little appreciation
for their resource needs or impact on other projects. The result is a total *lack of
focus*: far too many projects for the available resources.

The problems don't stop here. A lack of focus and too many active projects
mean that resources and people are *too thinly spread.* As a result, projects end up
in a queue—serious logjams in the process—and cycle time starts to increase.
Suddenly there are complaints about projects taking *too long to get to market.* But
worse: with resources and people thinly spread, everyone starts to scramble—too
many balls in the air. And the result is predictable: *quality of execution starts to
suffer.* For example, the essential up-front homework isn't done, and needed market studies designed to build in the voice of the customer are left out due to lack
of time and people. Poor-quality execution of these and other tasks, steps, and
stages in the new product process means an *increase in failure rates.*[7] So, not only
are projects late to market, but their success rates drop!

There's even more. Lacking effective portfolio management, there are no rigorous and tough decision points, which in turn leads to poor project selection decisions. One common result is *too many mediocre projects* in the pipeline: too
many extensions, minor modifications, and defensive products, which yield marginal value to the company. And so, many of the launches yield disappointing and
"ho-hum" results: there is a noticeable *lack of stellar new product winners.* Even
more insidious, the few really *good projects are starved* for resources, so that
they're either late to market or never achieve their full potential. And that creates
a huge opportunity cost, which never appears on the profit and loss statement!

The problems don't end there. Without a rigorous portfolio method, the *wrong
projects* often get selected and for all the wrong reasons. Instead of decisions
based on facts and objective criteria, decisions are based on politics, opinioneer-
ing, and emotion. Too many of these ill-selected projects simply fail!

The final negative result is strategic: without a portfolio management method,
strategic criteria for project selection are missing, and so there is *no strategic direction* to the projects selected. After all, new products are the leading edge of
business strategy. They define tomorrow's vision of your company! But without a
portfolio method, projects are *not strategically aligned* with the business's strat-

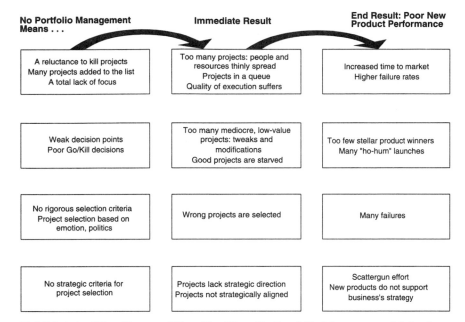

No Portfolio Management Means . . .	Immediate Result	End Result: Poor New Product Performance
A reluctance to kill projects Many projects added to the list A total lack of focus	Too many projects: people and resources thinly spread Projects in a queue Quality of execution suffers	Increased time to market Higher failure rates
Weak decision points Poor Go/Kill decisions	Too many mediocre, low-value projects: tweaks and modifications Good projects are starved	Too few stellar product winners Many "ho-hum" launches
No rigorous selection criteria Project selection based on emotion, politics	Wrong projects are selected	Many failures
No strategic criteria for project selection	Projects lack strategic direction Projects not strategically aligned	Scattergun effort New products do not support business's strategy

Exhibit 1.1   What Happens When You Have No Portfolio Management Method

egy, and many strategically unimportant projects find themselves in the pipeline. The end result is a *scattergun effort* that does not support the business's strategic direction.

The price for not having an effective portfolio management and project selection method for new products is very high. If your business faces any of these problems—a lack of stellar new products, long cycle times, a high failure rate, and lack of strategic alignment—perhaps the root causes can be traced back to ineffective portfolio management. So read on and find out what others are doing about the challenge and, most important, what *your* company can do!

A Road Map of the Book

This book begins with the results of an intensive study of portfolio management as currently practiced in industry. Note that formal portfolio management for new products is a relatively recent practice. Thus, perhaps the best place to start out on our journey is with a thorough understanding of the "what is"—the current situation. The purpose of our study was to investigate the current state of portfolio management, that is, how leading firms manage their new product portfolios and whether these approaches are really working. A second goal of the study was to identify best practices—what methods seem to work, and why. This investigation provides key insights that enable us to make concrete recommendations about how firms should be going about managing their R&D (or new product development) portfolios.

The format of this book is as follows:

1. The balance of this chapter provides background on the topic of portfolio management, helps shed light on why so many firms face difficulties in their attempts to allocate R&D resources, and defines the requirements for an *ideal* portfolio management approach. The chapter ends with some immediate conclusions from the study and briefly looks at the three goals in portfolio management.
2. Next, we provide a close look at the methods that leading corporations employ to manage their new product project portfolios and allocate their R&D resources. We also note the perceived strengths and weaknesses of:
   - approaches used to maximize the value of a portfolio (Chapter 2)
   - approaches used to achieve a balanced portfolio (Chapter 3)
   - approaches used to develop a strong link to strategy (Chapter 4)
3. Concluding observations are made regarding what appears to work in portfolio management and what doesn't, and the pitfalls, hurdles, and concerns management is addressing (Chapter 5).
4. Next, we recommend ways in which portfolio management can be made more effective in your organization, and we propose some techniques and methods to make this happen (Chapters 6 and 7). Our recommended Portfolio Management Process, along with a number of options and alternatives to consider, is outlined in these two chapters.
5. Finally, we provide an approach for the design and implementation of a Portfolio Management Process—the step-by-step procedure (Chapter 8).

Throughout the book, we use examples drawn both from our research study and from companies we have tried to help. These we hope yield additional insights and help clarify this challenging topic. Additionally, we provide "pauses" or reflection points throughout the book—"Points for Management to Ponder"— in the hope that you'll put the book down for a moment and think about how the material presented applies to your own business.

Three Decades of R&D Portfolio Methods: What Progress?

The challenge of portfolio management in product development is not new. Over the decades, the topic has surfaced under various guises, including "R&D project selection," "R&D resource allocation," "project prioritization," and "portfolio management." By the early 70s, dozens of articles had appeared on the topic, with most authors only making one stab at the subject before moving on to more fruitful fields. The majority of these early proposed methods were *management science, optimization techniques.* To the management scientist, this portfolio management problem was one of constrained optimization under conditions of uncertainty: a multiproject, multistage decision model solved by mathematical programming. Thus, the original portfolio selection models were highly mathematical and employed techniques such as linear, dynamic, and integer programming. The objective was to develop a portfolio of new and existing projects to maximize some objective function (for example, the expected profits), subject to a set of resource constraints.

Anyone familiar with these programming techniques will immediately recognize the hurdles that the mathematician and management scientist would have solving this portfolio problem. Further, in spite of the many methods proposed in the early days, there was a remarkable lack of follow-up: for example, few authors ever described attempts to actually implement their methods and to gauge their feasibility; indeed, the articles appear to be largely the result of academics writing to and for each other. In spite of the importance of the topic, no guru or "dominant school of thought" emerged, perhaps an indication of the frustrations faced in seeking solutions.[1,2,3,12,20]

More recent years have witnessed a number of other proposed new product portfolio methods. These include, for example,

- financial models and financial indexes, ranging from traditional net present value (NPV), return on investment (ROI), and payback methods to various financial ratios (such as the Productivity Index)[4,22]
- scoring models and checklists, where projects are rated and scored on a variety of qualitative questions (in some cases, the project score becomes the criterion for project prioritization)[16,25,32]
- probabilistic financial models, including Monte Carlo simulation and decision trees[27]
- behavioral approaches, designed to bring managers to a consensus (or to individual decisions), such as Delphi, Q-Sort, and analytic hierarchical modeling (paired comparisons)[21,27,33]
- mapping approaches, essentially extensions of the original strategic business unit (SBU) portfolio models (the Boston Consulting Group [BCG] model: stars, cash cows, dogs, wildcats; or the GE/McKinsey model), where various parameters are plotted against each other in a bubble diagram format—plots such as reward versus probability of success.[22,25]

Major Gaps between Theory and Practice

In spite of all the proposed solutions, management has been slow to adopt new and better project selection and portfolio management approaches. One of our recent benchmarking studies points to *project selection* and *project prioritization* as the weakest facet of all new product management activities.[9,10] Management in the 161 business units studied rated themselves very low in terms of:

- achieving the right balance between numbers of active projects and available resources (too many projects)—a poor "proficiency rating" of 51 points out of a possible 100
- undertaking solid ranking and prioritization of projects—an even poorer proficiency rating of only 49 points out of 100

Overall, managers confessed to making minimal attempts at portfolio management.

One result is that projects tend to take on a life of their own! In too many companies we investigated, projects move too far along in the process without being subjected to serious scrutiny. And it was only as these projects approached commercialization that the hard truths were recognized: that the market wasn't quite as large as expected; or that manufacturing costs were higher than anticipated; and so on.

Example: As one executive in a major biotechnology firm observed: "We claim to have a process with lots of screens or gates; we even show our new product process in the shape of a funnel—it's supposed to weed out poor projects along the way. But that's not happening. Once a project receives an initial "Go" decision, nothing can stop it. . . . Project reviews aren't Go/Kill decisions; they're progress review meetings! Nothing stops the project."

The lack of tough Go/Kill decision points means too many product failures, resources wasted on the wrong projects, and a lack of focus. The result is too many marginal projects in the pipeline, while the truly meritorious projects are starved.

There is a major gulf between theory and practice in portfolio management. While the published literature over the past 30 years outlines many approaches for portfolio management and project selection, there is very little evidence regarding the actual transfer of these techniques into management practice. It is not surprising to find that companies continue to flounder here. Thus, the question remains: How do and should companies select the appropriate portfolio of new product investments?

POINTS FOR MANAGEMENT TO PONDER

Does your company have effective new product project selection and portfolio management? Or do you suffer from many of the same ailments we found in our benchmarking studies? Do you have explicit criteria for making Go/Kill and prioritization decisions on projects at various points in the process from idea to launch? Or does your new product process resemble the biotechnology firm's cited above, with no projects ever killed once they receive initial approval? If you're uncomfortable about the answers to these questions, then perhaps it's time to find out why: undertake a *retrospective analysis of past projects*. That is . . .

- Identify a number of new product projects undertaken in the past few years in your company.
- Assemble the project teams that worked on each project.
- Have each team map out from beginning to end what happened on the project—from idea to launch.
- Require that they rate the "goodness" or proficiency of each major activity and all the key Go/Kill decision points in the process (pay special attention to the decision points).
- Determine where decision points were substandard, or worse yet, missed altogether, and find out why.
- Identify where activities or stages were weak, and probe why (for example, poor prioritization, a lack of focus, too many projects and not enough time, a lack of resources?).

Portfolio Management: It's Not So Easy

New product portfolio management sounds like a fairly deliberate exercise of decision-making and resource allocation. Why, then, has the goal of an effective portfolio management process been so elusive? One reason is that there are many unique facets of the problem that make it perhaps the most challenging decision-making task faced by the modern business.

▶ First, unlike traditional portfolio approaches, which allocate resources across business units (for example, the BCG or GE/McKinsey models), R&D portfolio management focuses on *what might be*—new opportunities, new products, new ventures. We witnessed much confusion between traditional portfolio methods—the well-known "stars, cash cows, dogs" models—and portfolio models for R&D or new product projects. The confusion is compounded because some of the diagrams, such as bubble diagrams, look much the same. But that's where the similarities end! Note that traditional portfolio models focus on *what is,* namely, existing businesses or SBUs, and allocate resources across these businesses. By contrast, *new product portfolio models* plot new products on a map—entities that don't even exist yet—and allocate resources to these.

Because new product portfolio management deals with *future events* and opportunities, unlike traditional portfolio models, much of the information required to make project selection decisions is at best *uncertain* and at worst *very unreliable*. But even with this doubtful information, the resource allocation decisions still must be made!

▶ Second, the decision environment is a very *dynamic* one. The status and prospects for projects in the portfolio are ever-changing, as results of new studies become known, market or technical tests are completed, and new competitive and market information emerges. What looked like an excellent project just six months ago is suddenly not so promising. Additionally, new opportunities are constantly being discovered—opportunities that vie for resources and compete with existing projects.

Example: A major Boston telecommunications hardware and software firm undertakes fairly high-risk and exciting projects, whose outcomes are often quite uncertain. Projects are commissioned with the full expectation that they'll be successful. But some months later, after the market studies are undertaken and the technical appraisals are completed, a very different picture often emerges: the market is smaller than anticipated; pricing is problematic; there are unforeseen and costly technical challenges; and so on. This new information dramatically changes the relative attractiveness of the project, and may even result in its deprioritization or outright cancellation. The point is that this business's portfolio is in a *constant state of flux* as the result of new information.

▶ Next, projects in the portfolio are at *different stages* of completion. Some are at the early stages, where little is known about them. Others are approaching commercialization and launch, where forecasts and data are somewhat more reliable. The dilemma is that all projects compete against each other for resources, so that comparisons must be made between projects at different stages, each with different amounts and "goodness" of information.

Example: At one firm, we sat in on a portfolio review meeting where management was trying to select and prioritize new product projects. Projects under consideration ranged from those well into the development and commercialization stages to projects at the idea stage; some were little more than a gleam in people's eyes. It was an almost impossible task to compare the merits of these early-stage projects—they were so ill-defined—with those at later stages. What management quickly discovered was that, with differing amounts and quality of project definition and information, idea-stage projects cannot be directly compared or prioritized against later-stage projects; but resources must still be allocated!

▸ The problem is made more complex by recognizing that *resources* to be allocated across projects are *limited*. A decision to fund one project may mean that resources must be taken away from another. Additionally, projects are not totally independent of each other: for example, the talents needed to work on one project may also be vital for another; conversely, undertaking one project may actually facilitate another   there exist synergies between projects. Finally, resources are not infinitely flexible: unlike money, people cannot always be immediately transferred between projects in a seamless fashion.

▸ The final facet of portfolio management that makes the decision process so difficult is that portfolio management is critically important. At one time, new product project selection and allocation of R&D resources was thought to be "an R&D thing," and was left largely in the hands of the technical community. Not so today, as senior management recognizes that new products are the leading edge of business strategy, and so new product choices are virtually synonymous with strategic choices.

Requirements for an Effective Portfolio Management Process

Progress in some areas of portfolio management has been achieved over the past 30 years. Given the lackluster performance of many existing portfolio management approaches, coupled with the reluctance of industry to adopt most of the methods, there is no shortage of prescriptions about what the ideal portfolio management method should be and do. The literature, while short on practical tried-and-proven solutions, offers myriad suggestions and insights into *portfolio management requirements*. Reflect for a moment on some of these requirements, especially as we get set to review the many portfolio methods in use in industry in the next three chapters.

1. *Corporate goals, objectives, and strategies must be the basis for new product (or R&D) portfolio selection.*[12,13,14,16,18,19,27,29,30]

More than ever, the management of technology and R&D is viewed as *strongly linked to corporate strategy* and a firm's competitive success.[12] This is especially true for multinational corporations, which face a much broader scope of possible strategic directions: portfolio management must be congruent with the overall strategy of the business;[14] indeed, it is the embodiment of that strategy! Portfolios in many Japanese firms, for example, tend to stress continual technological improvement (a long-term strategy) aimed at constant product improvement (incrementalism, a major aspect of the R&D effort), and have resulted in positive performance.[11] Portfolio analysis and resource allocation must be intimately linked to strategy formulation.[32]

2. *Senior management is the driver of strategy and hence must be closely involved in new product (or R&D) project selection decisions.*[5,8,11,12,16,18,19,32]

This is a parallel theme. Traditionally, senior management has been involved in R&D to the extent that they periodically review research programs, projects, and staff to assess progress and to determine the contribution that each makes to the corporate goal.[4] Today, however, there is a *need to go beyond this,* given that technology and strategy are inseparable.[7] Thus, the organizational context in which R&D project selection and resource allocation occurs must be considered when one develops appropriate project selection methods.[19] This means that the cooperation and active involvement of top management, who direct the long-term strategy, are essential if R&D efforts are to be properly focused.[19]

3. *Better communication and understanding must exist between senior corporate management and R&D management.*[12,27,28,34]

One problem with the adoption of some of the more sophisticated and quantitative portfolio models is the gulf between R&D management and senior corporate management. Senior executives often lack a strong research background, while R&D personnel lack the skills to communicate with senior executives in an understandable and credible fashion. This communication impasse mandates a portfolio selection method that not only effectively selects projects, but also manages R&D programs and projects *and their communication* to top management.[12] Senior personnel must have consensus on key issues (for example, new product goals or project priorities)—something that is often lacking—and ensure that this common position is understood lower down in the firm.[28]

4. *Portfolio methods must mesh with the decision framework of the business.*[4,14,16,19,27,29]

The organizational context in which new product or R&D project selection and resource allocation occurs is a fundamental consideration in the development of appropriate decision methods.[19] For example, there is growing recognition that project selection tools should be used to ask questions of the entire organization. "Picking the right projects" is a meaningless exercise unless the whole organization is involved and emotionally committed to the final set of selected projects.[27] For large multinational corporations, the problem is even more complex. Here portfolio decisions must be made seeking buy-in from multiple business units, across geographic boundaries, and at the corporate level.[14] One way to involve senior management in the decision process is by integrating selection models into interactive decision support systems.[19]

> 5. *Portfolio methods should be used for information display only, and not yield an optimization decision.*[4,5,13,16,29]

This conclusion almost flies in the face of logic. In the early days, the assumption was that management wanted the portfolio model to yield a decision recommendation (for example, a *prioritized list of the right projects*). The fact is that managers are less interested in the final result of the method than in the *process* itself. The value for them is in systematically stepping through each project and assessing its status as a project and how it fits with the corporate strategy and objectives.[4,5] For example, the provision of a risk–reward (or risk–return) map or matrix, often obtained via highly subjective methods, does not yield an optimum solution (for example, no list of best projects) or even an analytical tool to arrive at such a solution. But it is recommended as an effective tool and guideline for managers—a visual representation of the entire set of possible projects—for use throughout the whole process of portfolio selection.[13] Yet another recommended approach is *fuzzy modeling,* whose flexibility permits switching from maximizing behavior to *satisficing behavior* with respect to some or all goals.[29] This method permits the manager to investigate, in an interactive fashion, different scenarios in response to various new product aspirations.

> 6. *The selection method employed must accommodate change and the interaction of goals and players.*[13,26,29,30]

Portfolio methods must be able to deal simultaneously with resource interaction, benefit interaction, and outcome interaction among and between projects. To date, *no model has been proposed* that can do all three.[26] Further, the system must be flexible. It must adapt to the reality that goals, requirements, and project characteristics change during the lifetime of projects.[13] For example, if the manager modifies his or her aspirations, the system must adjust and compute a new compromise solution.[29] Finally, the system must enable managers to plan how the active project list evolves over time: which new projects are added to the list, when, and what role each should play in the total portfolio.[30]

> 7. *The portfolio selection method must accommodate decision-making at different levels in the organization.*[6,19,30]

Project selection decisions are made at different levels in major corporations. Some projects conducted within business units are independent or stand-alone efforts; others, such as platform programs or cross-SBU projects, involve several business units or divisions, and so subprojects within each business unit are highly interdependent. Clearly, the selection approach used must be able to handle both types.[6] The choice of levels in the problem hierarchy for R&D project selection must consider the organization structure and the nature of the decision-making process for these various types of projects.[19]

8. *Risk must be accommodated by the selection technique.*[17, 23,28,31]

One facet of strategy is deciding on the acceptable risk level within a chosen portfolio and then finding ways to minimize (or manage) risk.[28,31] Therefore, risk, uncertainties, and probabilities of success must be somehow built into the portfolio model and be visible in the project selection process.[23] Another way of handling risk is via diversity; and so diversity or portfolio balance must also be a consideration.

Where We Stand

In spite of the challenges outlined above, progress has been made!

▶ Classical methods, such as *scoring and sorting models,* have been modified and adapted to become more relevant as portfolio selection aids. While useful for ranking projects on financial, strategic, and other criteria, however, they often fail to capture concerns about the *right balance of projects in the portfolio.*
▶ New *mapping approaches* and bubble diagrams have gained adherents because they greatly simplify the portfolio problem and provide a visual representation of the choices faced. Mapping is perhaps too new for us to be able to assess its impact, but there are already some problems: mapping projects on a two-dimensional matrix may be a little too simplistic (after all, portfolio management is a complex problem, difficult to boil down to a few maps and a handful of dimensions); the maps that focus on financial rewards have been criticized for being too financially driven, while maps that consider numerous strategic and other qualitative factors are far too numerous for the executive to digest.
▶ *Mathematical programming* portfolio and project selection models have become more realistic in recent years.* Such models are now able to integrate multiple constraints, multiple time periods, differing goals and objectives, and other parameters into a single-choice model.
▶ Finally, there is the recognition that no one model gives the *right answer.* Instead, hybrid approaches are being developed that permit a more tailored approach to portfolio selection.

New product portfolio selection has become a central management issue. Today's business climate requires faster decisions, better allocation of scarce resources, and clearer focus. Given that corporate revenue streams are heavily dependent on successful new products and that technology strategy is intimately

---

*See, for example, 4, 6, 16, 19, 26, 29.

linked to corporate strategy, *effective portfolio management is more than ever central to corporate prosperity.*

POINTS FOR MANAGEMENT TO PONDER

With no clear answers available from the literature and strong evidence to suggest that management has rejected many of the proposed approaches, a number of provocative questions remain. For example, what is the current state of portfolio management in industry today and in your own business? How do senior managers handle the portfolio question inside their organizations? What about yours? How are they linking strategic direction to R&D decisions? Are the approaches that companies employ, including your own, producing the desired results? And what are the strengths and weaknesses of these approaches?

Portfolio Management Practices in Leading Firms: Challenges and Problems

How do various firms handle portfolio management? The next three chapters tackle this topic and begin to portray portfolio methods used by a selection of companies that are known to be actively using or developing and implementing a portfolio management approach. Before we delve into the details of these models, let's first consider some of the important research results that are immediately evident—conclusions regarding project selection and some of the problems these companies faced (or had faced) when it came to new product project selection and portfolio management.

- *A critical problem:* Every company we interviewed believed the portfolio management, project selection, and resource allocation problem to be critical to new product success. Virtually all companies had experienced considerable problems regarding project selection. And with resources tighter than ever, the issue of proper resource allocation and picking the right projects is paramount. Further, the desire to see the business's strategy reflected in its portfolio of R&D investments is another driver of improved portfolio management techniques. As a result, many of the firms contacted are devoting a considerable amount of effort to solving the portfolio problem.

POINTS FOR MANAGEMENT TO PONDER

Have you identified portfolio management for new products as a key issue in your business? And does the leadership team of your business play an active role in these portfolio decisions? If new products are vital to your future, then the *most important decisions your business faces concern portfolio management*—how you allocate your new product resources. Senior management must lead here! Make it a top-priority issue.

The Research That Underlies This Book

Many of the techniques, approaches, and insights we outline in this book are based on our extensive investigation into portfolio management in industry. Here, interviews were conducted in leading firms in various industries. Some companies were singled out for in-depth interviews on the basis of the uniqueness and proficiency of their portfolio approach. (For example, two companies had an ongoing task force in place for more than a year to "solve" the portfolio management problem; another company we interviewed in-depth had spent more than $500,000 on external consultants to arrive at their "portfolio solution.")

The companies, although quite willing to share the details of their portfolio approaches with us, were promised that we would not reveal any details of any project under development—all examples use disguised projects. Note that the method of sample selection was purposeful (not random). We deliberately selected firms according to their experience, proficiency, and ability to provide insights regarding portfolio management. During the in-depth interviews, the details of the portfolio approaches used, rationale, problems faced, and issues raised were all investigated.

Our investigation identified some of the specific problems faced by companies in project selection and portfolio management, problems that are creating the sense of urgency:

- *Does not reflect strategy:* Many businesses or SBUs we investigated had enunciated business strategies. In some cases, they had even developed new product strategies for the business—strategies that defined the goals for new products (for example, by year 5, 32% of our sales revenue will be generated by products we do not now have); the role that product development would play in achieving overall business goals (for example, 60% of our SBU's growth will come from new products; another 30% from market developments; and 10% from market size increases); and even strategic arenas of focus—what product types, markets and technologies (or platforms) would generate these new products. The problem lies in *linking these strategies—* business and new product—*to spending* on R&D projects. The breakdown of R&D spending by project type often revealed serious disconnects between the goals/strategies of the business and where the money was spent.

POINTS FOR MANAGEMENT TO PONDER

Does your portfolio reflect and *support your business's strategy?* Find out by doing what the plastics business unit general manager did earlier in this chapter. Undertake a portfolio review of all your active projects. Are they all on-strategy—that is, within product, market, or technology areas defined as areas of focus? Then undertake a breakdown of spending on the projects. Do the resulting splits reflect your strategic priorities? Are your spending breakdowns consistent with your business's strategy?

- *Poor-quality portfolios:* Executives are generally displeased with, or at best doubtful about, their firms' current portfolio of projects. Many new product projects are thought to be weak or mediocre ones; others are considered unfit for commercialization; and success rates in the marketplace are less than adequate. As one executive put it: "We implemented our portfolio management approach [a risk–reward bubble diagram model], and the first thing that became evident was that half our projects were in the wrong quadrants, including some of our big ones! By the end of the year, the list of projects had been cut in half." Similar audits had resulted in similar cuts in other firms, leading one to doubt the quality of current portfolios.

Key Problems Faced in Portfolio Management and Project Selection: Highlights

Portfolio management, project selection, and resource allocation were deemed critical to new product success by all firms in the study. But all were facing problems:

1. The portfolio of projects does not reflect the business's strategy: too many projects are off-strategy; and there are disconnects between spending breakdowns on projects and the strategic priorities of the business.
2. The portfolio's quality is poor: there are too many unfit, weak, and mediocre projects; and success rates at launch are inadequate.
3. Firms' new product processes are tunnels when they should be funnels. The Go/Kill decision points are weak; projects tend to take on a life of their own; and poor projects are often not killed.
4. Resources are scarce, and there is a lack of focus: most firms confess to having far too many projects for the available resources. Cycle times and success rates are suffering as a result.
5. Some firms admitted to having too many trivial projects in their new product pipeline—modifications, updates, and extensions—and too few of the projects needed to yield major breakthroughs and real competitive advantage. This is the result of the quest for cycle time reductions coupled with too few resources.

- *Tunnels, not funnels:* Another related problem is that Go/Kill decision points—the gates in new product processes—are often perceived to be ineffective. In too many companies, projects tend to take on a life of their own, and little can stop them once they gain momentum. In one leading firm, an internal audit of 60 current projects revealed that 88% resembled an express train "slowing down at stations [project reviews], but never with the intention of being stopped!" Only 12% were handled in a thoughtful way with rigorous Go/Kill decision points. Even when killed, some projects have a habit of being resurrected, perhaps under a new name.

MORE POINTS FOR MANAGEMENT TO PONDER

What is the *quality of your portfolio?* Are most of the projects solid ones? Are they high-value ones to the business? And is the economic value of your total portfolio considerably higher than what you've spent on it? Perhaps it's time to undertake a critical portfolio review, place a value or "economic worth" on each project, and cull out the mediocre projects.

We observed that criteria for making Go/Kill decisions are inadequate or not used, and often a mechanism for rating, prioritizing, or even killing projects is lacking. As one frustrated manager exclaimed: "We talk about having a funneling process which weeds out poor projects; heck, we don't have a funnel, we have a tunnel. Ten concepts enter the process, ten go into development, ten go to launch—and one succeeds!"

STILL MORE POINTS FOR MANAGEMENT TO PONDER

Do you have a *funnel*—where you start with a number of concepts, and via successive and tough screens at multiple stages in your new product process, you narrow the list down to the very best project: skimming the cream off the top? Or, once projects start, is there very little chance they'll ever be killed?

Suggestion: Undertake a review of the *attrition curve* of projects. If you keep records of project decisions, go back and find out how many projects (what proportion) were actually killed at each of your Go/Kill decision points. If very few were killed, then you have a tunnel, not a funnel!

- *Scarce resources, a lack of focus:* Resources are too scarce to waste on the wrong projects. Indeed, a common complaint is that product development suffers from lean resources, especially in areas such as marketing and manufacturing/operations. Most firms confessed to having far too many projects for the available resources. The result is that resources are spread very thinly across new product projects, so that even the best projects are starved for people, time, and money. The end result is that projects take too long to reach the market. Many key activities—such as up-front homework; getting sharp, early product definition; and building in the voice of the customer— are not executed as well or as consistently as they should be. The bottom line is that there is a lack of focus, which creates a plethora of other problems.

STILL MORE POINTS FOR MANAGEMENT TO PONDER

Are your new products reaching the market on time—when they were promised? Are projects being done in a time-efficient manner? And are your success rates and profit performance results consistent with expectations? These are metrics that you should track:

- on-time performance (measured at key review points and at launch)
- time efficiency (actual time to market versus fastest possible)
- success rates of launched products (met or exceeded financial hurdles, gauged one to two years after launch)
- profitability of projects versus forecast profits.

If these metrics are less than satisfactory, then find out why. Often the causes have their roots in faulty portfolio management: too many projects and people spread too thinly.

- *Trivialization of product development:* A final problem brought on by a lack of resources (or a lack of focus) is the trivialization of product development in some firms. The quest for cycle time reduction together with the desire for more new products than ever, when coupled with the resource constraint, leads many firms to do the obvious: pick "low-hanging fruit"—projects that can be done quickly, easily, and cheaply. Often these projects are trivial ones (modifications, extensions) while the significant products, which are the ones needed to yield real competitive advantage and major break-throughs, are placed on the back burner. The net result is a portfolio of projects that is very short-term, while projects designed to create tomorrow's winners or technology platforms for growth are missing.

ONE FINAL SET OF POINTS TO PONDER

Is your new product portfolio too heavily weighted to low-value, trivial, small projects? Is the problem of too many projects in the pipeline and excessive time pressures causing you to elect to run with too many short-run, quick hits? Again, we urge you to undertake a portfolio review and measure the split in resources across project types. Then compare this to the desired split.

Words of Warning

Before we commence our review of portfolio methods, we have several words of caution.

First, no company we interviewed has totally resolved the portfolio manage-ment problem. In spite of all that has been written, there are *no magic answers.* Moreover, there is not even a "preferred" or dominant method. The fact that lead-ing companies are trying many and varied approaches to portfolio management points to two conclusions:

- The right answer has not yet been discovered.
- There might not even be one right answer!

So the quest for the ideal portfolio management and project prioritization and se-lection method continues.

Second, many of the techniques presented in this book are quite new to the companies involved. For example, a major consumer goods company and a large materials firm had both set up task forces to deal with the problem a year before our interviews, and even at the time of the interviews, were only in the early stages of implementation. We saw much the same in other firms as well—new, relatively untried methodologies being implemented. Thus the reader should treat some of the techniques described as "exploratory" and "experimental" rather than "tried-and-proven" methods.

Third, portfolio management is not a panacea: it is not the single answer to everything that ails your new product efforts. True, portfolio management is a critical issue and is certainly worthy of top management's attention. But some firms had taken this too far. It was as though portfolio management *held all the answers* to effective product development. As we shall see in Chapter 5, there is much more to achieving a steady stream of successful new products than merely implementing a solid portfolio management approach!

Portfolio Practices in Leading Firms:
Three Goals in Portfolio Management

While the portfolio methods employed in firms vary greatly, the common denominators across firms are the goals management is trying to achieve. One or more of *three high-level or macrogoals* dominate the thinking of each firm we studied, either implicitly or explicitly. The goal most emphasized by the firm seems to influence the choice of portfolio method. These three broad or macrogoals are as follows:

1. *Maximization of Value:* To some firms, the preoccupation is to allocate resources so as to maximize the value of the portfolio in terms of some company objective (such as long-term profitability or return on investment, likelihood of success, or some other strategic objectives). These *maximization of value* methods are outlined in Chapter 2.

   Example: One major U.S. consumer goods firm uses a relatively simple financial index to rate, rank, and prioritize new product projects: NPV/investment. This is the ratio of the project's NPV to the total investment remaining in the project (R&D, capital and launch costs). The finance guru in product development was quick to point out that this method of trying to maximize the portfolio's value was fraught with deficiencies, but at least did place some of the obvious higher-value projects at the top of the list.

2. *Balance:* Here the principal concern is to develop a balanced portfolio—to achieve a desired balance of projects in terms of a number of parameters. For example, the right balance in terms of:
   - long-term projects versus short, fast ones
   - high-risk long shots versus lower-risk sure bets
   - the various markets the business is in (one doesn't want all one's new product resources targeted at only one market)
   - different technologies or technology types (for example, embryonic, pacing, base)
   - different project types: new products, improvements, cost reductions, fundamental research.

Portfolio methods aimed at securing the *right balance* of projects are the topic of Chapter 3.

Example: One SBU at Mobil Chemical uses four categories[*] of development projects:

---

[*]Slightly disguised project categories.

- Type I: cost reductions and process improvements
- Type II: product improvements, product modifications (visible to the customer), and customer satisfaction projects (product changes in response to customer requests)
- Type III: new products
- Type IV: new platform projects and fundamental/breakthrough research projects.

Additionally another two categories of work are also identified: plant support and technical support for customers. Senior management at this Mobil Chemical SBU reviews the spending split across these six types—the *what is*—and compares this to the target breakdown—the *what should be.*

3. *Strategic Direction:* The main focus here is to ensure that, regardless of all other considerations, the final portfolio of projects is strategically aligned and truly reflects the business's strategy—that the breakdown of spending across projects, areas, markets, and so on, is directly tied to the business strategy (for example, to areas of strategic focus that management had previously delineated); and that all projects are on-strategy. Chapter 4 highlights these *strategically oriented* portfolio methods.

Example: The Privat division of Telenor, Norway's national telephone company with annual revenues of 22 billion kroner (about 4 billion U.S.$), sells a multitude of products in many different market segments. In order to help direct the division's new product portfolio, the business's new product strategy was first developed. This included the development of a *product/market matrix,* identifying many possible *strategic arenas* to focus new product efforts on. These arenas were prioritized using traditional planning and portfolio techniques. Some arenas, such as Internet[*] services to the small office/home office (SoHo) segment, were accorded top priority.

The company also employs a stage-and-gate new product process, with gates acting as Go/Kill decision points. Important criteria at these gates include "strategic alignment" and "strategic importance." As a result, new product projects that are targeted at the Internet/SoHo arena score more points—hence they have a higher likelihood of passing each gate, and are also prioritized higher on the active list. Periodically, management also conducts a portfolio review, to ensure that spending across projects reflects strategic priorities (for example, that the funding for projects within the Internet/ SoHo arena adds up to a substantial proportion of total project funding). Although some of these processes are quite new at Telenor, over time the new product project portfolio is slowly achieving strategic alignment.

What becomes clear is the potential for conflict among these three high-level goals. For example, the portfolio that yields the greatest NPV or ROI may not be a very balanced one (it may contain a majority of short-term, low-risk projects, or

[*]Telenor is also an Internet provider in Europe.

it may be overly focused on one market). Similarly, a portfolio that is primarily strategic in nature may sacrifice other goals (such as likelihood of success). What also became clear in our interviews is that although executives did not explicitly state that one of the goals took precedence over the other two, the nature of the portfolio management tool elected by that firm certainly indicated a hierarchy of goals. This is because certain portfolio approaches uncovered are much more applicable to some goals than others. For example, the visual models (such as maps or bubble diagrams) are most amenable to achieving a balance of projects (visual charts being an excellent way of demonstrating balance); scoring models tended to be very poor for achieving or even showing balance, but most effective if the goal is maximization of value against an objective. Thus the choice of the "right" portfolio method depended on which goal management had explicitly or implicitly focused on.

POINTS FOR MANAGEMENT TO PONDER

How does your current portfolio of new product or R&D projects rate against these three goals?

- maximizing the value of the portfolio—for example, in financial or strategic terms
- optimal balance—the right mix and balance of projects
- strategic alignment—all projects on-strategy and spending reflects strategic priorities.

Has your business consciously considered the various goals it seeks for its new product portfolio? What methods have you adopted to achieve these various goals?

Some Definitions

Before we lower the microscope on leading firms' current portfolio practices, here are some definitions of terms we use throughout this book:

Stage-Gate™ Process*: This is the formal process, or road map, which firms use to drive a new product project from idea to new product launch. This process typically has multiple stages, together with gates or decision points. A Stage-Gate process has many variants; it is also called the *new product process, gating process,* or *phase-review process.* Such a process is important to portfolio management because the gates are where Go/Kill decisions are made on individual projects, and hence where many of the resources are allocated. If your company has such a Stage-Gate process, then it must be included as an integral facet of the total portfolio approach.

Portfolio Review: This is the periodic review of the portfolio of all projects. It may take place annually, biannually, or quarterly. Here all projects—active

---

*Stage-Gate™ is a trademark of R. G. Cooper.

projects and even those on hold—are reviewed and compared against each other. This Portfolio Review often uses portfolio models (defined below) to display lists or maps of the current portfolio. The vital questions in the portfolio review are: Are the active projects the right ones? Do you have the right combination or mix of active projects here? Is this really where you want to spend your money?

Portfolio Models: These are the specific models or tools used to select projects or review the portfolio. They include scoring models, bubble diagrams and maps, various charts, financial models, and strategic approaches. These are outlined in Chapters 2, 3, and 4.

Portfolio Management Process (PMP): This is the *entire method* of project selection and portfolio management. It includes all of the components defined above.

Business Unit (BU) or (SBU): This is the smallest unit in the company for which portfolio management is undertaken. Usually a BU (or SBU) is a semiautonomous, self-contained business with its own goals, strategy, and resources. For example, a BU likely has its own R&D budget. For smaller firms, the BU may be the entire company.

Business Strategy: This is the strategy for the BU. It specifies the goals, direction, and areas of focus for the BU.

New Product Strategy: This is a component of (or flows from) the BU's business strategy. It specifies the BU's new product goals, direction, and areas of focus (that is, areas where the BU will focus its product development efforts). It may even specify desired levels of R&D and new product spending in specific arenas of focus (for example, how much to spend in certain markets or product categories).

Now, read on and learn the details of the portfolio approaches that we found to be the most effective in achieving the three goals of portfolio management.

CHAPTER 2

Portfolio Management Methods: Maximizing the Value of the Portfolio

Goal 1: Maximizing the Value of the Portfolio

The first goal of most firms we studied is to maximize the value of the portfolio of projects against one or more business objectives (such as profitability; strategic; acceptable risk; and so on). A variety of methods are used to achieve this goal, ranging from financial methods to scoring models. Each has its strengths and weaknesses.

The end result of each maximization method in this chapter is a rank-ordered list of projects. The projects at the top of the list score highest in terms of achieving the desired objective(s), and so the value of the portfolio against that objective is maximized. The challenge is to arrive at the appropriate criteria and method for rating and ranking the projects. This chapter provides the approaches.

Throughout this chapter, we refer to two decision processes: project Go/Kill decisions or *gate decisions* (here the focus is on individual projects); and *portfolio reviews* (where the entire portfolio of projects is considered—all projects together). These are important distinctions that are sometimes missed.

Expected Commercial Value

The Expected Commercial Value (ECV) method seeks to maximize the value or *commercial worth* of the portfolio, subject to certain budget constraints. This approach is one of the more well-thought-out financial models. It features several new twists that make it particularly appropriate to portfolio management. We found it in use at a major U.S. producer of clay and materials, English China Clay:

Example: ECC International (English China Clay) is the world's largest producer of clay and clay-related products, with annual sales revenues of about $4 billion

(U.S.). U.S. operations are headquartered in Atlanta, Georgia. Clay products have myriad markets and applications, including fine paper (clay is what makes paper white and bright), and extenders and fillers for plastics, paints, and other materials. Even though clay is a rather mature business, ECC's aggressive management has an objective of a 30% increase in revenue derived from new products over the next five years.

In this ECV method, English China Clay determines the value or commercial worth of each project to the corporation, namely, its Expected Commercial Value. This approach is based on a decision tree shown in Exhibit 2.1; it considers the future stream of earnings from the project, the probabilities of both commercial and technical success, along with both commercialization and development costs. ECC's version of the ECV method also incorporates the *strategic importance of the project,* a feature the company added to the general ECV model in Exhibit 2.1.

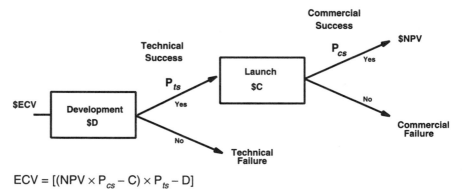

$$ECV = [(NPV \times P_{cs} - C) \times P_{ts} - D]$$

ECV = Expected Commercial Value of the project
P_{ts} = probability of technical success
P_{cs} = probability of commercial success (given technical success)
D = development costs remaining in the project
C = commercialization (launch) costs
NPV = net present value of the project's future earnings (discounted to the present)

Exhibit 2.1   Determination of Expected Commercial Value of Project

Note: ECC uses a slightly modified version of this exhibit.

An Explanation of the Decision Tree in Exhibit 2.1

- Begin at the left side of the exhibit.
- First, one must develop the product (development box); this costs $D.
- There is a probability of technical success, however (branch exiting the development box), with P_{ts} being that probability.
- If technically successful, the project moves into launch (launch box), where the capital and marketing costs are $C.

- But there is a probability of being commercially successful (branch exiting the launch box), namely, P_{cs}.
- If commercially successful, the product will generate an income stream (sales less operating costs) which, when present valued, is NPV.
- Tracing all these events, costs, incomes, and probabilities through the diagram yields the ECV—see formula.

Based on a decision tree analysis (see Exhibit 2.1), the formula for the ECV is

$$ECV = (NPV \times SI \times P_{cs} - C) \times P_{ts} - D$$

where:

NPV = net present value of 10-year cash flow, after launch (none of the project costs—development, capital, and so on—has been subtracted from this stream; this NPV is strictly the income stream)

SI = strategic importance index, which has three levels, depending on the strategic importance of the project (high, medium, low = 3, 2, 1)

P_{cs} = probability of commercial success (from 0.2 to 1.00, in increments of 0.2, based on established criteria)

C = commercialization (launch) costs (capital costs, customer trials, marketing costs)

P_{ts} = probability of technical success (again 0.2 to 1.00, in increments of 0.2, based on established criteria)

D = development costs (remaining in the project)

A sample calculation is given in Exhibit 2.2, with disguised projects from the company. Note *how different the ECV is from the NPV;* for example, Project Alpha's NPV is $30 million; after subtracting development and commercialization costs, its value becomes $22 million. Thus, at first glance, one might be tempted to place a commercial worth of $22 million on Project Alpha. But not so, according to the ECV method: the *real value* of the project is only $5 million—a major difference from the $22 million! The point is that merely rating or ranking projects according to NPV could be very misleading.

In order to arrive at a prioritized list of projects, ECC considers scarce resources: in their case, capital resources are thought to be the constraining or scarce resource (note that many of ECC's projects are very capital-intensive; for example, requiring new plant equipment). Other companies may choose to use

Project Name	NPV	Probability of Technical Success	Probability of Commercial Success	Develop-ment Cost*	Commercial-ization Cost*	ECV
Alpha	30	0.80	0.50	3	5	5.0
Beta	63.75	0.50	0.80	5	2	19.5
Gamma	8.62	0.75	0.75	2	1	2.1
Delta	3	1.00	1.00	1	0.5	1.5
Echo	50	0.60	0.75	5	3	15.7
Foxtrot	66.25	0.50	0.80	10	2	15.5

Exhibit 2.2   ECC's Determination of Expected Commercial Value

*Development cost (or commercialization cost) remaining in project.

R&D people or work-months, or R&D funds, as the constraining resource. Most firms have a finite annual R&D budget and finite number of people. In the example borrowed but disguised from ECC, we've used R&D dollars as the constraint and have set a budget of $15 million as a dummy figure to illustrate.*

ECC then takes the ratio of what it is trying to maximize (the ECV) *divided by the constraining resource* (the annual R&D spending proposed per project). Projects are rank-ordered according to this ratio, thereby ensuring the greatest "bang for buck"; that is, the ECV is maximized for a given R&D budget.** Exhibit 2.3 shows the final prioritized list, with a horizontal line noting the point where the budget of $15 million is exceeded. Projects above the line are considered "active and in the portfolio"; those below the line are placed on hold.

Note that had ECC's projects simply been rank-ordered according to the ECV alone (rather than the ECV/R&D ratio), the prioritized list would have been quite different. And, most important, the *value of the total portfolio would have been inferior:* that is, the resulting project list would have yielded a lower total ECV value for a given R&D budget!

This ECV model has a number of attractive features. Because this formula is based on a decision tree approach, it recognizes that if a project is halted partway through, certain expenses are not incurred, and that the Go/Kill decision process is a step-wise or incremental one. (For example, the simplistic route adopted by some—multiplying the NPV of a project by its probability of success—fails to capture this subtlety. This method distorts the value of projects, and in particular, overpenalizes projects with high capital or commercialization costs and low prob-

Project Name	ECV	Development Cost (Dev)	ECV/Dev	Sum of Dev
Beta	19.5	5	3.90	5.0
Echo	15.7	5	3.14	10.0
Alpha	5.0	3	1.67	13.0
Foxtrot	15.5	10	1.55	(23.0)
Delta	1.5	1	1.50	14
Gamma	2.1	2	1.05	15

Exhibit 2.3   ECC's Rank-Ordered List According to ECV/Dev

Note: Total development budget of $15 million.

Criterion: Ratio of what you are trying to maximize divided by constraining resource (yields maximum "bang for buck").

---

*Note that ECC uses exactly the same routine to maximize the portfolio's value, except with capital as the constraint.

**This decision rule of "rank order according to the ratio of what one is trying to maximize divided by the constraining resource" seems to be an effective one. We did simulations with a number of random sets of projects (much like the disguised list in Exhibit 2.2), and found that this decision rule worked very well—truly giving "maximum bang for buck"!

ability of technical success.) Note that the ECV method recognizes that management has Go/Kill options along the way; that these options reduce the risk of a project; and that the "correct valuation" of a project should be via a decision tree approach, as in Exhibit 2.1 (see box entitled "Options Pricing Theory versus NPV").

A second feature is that all dollar amounts are discounted to today (not just to launch date), thereby appropriately penalizing projects that are years away from launch. A third benefit is that sunk costs—money already spent on R&D or commercialization—are not considered. Another feature is that the model, although largely financially based, does consider the strategic importance of projects. Finally, the model recognizes the issue of constrained resources and attempts to maximize the value of the portfolio in light of this constraint: the notion of "maximum bang for buck" rather than just "maximum bang."

A careful review of the equation in Exhibit 2.1 and the rank-ordering model in Exhibit 2.3 reveals that certain types of projects will be appropriately favored by this ECV model. Projects that this model will prioritize more highly:

- are those closer to launch (distant projects are penalized)
- have relatively little left to be spent on them—all money spent so far is a sunk cost, and hence not relevant to the ranking decision
- have higher likelihoods of success (commercial and technical probabilities) and a higher stream of earnings
- utilize less of the scarce or constraining resource (in ECC's case, projects with smaller R&D annual costs and lower capital requirements[*]).

The major weakness of the method is the *dependency on financial and other quantitative data.* For example, accurate data on all projects' future streams of earnings, on their probable commercialization (and capital) expenditures, on their development costs, and on probabilities of success must be available. Often these estimates are unreliable, leading to doubts about the validity of the ranking method; or these estimates are simply not available early in the life of a project and hence the method can only be used for projects past a certain point in the process (for example, after a full financial business case has been developed). A second weakness is the *treatment of probabilities.* How does one quantitatively estimate probabilities of success?[**] One seasoned executive took great exception to multiplying two very uncertain probability figures together: "This will always unfairly punish the more venturesome projects!" A third weakness is that the method does not look at the balance of the portfolio—at whether the portfolio has the right balance between high- and low-risk projects, or across markets and technologies. A final weakness is that the method considers only a single criterion—the ECV—for maximization (although, admittedly, this ECV is comprised of a number of parameters).

---

[*]But this could be any constraining resource, such as full-time equivalent people (FTEs). The same type of calculations would apply.

[**]There are methods for estimating probabilities of success, which are described later in this chapter.

POINTS FOR MANAGEMENT TO PONDER

If

+ your company is very financially oriented
+ good financial data and profitability estimates are available fairly early in the life of a project (that is, profitability and commercial assumptions are typically fairly predictable)
+ and there is a major constraining resource (so that maximization of bang for buck is the goal)

then the ECV method has many merits. We recommend that you at least consider it over other, more simplistic financial methods.

Productivity Index

The *productivity index* (PI) is similar to the ECV method described above, and shares many of its strengths and weaknesses. The PI also tries to maximize the financial or economic value of the portfolio for a given resource constraint. We saw the method in use in two firms—a medical products firm in the United States and a nuclear firm in the United Kingdom. The method has been popularized by Strategic Decision Group (SDG).[3]

The Productivity Index is:

$$PI = [ECV \times P_{ts} - R\&D] / R\&D$$

Here, *ECV* is a probability-weighted stream of cash flows from the project, discounted to the present and assuming technical success.[*] P_{ts} is the probability of technical success, while *R&D* is the R&D expenditure remaining in the project (note that R&D funds already spent on the project are sunk costs and hence are not relevant to the decision). Projects are rank-ordered according to this index in order to arrive at the preferred portfolio.

Example: In the U.K. nuclear firm, each project has its productivity index calculated according to the above formula. The projects are then rank-ordered on a list, those with the highest productivity indexes at the top. Lower-ranked active projects are flagged for immediate review. Several projects with lower productivity indexes had already been cancelled within months of implementation of the method.

Example: A major U.S. consumer goods firm uses a variant of the productivity index. Here the denominator, instead of being just R&D costs, is *all investment remaining* in the project (R&D, capital and launch costs). While considered to be a sound technique for driving obvious high-value projects to the top of the list, management is concerned that certain dramatic breakthroughs, with uncertain estimates, will not score well using this method. One of the firm's major success stories in the hair care field would likely never have never made it through to de-

---

[*]Note that the definition of *expected commercial value* here is different than that used by English China Clay (Exhibit 2.1).

velopment had this productivity index been rigorously applied, according to one senior executive.

Options Pricing Theory versus NPV

In recent years, some financial experts have recognized that the assumptions underlying traditional discounted cash flow (DCF) analysis (including NPV and internal rate of return [IRR]) are invalid in the case of new product investments. The net result is that NPV analysis *unfairly penalizes* certain types of projects, and by a considerable amount. Here's why:

In DCF analysis, the assumption is that the project is an "all or nothing" investment—a single and irreversible investment expenditure decision. In reality, however, investments in new product projects are made in increments: that is, management has a series of Go/Kill options along the way. As new information becomes available, the decision is made to invest more or to halt the project. These Go/Kill options, of course, reduce the risk of the project (versus an "all or nothing" approach). When DCF is used, this lost option value is an opportunity cost that should be incorporated when the investment is analyzed.[11] But traditional spreadsheets used to generate NPVs do not!

By contrast, options pricing theory (OPT) recognizes that management can kill a project after each incremental investment is made—that management has options along the way. Options pricing theory is thus claimed to be the correct evaluation method, and a number of pundits have argued that NPV or DCF is "misused." Senior management at Eastman Kodak go further and state that "the use of options pricing theory concepts brings valuable insights into the R&D valuation process" and that "an options approach often yields a substantially higher valuation than a DCF approach."[12] We have done a number of simulations, and conclude that the Kodak view is correct: when the project is a high-risk one—that is, when the probability of technical or commercial success is low and the costs to undertake the project are high—then DCF and NPV *considerably understate the true value* of the project. This means that you will tend to kill otherwise valuable projects if you use the traditional NPV!

One way to approximate an OPT approach is to structure the decision problem via a decision tree, much like the ECV method (Exhibit 2.1), according to Kodak.[12] A more realistic representation than Exhibit 2.1 might be to use three, four, or five stages and Go/Kill options along the way; but at least the ECV method does begin to incorporate the notion of options, and hence yields the more correct project valuation than does straight DCF or NPV.

POINTS FOR MANAGEMENT TO PONDER

Have you ever determined what the *economic value or worth* of your business's new product or R&D portfolio is? Most managers have a fairly good idea of how much they have spent on the portfolio over the past few years, but ironically they have very little idea about its *current value*. The analogy is that of stock market portfolio managers knowing how much they paid for the shares they own, but having no idea of their current value. We'd fire them!

Yet many businesses are guilty of the same crime: they have no idea what the economic value of their portfolio of projects is. Perhaps it's time to undertake this task now. In doing so, assess the economic value or worth of each project in the portfolio, using the ECV method (Exhibit 2.1) or the probability-weighted NPV seen in the PI method above (more details in the next chapter). Then add up the values of the projects. You may be shocked at the worth of your portfolio versus what you've spent to get there!

Dynamic Rank-Ordered List

The next method overcomes the limitation of relying on only a single criterion to rank projects. We've labeled it the Dynamic Rank-Ordered List approach, although Company G[*] simply called it their "portfolio model." This method has the advantage that it can rank-order according to several criteria concurrently, without becoming as complex and time-consuming as the use of a full-fledged, multiple-criteria scoring model. These criteria can include, for example, profitability and return measures; strategic importance; ease and speed; and other desirable characteristics of a high-priority project. Exhibit 2.4 provides an illustration using disguised projects and data from Company G. The four principal criteria used by this company are:

- The *NPV* of the future earnings of projects, less all outstanding expenditures. This NPV value is considered an important objective by Company G, in that it captures both the fact that the project exceeds the acceptable hurdle rate and also denotes the sheer magnitude or impact of the project on the company—the "bang." Note that the NPV has built into it probabilities of commercial success (in the calculation of the NPV, sales revenues, margins, and so on, have all been multiplied by probabilities to account for uncertainties).
- The *IRR* or *ROI* is calculated using the same data as the NPV, but gives the percent return. This is an equally important criterion for Company G, as it captures the efficient utilization of capital—namely, "bang for buck."
- The *strategic importance* of the project—how important and how aligned the project is with the business's strategy—is a key criterion to rank projects at Company G. Importance is gauged on a 1–5 scale, where 5 is "critically important."

Project Name	IRR[*] (%)	NPV ($ millions)	Strategic Importance[**]	Probability of Technical Success
Alpha	20%	10.0	5	80%
Beta	15%	2.0	2	70%
Gamma	10%	5.0	3	90%
Delta	17%	12.0	2	65%
Epsilon	12%	20.0	4	90%
Omega	22%	6.0	1	85%

Exhibit 2.4   Company G—Dynamic Rank-Ordered List

[*]The hurdle rate is 10% IRR.

[**]Strategic importance scale is a 1–5 rating, where 5 = critically important.

[*]Some companies preferred not to have their names mentioned.

⯈ The *probability of technical success* is also an important consideration in ranking projects for Company G, as some projects are very speculative technically.

How are projects prioritized or ranked on four criteria simultaneously? First, the probability of technical success is multiplied by each of the IRR and NPV to yield an adjusted IRR and NPV (see Exhibit 2.5). Next, projects are ranked according to each of the three criteria: IRR adjusted; NPV adjusted; and strategic importance. Exhibit 2.5 shows this procedure, with the numbers in parentheses showing the rank orders in each of the three columns. The overall rankings—the far right column in Exhibit 2.5—are determined by calculating the *mean of the three rankings*. For example, in Exhibit 2.5, for Project Alpha, which scored first on strategic importance and second on each of the IRR and NPV, the mean of these three rankings is 1.67, which places Alpha at the top of the list. Simple perhaps, but consider the disguised list of projects in Exhibit 2.5 and try to come up with a better ranking yourself—one that maximizes against all three criteria!

POINTS FOR MANAGEMENT TO PONDER

Several financial and strategic criteria might be the goal in your portfolio management approach. Do consider this Dynamic Rank-Ordered List approach. It certainly is simple, and it considers not only the NPV but also the efficiency of funds employed, namely, the IRR. Strategic importance and probability of success are also built in. We suggest that if this method is of interest, you consider modifying it by considering key ratios (such as NPV/R&D costs) rather than just NPV to do the ranking (much like the ECV and PI methods do).

The major strength of this dynamic list is its sheer simplicity. Rank-order your projects on each of several criteria, and take the means of the rankings. Another

Project Name	IRR × PTS	NPV × PTS	Strategic Importance	Ranking Score*
Alpha	16.0 (2)	8.0 (2)	5 (1)	1.67 (1)
Epsilon	10.8 (4)	18.0 (1)	4 (2)	2.33 (2)
Delta	11.1 (3)	7.8 (3)	2 (4)	3.33 (3)
Omega	18.7 (1)	5.1 (4)	1 (6)	3.67 (4)
Gamma	9.0 (6)	4.5 (5)	3 (3)	4.67 (5)
Beta	10.5 (5)	1.4 (6)	2 (4)	5.00 (6)

Exhibit 2.5   The Six Projects Rank-Ordered

Note: Both IRR and NPV are multiplied by probability of technical success. Projects are then ranked according to the three criteria. Numbers in parentheses show the ranking in each column. Projects are rank-ordered until there are no more resources.

*The final column is the mean across the three rankings. This is the score that the six projects are finally ranked on. Project Alpha is number 1 while Project Beta is last.

strength is that the method can handle several criteria concurrently without becoming overly complex. Its major weakness is that the model does not consider constrained resources (as did the ECV model, although conceivably Company G could build this into its rank-ordering model), and, like the ECV and PI models, it is largely based on uncertain, often unreliable financial data. Finally, it fails to consider the appropriate balance of projects.

The Dark Side to the Financial Approaches to Project Evaluation

Virtually all firms we interviewed employ financial methods of one form or another—either at gate reviews or at portfolio review meetings—to attempt to maximize the economic value of the portfolio. The rigor and toughness of financial methods, coupled with the fact that the assessment boils down to a few key numbers, are positive features.

One concern that was consistently heard in our study, however, is that an overreliance on strictly financial data and criteria may lead to wrong portfolio decisions, simply because the financial data are often wrong! And there is indeed evidence to support this view.

▶ More's study of firms' abilities to estimate expected new product sales revenues showed that there were orders of magnitude errors, on average.[4]

▶ Another study also echoes the concerns of overreliance on net present value techniques.[5]

▶ One company had tracked NPV estimates over the life of a project for a set of 30 projects.[6] (Most managers had no idea how accurate their NPV and financial estimates had been!) In that firm, the sum of the NPVs across the 30 projects showed a marked decline as the projects progressed from predevelopment through to postlaunch: on average, financial prospects are very much overestimated! Unfortunately, while the *average of the 30 projects* followed the shape of a predictable, smooth curve downward, *plots of individual projects' NPVs* over time were more erratic, thus ruling out the use of a standard "correction factor" that could be applied to early NPV estimates.

One reason for this unreliable financial information is the continuing reluctance on the part of senior management to insist that solid up-front homework and good market information be part of every project at the "Go to Development" decision point (our recent benchmarking studies reveal that up-front homework and solid market information remain critical weaknesses[7]). Some senior people seem to be in such a hurry that they are prepared to sacrifice project quality, and then are disturbed when everything starts to go wrong! Other reasons are that many financial variables remain uncertain until later stages of a project and well into the development stage (for example, manufacturing costs or capital requirements).

A second and more subtle concern about an overreliance on financial data to make project Go/Kill and portfolio decisions is the belief that *major breakthrough projects will be penalized,* while minor modifications and small, low-risk initiatives will score higher. One reason for this is the "all or nothing" investment assumption made in traditional NPV calculations; in reality, however, management has Go/Kill options in projects: options reduce the risk of projects and hence portray particularly high-risk projects in a more favorable economic light than does NPV (see box entitled "Options Pricing Theory versus NPV"). Another reason why breakthrough projects are penalized is that the expected outcomes and payoffs from breakthrough projects are harder to quantify and prove, especially in a project's early days.

POINTS FOR MANAGEMENT TO PONDER

If you use financial data and criteria to make Go/Kill and portfolio decisions in the early stages of a project, you're using *a very rubbery meter stick*. Not surprisingly, many of your decisions will be wrong ones! With the exception of close-to-home, well-defined projects, financial estimates made for many new product projects are highly uncertain, especially when made prior to the beginning of the development phase. The dilemma is that this is precisely when portfolio and project selection decisions are required.

Suggestions:

▶ Do consider the financial data and financial criteria at these early decision points. But don't base the entire decision on these. Go beyond the financial methods and use some of the nonfinancial methods to gauge reward and make decisions on projects. These are outlined in the rest of this chapter and in the next.
▶ Demand that the quality of information, especially market information, be improved, notably at the "Go to Development" decision point. Insist on solid up-front homework!
▶ Start tracking your financial estimates over the life of a project. Be sure to build in a postlaunch review (perhaps 12 to 18 months after launch), where the actual results can be compared to those forecast when the project was approved. This way you can determine the reliability of financial estimates made early in the life of a project.

Estimating Probabilities of Success

The three value maximization methods outlined so far—the ECV, the PI, and the Dynamic Rank-Ordered List—all require quantitative estimates of probabilities of success (as a percent). These are difficult numbers to estimate; moreover, small variations in these numbers can cause major changes in the attractiveness scores of projects and hence their relative ranking. For example, in the ECV method, two probabilities are multiplied together; if these two numbers are somewhat wrong, then the final ECV number is *very wrong*—the error is magnified. This is one of the reasons some managers we interviewed were skeptical about using these financially based models in project selection and portfolio management.

Some companies employ techniques that render the estimation of probabilities of success at least somewhat more objective and reliable. Consider these approaches:

1. Delphi consensus approach: At the project review meeting, management is asked to consider the probability of technical success. Each senior person writes a number on a piece of paper representing the probability of technical success. These estimates are collected and then displayed anonymously on an overhead projector screen. On occasion, there is total agreement! Most often, there is a range of estimates from the evaluators in the room. Then discussion ensues, with each decision-maker listening to the others' points of view. A second round follows, whereby each person submits a revised estimate of the probability. By the end of the third round, there is consensus. Experiments done in psychology suggest that this method not only yields consensus; it usually yields an answer very close to the truth!

2. *Matrix approach:* Rohm and Haas, a U.S.-based chemical company, uses a matrix to determine probabilities of commercial and technical success. The *commercial success probability* is decided via a two-dimensional matrix chart, whose axes are:

▶ market newness, ranging from "current market" to "new to world"
▶ degree of competitive advantage, ranging from "me-too product" to "enabling benefit that opens up significant business opportunities"

The theory here is that the likelihood of commercial success decreases with increasing market newness and increases with competitive advantage. Different probabilities of commercial success have been developed for the 12 cells in the chart (see Exhibit 2.6).

The *probability of technical success* is also based on a matrix with two dimensions. These two dimensions both capture the newness of the technology to the company—product technology and process technology. For both dimensions,

▶ very high probability is defined as "solution already demonstrated; need only final engineering; repackage"
▶ very low probability is defined as "probably beyond current technology or don't know how to approach; need to import new technology

Exhibit 2.7 provides a matrix of probabilities. The product of the commercial and technical probabilities provides an overall probability of success that may change as the product moves through the development process.

3. *Scoring method:* Hoechst-U.S. uses much the same approach in estimating the probability of technical success, but considers different parameters. The company employs a four-item scoring method to determine a probability of *technical success score* (see next section; also Exhibit 2.8, first chart). The 1–10 score on this factor can be translated into a probability of success from Hoechst's summary table (Exhibit 2.8, final chart).

4. *NewProd model.** Procter & Gamble, Exxon Chemical, and others use the NewProd model to estimate probabilities of commercial success. This is an empirically based computer model that has been customized to each user firm.

*NewProd was developed by one of the authors.[8] For more information on NewProd, see Web page at www.prod-dev.com.

Market	Probability Scores			
Current	0.5	0.6	0.85	0.95
New to R&H	0.1	0.2	0.5	0.7
New to World	0.05	0.05	0.1	0.2
	Low	Moderate	High	Very High
	Competitive Advantage			

Note: For example, a current market and a product with a low competitive advantage would score 0.5.

Definitions for Competitive Advantage Scale	
Low	Me-too or catch-up product; minor cost reduction; benefits cannot overcome significant switching costs.
Moderate	Benefit seen as marginally great enough to switch in absence of other factors.
High	Benefit perceived to justify switching costs in the context of all competing demands.
Very High	Enabling benefit that opens significant new business opportunities for the customer.

Exhibit 2.6   Rohm and Haas—Matrix for Commercial Success

Process	Probability Scores				
Very High	0.2	0.5	0.75	0.9	0.95
High	0.15	0.4	0.65	0.8	0.9
Moderate	0.15	0.3	0.5	0.65	0.75
Low	0.1	0.2	0.3	0.4	0.5
Very Low	0.05	0.1	0.15	0.15	0.2
	Very Low	Low	Moderate	High	Very High
	Product				

Note: For example, probability of technical success for process (very high) and product (very low) would be 0.2.

Definitions for Technical Success	
Very High	Solution already demonstrated; need only final engineering; repackage.
High	Prototype in hand demonstrating all necessary characteristics, but need to optimize performance.
Moderate	Prototype not yet in hand, but good lead within current technology; experts believe this can be done.
Low	Technology route/lead not well established; scouting work to be done; experts think this probably can be done with available technology.
Very Low	Probably beyond current technology or don't know how to approach; need to import new technology.

Exhibit 2.7   Rohm and Haas—Matrix for Technical Success

Users simply answer approximately 30 key questions (0–10 scales); the answers from a variety of people are combined; and the resulting "profile of the project" is compared to profiles already in the model's database to predict whether it will be a winner.

The advantage is that the model is based on many past new product cases, some drawn from within the company, others from available databases. The commercial outcomes—success or failure—of these projects in the database is known. The probability of success is then linked via statistical analysis to a number of potential driver variables. Procter & Gamble claims an 85% predictive ability using this model,[9] while a Dutch study reports similar positive results in Europe.[10] The best experience has been where users have had the model customized to incorporate their own data and cases or have developed industry-specific versions of the model (as in P&G's case).

None of the methods above is a perfect estimator of success probabilities. But each brings some degree of objectivity and validity to these estimates. Nonetheless, all the financial methods suffer due to the problem of obtaining reliable estimates of success probabilities; the exceptions, of course, are those projects that are well defined and known entities, where the probability of success is 100%!

POINTS FOR MANAGEMENT TO PONDER

If you do choose to use one of the financial methods above, be careful about how you handle the probabilities of both commercial and technical success. First, you cannot ignore probabilities: most projects have a less than 100% chance of success. Failure to build this reality into your method will lead to the wrong project prioritizations. Second, adopt one of the more objective methods for estimating probabilities we outlined above—not perfect, but better than guesses. Additionally, the next chapter shows how some firms build uncertainty and risk directly into their NPV calculations.

Nonfinancial Value Maximization Methods: Scoring Models

Scoring models have long been used for making Go/Kill decisions at gates; they also have applicability for project prioritization and portfolio management. Here, a list of criteria is developed to rate projects—criteria that are thought to discriminate between high-priority and low-priority projects. Projects are then rated by evaluators on each criterion, typically on 1–5 or 0–10 scales with anchor phrases. Next, these scores are multiplied by weightings and summed across all criteria to yield a project score for each project.

Although many firms we interviewed professed to be using such scoring models, either they were poorly crafted models (for example, inappropriate criteria) or there were serious problems in the actual use of the model at management decision meetings. Hence such models often fell into disuse. The key seems to be in the construction of an appropriate list of scoring criteria—ones that really do separate winners from losers—and a procedure to gather the data and use the model at a management meeting.

Two firms we interviewed had developed particularly effective scoring models, which they both used for portfolio management: Hoechst-U.S. Corporate Research & Technology (Hoechst) and the Royal Bank of Canada (RBC). Hoechst had constructed one of the best scoring models we've seen: it took several years of refinement, but the eventual model is so well conceived that we report it here. Additionally, RBC's scoring model is reported later in the chapter, as it provides a solid example of a shorter scoring model and an example of one appropriate for the service sector.

Example: Hoechst-AG is one of the largest chemical companies in the world, with annual sales in excess of $30 billion U.S. The particular unit studied was the Corporate Research & Technology in the U.S. (HCRT), a research- and technology-intensive unit within the corporation whose special mandate is to develop and commercialize new products that lie outside the scope of the traditional business units. It tends to focus on larger, higher-risk, more step-out and longer-term major projects (as opposed to projects designed to maintain and renew a business unit's existing product line). Hoechst-U.S. spends approximately $300 million on R&D, of which a significant portion goes to HCRT. It also uses a Stage-Gate new product process—a five-stage and -gate process designed to move projects from the idea stage through to commercialization.

The scoring portfolio model comprises a list of 19 questions within five major categories. Each question or criterion had been carefully selected and worded, operationally defined, and tested for validity and reliability over several years. We offer their model in Exhibit 2.8 as an example to other companies.

The five major factors Hoechst considers in prioritizing projects are:

- probability of technical success
- probability of commercial success
- reward (to the company)
- business strategy fit (fit with the business unit's strategy)
- strategic leverage (ability of the project to leverage company resources and skills).

Within each of these five factors are a number of specific characteristics or measures (19 in total), which are scored on 1–10 scales by management. The 19 scales are anchored (scale points 1, 4, 7, and 10 are defined) to facilitate discussion (see Exhibit 2.8 for the questions and their operational definitions).

Simple addition of the items within each factor yields the five factor scores. Then the five factor scores are added together in a weighted fashion to yield an overall score for the project, namely, the *program attractiveness* score. This final score is used for two purposes:

1. *Go/Kill decisions at gates:* Embedded within Hoechst's new product process are predefined decision points or gates. These gates are staffed by a

Factor 1: Probability of Technical Success

Key Factors	Rating Scale				Rating	Comments
	1	4	7	10		
Technical "Gap"	Large gulf between current practice and objective; must invent new science	"Order of magnitude" change proposed	Step-change short of "order of magnitude"	Incremental improvement; more engineering focus		
Program Complexity	Difficult to define; many hurdles	Easy to define; many hurdles	A challenge, but "do-able"	Straightforward		
Technology Skill Base	Technology new to the company; (almost) no skills	Some R&D experience, but probably insufficient	Selectively practiced in company	Widely practiced in company		
Availability of People and Facilities	No appropriate people/ facilities; must hire/build	Acknowledged shortage in key areas	Resources are available, but in demand; must plan in advance	People/facilities immediately available		

Exhibit 2.8 Hoechst-U.S.—Scoring Model

38

Factor 2: Probability of Commercial Success

Key Factors	Rating Scale				Rating	Comments
	1	4	7	10		
Market Need	Extensive market development required; no apparent need	Need must be highlighted for customers; product tailoring required	Clear relationship between product and need; one-for-one substitution of competitor's product	Product immediately responsive to customer need; direct substitute for existing company product		
Market Maturity	Declining	Mature/embryonic	Modest growth	Rapid growth		
Competitive Intensity	High	Moderate/high	Moderate/low	Low		
Commercial Applications/ Development Skills	Must develop; new to company	Must develop beyond current limited use	Need to tailor to proposed program	Already in place		
Commercial Assumptions	Low probability/ low impact	Low predictability/ low impact	High probability/ high impact	High predictability/ high impact		
Regulatory/Social Political Impact	Negative	Neutral	Somewhat favorable (for example, waste minimization, reduce hazardous materials in process)	Positive impact on high-profile issues (for example, plastics recycle)		

Exhibit 2.8   *(continued)*

Factor 3: Reward

Key Factors	Rating Scale				Rating	Comments
	1	4	7	10		
Absolute Contributions to Profitability (five-year cumulative cash flow from commercial start-up)	< $10 MM	$50 MM	$150 MM	> $250 MM		
Technology Payback	> 10 years	7 years	5 years	< 3 years		
Time to Commercial Start-Up	> 7 years	5 years	3 years	< 1 year		

Note: Payback = number of years needed for cumulative cash flow to equal all cash costs expended prior to start-up plus capital investment after start-up.

Exhibit 2.8 (*continued*)

Factor 4: Business Strategy Fit

Key Factors	Rating Scale				Rating	Comments
	1	4	7	10		
Congruence	Only peripheral fit with business strategies	Modest fit, but not with a key element of the strategy	Good fit with a key element of strategy	Strong fit with several key elements of strategy		
Impact	Minimal impact; no noticeable harm if program dropped	Moderate competitive, financial impact	Significant impact; difficult to recover if program unsuccessful or dropped	Business unit future depends on this program		

Exhibit 2.8 (continued)

Factor 5: Strategic Leverage

Key Factors	Rating Scale				Rating	Comments
	1	4	7	10		
Proprietary Position	Easily copied	Protected, but not a deterrent	Solidly protected with trade secrets, patents; serves captive customer	Position protected (upstream and downstream) through a combination of patents, trade secrets, raw material access, and so on		
Platform for Growth	Dead end/one-of-a-kind	Other opportunities for business extension	Potential for diversification	Opens up new technical and commercial fields		
Durability (Technical and Market)	No distinctive advantage; quickly "leap frogged"	May get a few good years	Moderate life cycle (4–6 years) but little opportunity for incremental improvement	Long life cycle with opportunity for incremental improvements		
Synergy with Other Operations within Corporation	Limited to single business unit	With work, could be applied to another SBU	Could be adopted or have application among several SBUs	Could be applied widely across the company		

Exhibit 2.8 (continued)

Program Attractiveness Score: Summary of Scores on Five Factors
Abbreviated Form

Key Factors	Rating Scale				Rating	Comments
	1	4	7	10		
Probability of Technical Success	< 20% probability	40% probability	70% probability	> 90% probability		
Probability of Commercial Success	< 25% probability	50% probability	75% probability	> 90% probability		
Reward	small/breakeven	Payback > 7 years	Payback = 5 years	Payback < 3 years		
Business Strategy Fit	R&D program is independent of business strategy; also low SBU impact	Somewhat supports SBU strategy; moderate impact	Supports SBU strategy; moderate impact	Strongly supports SBU strategies; high impact		
Strategic Leverage	"One-of-a-kind"/ dead end	Several opportunities for business extensions	Opportunities to transfer to another SBU	Vast array of proprietary opportunities		

Exhibit 2.8 (*continued*)

group of senior managers and executives, who review the projects under consideration and make Go/Kill decisions. The *program attractiveness score* is one input into the Go/Kill decision at each gate: a score of 50% of maximum is the cutoff or hurdle. Note that the decision is not quite as simple as a "Yea/Nay" based on this score. There are animated discussions at the gate, where opinion and experience of managers surface and where other issues and qualitative factors not captured in the 19 measures are dealt with. These gate meetings take place about once a month and are facilitated by an outside "referee," who walks the gatekeepers through the scoring model and also computes and records the scores.

2. *Prioritization:* Immediately following the gate meeting, the portfolio of projects is reviewed. This is where the prioritization of "Go" projects from the gate takes place and where resources are allocated to the approved projects that were positively rated at the gate meeting. Here, the *program attractiveness* scores for the new projects (versus scores for already resourced projects) determine how the new projects are prioritized in the total list and whether these new ones receive resources or are placed on hold. Other considerations, besides the computed *attractiveness* score, are:

   ▶ appropriate balance or mix of projects
   ▶ resource needs of each project (people, money)
   ▶ availability of key people and money

Obtaining the Data for Scoring Models

The method of data collection for input to the portfolio model is relatively straightforward for the ECV, Productivity Index, and the Dynamic Rank-Ordered List techniques. All use largely financial data to rank projects. These financial data are usually presented at the Go/Kill or gate meeting as part of the project's business case. Moreover, there are usually only a few key criteria, such as NPV, ECV, or IRR, to be considered.

By contrast, scoring models use many more criteria (witness the 19 criteria used by Hoechst), and most of these are subjective in nature. This means the decision-makers themselves must "provide" much of the data (in the form of ratings based on subjective opinion) at the review meeting. As a result, one of the recurring and frequently mentioned problems with scoring models is the actual use of the model at a gate or portfolio meeting. The model can become cumbersome. Requiring decision-makers to rate and score projects at a meeting is time-consuming (and something many senior people are loathe to do), and collecting these data in a time-efficient manner during the meeting is difficult.

Several companies have solved some of this data collection problem by passing out a scorecard to the evaluators during the meeting. A facilitator walks the decision-makers through the criteria one at a time. After some discussion, the facilitator calls for each evaluator to score the project on that criterion (privately and independently), and then moves to the next criterion. The scorecards are collected after all criteria are evaluated, and are quickly tallied on an overhead transparency for display and discussion. Consensus or alignment is reached, and a decision on the project made. While not the neatest meeting format, this procedure does seem to work.

One major North American financial institution, the Royal Bank of Canada, also relies heavily on a scoring model—a much simpler one than Hoechst's—but the *scoring methodology* is sufficiently unique that it merits mention here.

Example: The Royal Bank of Canada (RBC) is the largest bank in Canada, and one of the largest financial institutions in North America. It is a multibranch bank with branches around the world, 50,000 employees, and assets of $120 billion (U.S.$). Although much of its business is retail (that is, to consumers), its *Business Banking division* is where significant advances have been made in new product and portfolio management.

The method involves the use of both a *sorting technique* and a *scoring model.* All the *new* and *existing* projects from the various product lines (product groups*) in RBC are considered—together and against each other—since they all compete for the same resource pie.

The portfolio analysis is a critical all-day meeting, to which the product group heads and other knowledgeable managers are invited. RBC is a heavy user of technology in meeting rooms, and the portfolio meeting is no exception. An electronic meeting room is used, where every attendee has a computer and keyboard in front of him or her; when issues arise, attendees can type in text, which then appears on the computer screens of others in the room. The facilitator can also call for votes on issues. For example, "Now that we've discussed the revenue potential of this project, I'd like you to vote on this, scoring it from 1 to 9, where . . ." Attendees then key in their scores; the results are tallied and displayed on each attendee's computer screen, including various statistics (means and deviations) or rank-ordered lists; some discussion takes place; and then the meeting moves to the next issue or vote.

This electronically based procedure has proven very effective in soliciting and integrating views from a diverse group of people (everyone gets a chance to be heard) and also for gaining closure on each issue in a time-efficient manner (via the electronic vote). Note that these are quite senior people, yet even they have adapted to the new meeting technology.

In RBC's process, almost 200 projects competing for the same pool of resources are under consideration. Almost half of these are relatively small, *nondiscretionary* projects—vital maintenance work, minor systems changes and upgrades, and necessity work—and are automatically "in the budget." The remaining budget must then be allocated across *discretionary* projects, both *new* and *existing* product development projects. Prior to the portfolio meeting, each product group meets informally to discuss its own list of priorities.

---

*Product groups in Business Banking are product lines, and include loans; deposits; electronic data interchange (EDI); payroll; trade products; cash management; and a host of other products/services provided by RBC to its corporate clients.

The main portfolio meeting begins with a brief description of each of the roughly 100 discretionary projects (attendees have received a listing of these and some description prior to the meeting). Voting begins via a *sorting technique*: the facilitator requests each attendee to select his or her top and bottom 15 projects (all votes are keyed in via attendees' computers). The results of this *sorting vote* are displayed on the screens. The usual pattern is this:

▶ A subset of the more obvious projects, including many which are well underway, receive quite a few positive votes each—there is general concurrence on these.
▶ Similarly, a subset receives a number of negative votes each—these are the obvious "kill" projects.
▶ A group of projects are in the middle—few votes and mixed positive and negative votes. These are flagged for discussion.

At this point, any attendee is allowed to *lobby* for any project in the *middle group*. Note that the very positive and very negative projects are not discussed as there was general concurrence on these. Only the uncertain ones (the exceptions) are debated.

Next, the facilitator calls for a *scoring vote* (1–9 ratings) for each project on each of two major factors, each of which contains three criteria:

Factor 1: project importance, consisting of

▶ strategic importance
▶ magnitude of impact on the bank
▶ economic benefits to the bank.

Factor 2: ease of doing, consisting of

▶ cost of doing (negative scale)
▶ complexity of project (negative scale)
▶ resource availability.

Exhibit 2.9 provides detailed definition of these six criteria.

Rating scores, averaged across evaluators, are now added for each project to yield the two factor scores, importance and ease. A total *project score* is also computed (the sum of these two factors), which is then converted to a percent. (At one time, RBC applied weights to its scoring criteria; however, the choice of weights caused much debate; thus more recent scoring sessions have simply assigned *equal weights* to all criteria.)

Following this sorting and scoring session, a prioritized list of projects is generated and rank-ordered *according to the project scores*. In this respect, the model so far is somewhat similar to the scoring approach used by Hoechst. Also shown on the list is the *expected annual expenditure* for this project, as well as the *cumulative spending* (the sum of all spending for all projects on the list, above and including this project; see sample using disguised projects in Exhibit 2.10). The

Decision Criteria in Portfolio Scoring:
Operational Definitions of Voting Criteria

Project Importance:

1. Strategic Importance
How well does the project fit the overall strategic direction? This is relative to the context, since certain goals and critical success factors have higher organizational impact.

9 = High	5 = Medium	1 = Low

2. Magnitude of Impact
Evaluate the project in terms of its impact on the organization. Major areas are customer, profitability, revenue, and productivity.

9 = High	5 = Medium	1 = Low

3. Economic Benefits
Assess a subjective rating based on total project costs to completion and perceived benefit, such as dollar savings, revenue growth, and business effectiveness.

9 = High	5 = Medium	1 = Low

Ease of Doing:

1. Cost of Doing
Evaluate the relative difficulty of funding the project in the current period.

9 = High (over $2MM)	5 = Medium ($250M–$2MM)	1 = Low (under $250M)

2. Project Complexity
Assess the degree of difficulty for design, development, implementation, and rollout.

9 = High	5 = Medium	1 = Low

3. Resource Availability
Skilled resources are critical to successful project implementation.

9 = None	5 = Partial	1 = Available

Exhibit 2.9   The Royal Bank of Canada

list goes on for several pages, with the cumulative amount becoming larger and larger; when the *cumulative amount* equals the *annual budget,* a line is drawn under that project. For this first pass, those projects *above the line* are tentatively "Go" projects; those below it are not, and are tentatively placed on hold.

Additionally, projects are also displayed on an *x–y* bubble diagram, where the two axes are ease and importance (see Chapter 3). Depending on which of the four quadrants each project is located in, different decisions and routings are decided (more on this in the next chapter).

A second meeting takes place, where managers reconsider the list of projects, particularly those projects close to the line or those that fall below the line yet might be important ones. Based on management judgment and experience, marginal and other projects can be shifted one way or the other. Also available at this

Rank Order	Project Name	Project Score (%)	Development Cost (S&T* dollars 000) (annual)	Cumulative Development Cost (000)
1.	RBCash	83	2,400	2,400
2.	CashCore	76	1,920	4,320
3.	EBX	76	1,800	6,120
4.	EBY	73	500	6,620
5.	BuyAct	73	6,000	12,620
6.	CorpPay	70	2,000	14,620
7.	Project A-PC	70	1,600	16,220
8.	PC-MD	68	7,500	23,710
.	.	.	.	.
.	.	.	.	.
.	.	.	.	.
26.	**Tiered/Interest Accounts**	**55**	**930**	**90,150****
27	Tiered	52	1,000	
28	Trade-AP	52	1,200	
29	ATM-Y	50	500	
.	.	.	.	.
.	.	.	.	.
.	.	.	.	.

Exhibit 2.10   The Royal Bank of Canada—Prioritized List of Projects

Note: The numbers and names of projects have been disguised.

*S&T: systems and technology, analogous to R&D.

**Budget is $90 million; project 26 takes the portfolio slightly over budget. A line is drawn after project 26.

meeting is a breakdown of the funded projects by product group, along with the total expected expenditure per group. This breakdown, together with the strategic role and mission of each group, is used to spot inconsistencies in resource allocation. For example, if a small business, whose mission is to "maintain and defend," was to receive a high proportion of funded projects and a significant percentage of the total development resources on this first pass, a flag is raised. This product group's projects are then reassessed. Ultimately, and after considerable discussion, the final and prioritized list of projects is agreed to.

Alternate Approaches to Obtaining Scoring Model Data

In an attempt to overcome the time inefficiencies of scoring right at the gate or portfolio meetings, some companies prescore projects. Neither method we outline below is strongly recommended, but we offer them as options.

Prescoring by gatekeepers: Project scores are generated before the review meeting even begins by management at National Sea Products, a major producer and marketer of branded seafood products. National Sea has a Stage-Gate new product process. At each gate or Go/Kill decision point, senior management (the gatekeepers) receive the deliverables on the project several days ahead. Each gatekeeper reviews the facts, and independently of others, *scores the project on 30 criteria several days before the meeting.* These criteria cover topics such as competitive advantage, market attractiveness, leveraging core competencies, and so on, and are scored on 0–10 scales. Additionally, each question or criterion calls for a confidence estimate—how sure evaluators are about their score on that question (again, 0–10).

The scorecards from this advance scoring are fed to the new product process manager, who integrates and analyzes them via a software package. By the time the gatekeepers arrive at the gate review meeting, a summary table of all their scores, confidences, and areas of disagreement is on the table, awaiting discussion.

One of the executives at National Sea did express some concerns about the technique, however: "The method is extremely efficient and cuts to the chase— we don't waste a lot of time discussing things we already agree on. The trouble is, it's almost too efficient. . . . The decision is almost made before the meeting starts. We miss the benefit of walking through each criterion, discussing it, and reaching a consensus based on that discussion."

Note that unlike RBC, but like Hoechst, National Sea uses these gate scores not only to make Go/Kill decisions at gates, but also to rate and rank projects against each other in periodic portfolio review meetings. This is a positive feature.

Prescoring by the project team: In yet another approach, the *project team itself* is asked to do the scoring of the project in advance of the project review meeting. The team then presents their scores to the senior management at the gate review, who either accept or refute the scores. Only a minority of firms have adopted this approach, their argument being that the project team is in a much better position to do the scoring than are senior people and that the gate decision process is more time-efficient. The counterargument (and majority view) is that the project team is not sufficiently objective to undertake the scoring (the "fox in the hen-house"); that they have a vested interest in seeing the project move ahead; and that senior management is not afforded the opportunity to walk through each criterion in depth: discussion and debate are shut down.

Assessment of Scoring Models

Are scoring model methods effective as portfolio management models? Scoring models are certainly popular: many firms use them at project gate meetings, and some at portfolio reviews. There are still some concerns voiced by senior people at Hoechst, Royal Bank, and other firms, however; and all confess that some "rough edges" have yet to be ironed out. But overall, users appear to be satisfied with the process and the apparent rigor of their decisions.

POINTS FOR MANAGEMENT TO PONDER

How are opinions of senior people and key decision-makers in your business captured in order to make project decisions? Is there any rigor to the way you solicit these "data" and incorporate them into a Go/Kill or prioritization decision? Or is the project review just a meeting of senior people with a rambling agenda?

If you adopt a scoring model approach, we recommend the following:

- The gatekeepers or senior people must do the scoring. Having the project team do the scoring introduces significant biases into the evaluation.
- The scoring should be done at the gate review meeting. A major payoff from using a scoring model is the *process itself*, namely, that senior managers review the project together, discuss each criterion, score the project on each, and reach a consensus.
- Use a scorecard at the meeting, where the decision-makers can record their scores for each question. Two companies we encountered—one in North America, the other in Sweden—use electronic voting machines in the meeting room: each decision-maker has a numerical keypad, and his or her answers are recorded instantly, fed into a computer, and the results displayed on a large projector screen.

Scoring models' major strengths are as follows:

- They do not place too heavy an emphasis on financial criteria, whose reliability is doubtful at the early stages of a project. Note that in Hoechst's 19-question model, *only two questions* deal with financial issues (see Exhibit 2.8).
- Scoring models capture multiple goals, such as strategic importance, competitive advantage, and market attractiveness.
- They reduce the complex problem of making Go/Kill and prioritization decisions to a manageable number of specific questions.
- Each project is subjected to assessment on a complete set of criteria, ensuring that critical issues are not overlooked (as so often happens in unstructured meetings).
- The method forces managers to consider projects in greater depth and provides a forum for discussion.
- Scoring models recognize that some questions are more important than others (via weights).
- They yield a single score, which is a useful input into a project prioritization exercise.

Perhaps most important, scoring models *seem to work:* that is, they yield *good decisions!* Witness the 85% predicative ability claimed by P&G using their computer-based scoring model and the Dutch study's results.[9,10] Further, an investigation of 26 project selection techniques, including scoring models and financial approaches, revealed that scoring models were rated best by managers in terms of cost and ease of use and that they were deemed "highly suitable for preliminary decisions" in the earlier phases of a project—namely, where the key selection and portfolio decisions are made.[11]

POINTS FOR MANAGEMENT TO PONDER

Scoring models are generally applauded by their users. We recommend that you take a close look at them if you're serious about getting better project prioritization decisions. Their big advantage is that they consider multiple goals and enable an escape from a preoccupation with financial data and ratios. The concern voiced about the financial methods—that financial models and ratios do a disservice to breakthrough projects—is a universal concern.

Scoring models work: they yield good decisions. And they provide an excellent agenda for discussion: the process of walking a group of senior people through the important project criteria is a positive facet. The major drawback is that scoring models are more time-consuming. If the decisions are important ones, however, maybe the extra time should be spent by senior management!

Managers did express some major concerns about using scoring models as prioritization methods, however:

1. *Imaginary precision:* While useful, a scoring model should not be overused nor its results necessarily believed. Certain senior people are concerned that using a scoring model imputed a degree of precision that simply did not exist. As one executive at Hoechst exclaimed: "They're trying to measure a [soft] banana with a micrometer!" Within the gate meetings themselves, there was also evidence of this imaginary precision. For example, one project with a score of 49.7% (a fraction below the hurdle of 50%) was allowed to pass while another with a score of 48.3% was killed. Missing the hurdle by 1.7% was enough to do the project in!

2. *Halo effect:* This is a concern at the Royal Bank of Canada, which over the years has whittled the list of scoring criteria down to six (see Exhibit 2.9). Why? Management argues that if a project scores high on one criterion, it tends to score high on many of the rest—a halo effect. RBC had started out with a list in excess of 15 criteria, but, via statistical analysis,* showed that this many criteria could be boiled down to a handful of key factors. Management in other firms did not share this view, however: numerous firms use scoring models, and the scores across criteria for the most part are thought to capture quite different facets of a project (no halo effect).

3. *Efficiency of allocation of scarce resources:* A final concern is that a missing ingredient in both Hoechst's and RBC's scoring model approaches is to ensure that the resulting list of "Go" projects indeed achieve the highest possible scores for a given total R&D expenditure. Recall that English China Clay in the ECV approach divided the parameter they were trying to maximize (the project's ECV) by the constraining resource in order to maximize "bang for buck." So did the PI method. The two scoring models shown here fail to do this. For example, one artefact

---

*RBC used correlational and factor analysis to reveal that the many scoring criteria they initially used were highly intercorrelated and could be greatly reduced to a subset of scoring factors.

of some firms' scoring methods is that much larger projects tend to rise to the top of the list; however, if the ranking criterion had been "Project Score/R&D Spend" instead of just "Project Score," then some smaller but efficient projects, requiring much fewer R&D resources, would have risen to the top.

Checklists as Portfolio Tools

Some firms use checklists instead of scoring models at their gate review or Go/Kill meetings. A good example of a checklist is shown in Exhibit 2.11 (from Milltronics Inc., a midsize and leading-edge producer of level-measuring instruments in the process industries). The main difference between scoring models and checklists is that, while the questions are similar, the scoring procedure and end result are quite different. In a checklist method, the answers are Yes/No. A single "No" answer is a knockout: it kills the project.

Exhibit 2.11   A Typical Checklist of Must-Meet Criteria (from Milltronics Inc.)

The following items are Yes/No. A "No" is a "kill."

√ *Strategic Fit:* The proposed project is aligned with the company's strategy and vision.

√ *Technical Feasibility:* There exists a reasonable likelihood of technical feasibility—that we can develop and manufacture the product—in light of the magnitude of the payoffs (no obvious reasons why it cannot be done).

√ *Competitive Rationale:* A competitive reason exists to undertake the project: either it is a necessary defensive or strategic product, or the product likely has significant competitive advantage (for example, is a unique, superior product; better value for money; and so on).

√ *Market Attractiveness:* The market is large and growing; the need for the product is significant; competition is vulnerable.

√ *Sustainable Competitive Advantage:* The product has a protectable advantage or raises barriers to entry to competitors.

√ *Synergies:* The project leverages (or builds from) our core competencies or strengths (marketing, technical, manufacturing).

√ *Commercial Attractiveness:* Given the market size, units, and price projections, there is a strong likelihood that we could make adequate profits here.

√ *Showstoppers:* There are no evident showstoppers or potential "killer variables" at this point.

POINTS FOR MANAGEMENT TO PONDER

If you are using a checklist method to make Go/Kill decisions on projects, that's fine. Many companies do. It won't be of value in project prioritization, however.

Suggestion: Use a checklist method as a culling tool at project review or gate meetings—to discard the obvious misfit projects; then a scoring model to rank and prioritize projects.

Checklists prove most effective at project review meetings as a culling tool—to weed out poor projects. But they are not useful for project prioritization, since there is no 0–100 total project score that facilitates rank-ordering projects.

Paired Comparisons

One method encountered infrequently is the paired comparison approach. This method might be useful, particularly at the very beginning of projects (idea stage), when almost no information is available.

In this approach, managers compare a pair of project ideas against each other, one pair at a time. Here the question is: "If you had a choice, which of the two projects would you do?" There is discussion, and a consensus vote is reached on each pair. Projects are then rank-ordered according to the number of times they receive a "Yes" vote in each paired comparison.

Example: One SBU within Telenor employed this method with mixed results. The business team regularly reviewed project ideas via paired comparisons, ranked the projects, and made Go/Kill decisions. While the method may have given good choices and yielded management consensus, it was criticized by those outside this team as being "soft, unstructured, political, emotional, and lacking rigorous criteria."

The method can also require considerable time. For example, if 10 ideas are considered, then a total of 45 paired comparison choices must be made!

Value Maximization Methods: Summing Up

Four very useful value maximization methods have been outlined in this chapter:

1. Expected Commercial Value: a financial method based on a decision tree, incorporating probabilities and resource constraints
2. Productivity Index: a financial ranking approach using expected commercial value, technical risk, and R&D expenditures
3. Dynamic Rank-Ordered List: a ranking technique that combines several criteria—NPV, IRR, and strategic importance—and ranks projects concurrently on each
4. Scoring model: a scoring technique that considers multiple criteria and combines ratings on these in a weighted fashion to yield an overall or project score

Two other methods—checklists and paired comparisons—were also outlined, but have limited use as portfolio tools.

The four main models have much to commend them. Specific weaknesses and problems—quantity of data required, reliability of data, dealing with multiple objectives, imaginary precision, and halo effects—have been outlined throughout the chapter. As a group, their greatest weakness is that they fail to ensure that the portfolio is on-strategy* or strategically aligned, or that it is even reasonably balanced. For example, the resulting list of projects from any of the methods in this chapter could maximize profits or some project score, but be a very unbalanced list of projects (for example, too many short-term ones) or fail to mirror the strategic direction of the business. These goals—balance and strategic alignment— are highlighted in the next two chapters.

In spite of these weaknesses, maximization of the portfolio's value is still a very worthwhile objective. We can argue about balance all we want and philosophize about the strategic direction of a portfolio, but if the projects in the portfolio are poor ones—poor profitability, low likelihoods of success, or poor attractiveness scores—then the rest of the portfolio exercise is rather academic. First and foremost, the portfolio must contain "good" projects, and that is where the maximization methods outlined in this chapter excel. You cannot ignore these methods. They must be part of your repertoire of portfolio models.

---

*Although as we shall see in Chapter 4, some firms have modified their scoring models to deal in part with the on-strategy issue.

CHAPTER 3

Portfolio Management Methods: A Balanced Portfolio

The second major goal of many firms is the desire to obtain a *balanced portfolio* of new product projects. The means to achieving this balance vary widely, however, from company to company, and as a result, many different and ingenious approaches were witnessed. In this chapter we explore the many portfolio management methods that can be used to reach the goal of a balanced portfolio of new product projects, and we provide some insights into the pros and cons of these methods.

Goal 2: Achieving a Balanced Portfolio

What is a balanced portfolio? It is a balanced set of development projects in terms of a number of key parameters. The analogy is that of an investment fund, where the fund manager seeks balance in terms of high-risk versus blue chip stocks, domestic versus foreign investments, and balance across industries in order to arrive at an optimally diversified investment portfolio. Note that one way of managing risk is through diversity of investments.

Visual charts are the most popular way to display balance in new product portfolios. These charts are favored for their ability to visually display the balance of projects in the portfolio, something that the ranked-ordered lists, financial methods, and scoring models in Chapter 2 fail to do. These visual representations include the popular portfolio maps or *bubble diagrams,* adaptations of the four-quadrant BCG and GE/McKinsey business strategy models. (The latter are the familiar star, cash cow, dog, wildcat models that have seen service as strategy models since the 70s.) We call these portfolio maps "bubble diagrams"—the description that most people are familiar with—simply because projects are shown as balloons or bubbles. Additionally, visual chart portfolio tools also include traditional histograms, bar charts, and pie charts.

Bubble Diagrams

A casual review of portfolio bubble diagrams will lead some to observe that these new models are nothing more than the old strategy bubble diagrams of the 70s.

Not so. Recall that the BCG strategy model, and others like it (such as the GE and McKinsey models), plotted SBUs on a *market attractiveness* versus *business position* grid. Note that the unit of analysis is the SBU, an existing business—*what is*—whose performance, strengths, and weaknesses are all known. By contrast, today's new product portfolio bubble diagrams, while they may appear similar, plot individual *new product projects*—future businesses or *what might be.* As for the dimensions of the grid, the "market attractiveness versus business position" dimensions used for existing SBUs may not be as appropriate for new product possibilities; so we saw other dimensions or axes extensively used.

What Dimensions to Consider?

What are some of the parameters that companies plot on these bubble diagrams to seek balance? Pundits recommend various parameters and lists, and even suggest the "best plots" to use. Here is a sample list of possible parameters to consider; any pair can be the *x* and *y* axes for a bubble plot:

- fit with business or corporate strategy (low, medium, high)
- inventive merit and strategic importance to the business (low, medium, high)
- durability of the competitive advantage (short-term, medium, long-term)
- reward based on financial expectations (modest to excellent)
- competitive impact of technologies (base, key, pacing, and embryonic technologies)
- probabilities of success (technical success and commercial success as percentages)
- R&D costs to completion (dollars)
- time to completion (years)
- capital and marketing investment required to exploit (dollars).[1]

Other useful descriptors we found in bubble diagrams that help characterize the portfolio and portray balance are:

- markets or market segments (market A, market B, etc.)
- product categories or product lines (product line C, product line D, etc.)
- project types (new products; product improvements; extensions and enhancements; maintenance and fixes; cost reductions; and fundamental research)
- technology or platform types (technology X, technology Y, etc.)

POINTS FOR MANAGEMENT TO PONDER

Have you considered what the *right balance of projects* for your new product portfolio is? Many managers had not. In fact, *they could not even tell us the current situation—* the current breakdown of either projects or spending: for example, what percent of funding was going to new products versus maintenance work versus fundamental research; or the R&D spending breakdown across markets or technologies? Perhaps the place to begin is with an assessment of the current situation: Where is the money being spent *now?*

Risk–Reward Bubble Diagrams

Perhaps the most popular bubble diagram is a variant of the risk–return diagram; two versions are proposed by two consulting firms. Here one axis is some measure of the reward to the company, the other is the probability of success—thus, *risk* and *reward.*

▶ Some firms use a *qualitative estimate* of reward, ranging from "modest" to "excellent." Management points out that too heavy an emphasis on financial analysis can do serious damage, notably in the early stages of a project. The other axis is the probability of overall success (probability of *commercial* success times probability of *technical* success). This is the view voiced by the consulting firm Arthur D. Little Inc. in their book, *Third Generation R&D.*[1]

▶ In contrast, other firms rely on quantitative and financial gauges of reward, namely, the risk-adjusted NPV* of the project. Here the probability of *technical* success is the vertical axis, as the probability of commercial success has already been built into the NPV calculation. Strategic Decision Group's method, for example, uses a quantitative, financial gauge of reward, namely, the shareholder value of the project.[2]**

A sample bubble diagram is shown in Exhibit 3.1 for a division of a major chemical company we label Company T. Note that NPV, adjusted for commercial risks, is the horizontal axis (reverse direction, from right to left) while the vertical axis is the probability of technical success. The size of each bubble shows the annual resources to be spent on each project. (In Company T's case, this is dollars per year. It could also be full-time equivalent people or work-months allocated to the project.)

The four quadrants of the bubble diagram model are as follows:

▶ *Pearls* (upper left quadrant): These are the potential star products—projects with a high likelihood of success—which are expected to yield very high rewards. Most firms wish they had more of these. Company T has two such Pearl projects, and one of them has been allocated considerable resources (denoted by the sizes of the circles).

▶ *Oysters* (lower left quadrant): These are the *long-shot* projects—projects with a high expected payoff, but with low likelihood of technical success. They are

*NPV: the net present value of the future stream of earnings (cash flow) from the project, less all development, capital, and launch costs. This is risk-adjusted as follows: by using a risk-adjusted discount rate; by applying probabilities to uncertain estimates in calculating the NPV; or by using Monte Carlo simulation to determine NPV. Later in this chapter, we outline options for incorporating uncertainty and probabilities into the determination of NPV and reward.

**Shareholder value is the expected commercial value multiplied by the probability of technical success, less expected remaining R&D investment (see Productivity Index, previous chapter). Uncertain commercial estimates—such as expected sales revenues—have probabilities built in; thus the commercial value has already been discounted for commercial uncertainty.

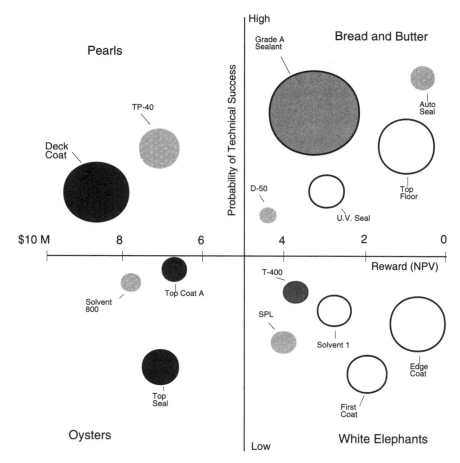

Exhibit 3.1   Risk–Reward Bubble Diagram for Company T: Chemical Company

Note: Size = resources (annual); color = timing (not shown); shading = product line.

Source: Adapted from Strategic Decisions Group model.[2]

the projects where technical breakthroughs will pave the way for solid pay-offs. Company T has three of these; none is receiving many resources.

▶ *Bread and Butter* (upper right quadrant): These are small, simple projects with a high likelihood of success, but low reward. They include the extensions, modifications, and updating of projects. Most companies have too many of these. Company T has a typical overabundance (note that the large circle here is actually a cluster of related product renewal projects). More than 50% of spending goes to these Bread and Butter projects in Company T's case.

▶ *White Elephants* (lower right quadrant): These are the low-success and low-reward projects. Every business has a few White Elephants, which inevitably are difficult to kill—projects that began life as good prospects, but over time, become less attractive. Company T has far too many. One-third of the projects and about 25% of Company T's spending fall in the White Elephant quadrant.

An attractive feature of a bubble diagram model is that it forces management to deal with the resource issue. The size of the circles denotes resource allocations per project, so that, given finite resources (for example, a limited number of people or money), *the sum of the areas of the circles must be a constant.* That is, if you add one project to the diagram, you must subtract another; alternatively, you can shrink the size of several circles. The elegance here is that the model forces management to consider the resource implications of adding one more project to the list—other projects must pay the price!

Also shown in this bubble diagram is the product line with which each project is associated (via the shading or cross-hatching). A final breakdown revealed by Company T via color is timing (although we could not show this in our black-and-white diagram). Hot red means "imminent launch" while blue is cold and means an early-stage project. Thus, this apparently simple risk–reward diagram shows much more than simply risk and profitability data. It also conveys resource allocation, timing, and allocations across product lines.

Using Risk–Reward Bubble Diagrams

How is the bubble diagram model used? Unlike the maximization models of Chapter 2, there is no prioritized list of projects produced. Bubble diagrams are very much an *information display* and not so much a *decision model* per se. Nonetheless certain quadrants have more preferred projects than others; and the balance across three of the better quadrants is also vital. From the example in Exhibit 3.1, management debates the appropriateness of the current portfolio and takes necessary action.

- To deal with the overabundance of White Elephants, the company initiated an immediate review of these five projects with the idea of pruning the list and reallocating resources to more deserving projects. Note that there were a number of fairly good projects on hold awaiting resources (these are not shown on the bubble diagram, but several companies we interviewed also produced bubble diagrams of the on-hold projects).
- Management felt that the three Oyster projects were about the right number, but decided to increase resources to move them along more quickly. Two in particular were being starved for resources.
- Projects in the upper right quadrant—the Bread and Butter ones, accounting for more than 50% of spending—were closely scrutinized. There was a general unease on the part of senior management about the high level of spending here (the business had been designated a "growth business"). There was also a concern about whether they were in danger of becoming "busy fools"—a lot of activity around a number of trivial projects. As a result, several projects were cancelled or postponed.
- Several projects in the hold vault were immediately activated (projects that had been placed on hold due to lack of resources—no people to work on them). People resources were made available by cutting back on the White Elephant and Bread and Butter projects.

Bubble diagrams find use in two settings. The first and most obvious is in portfolio review meetings, much like the situation described at Company T. Here the entire portfolio of projects is periodically reviewed (for example, semiannually or quarterly) and appropriate actions are taken, as described above. The second use of bubble diagrams—and indeed all the visual charts in this chapter—is at gate or project review meetings. One method is as follows:

▶ The one project under consideration is shown on a bubble diagram as a dotted circle (yet to be approved).
▶ The same bubble diagram displays the other projects currently underway—the active projects and current resource allocations.
▶ A second bubble diagram (optional) displays projects on hold and awaiting resources.

In this way, the project under consideration is compared to others in the queue as well as to active projects. Additionally, by showing the new project on the active bubble diagram, the impact that this new project has on the total portfolio—for example, what it would do to the balance or how it might fit into the portfolio—can be seen. Note that various software packages have been developed to assist in the construction of bubble diagrams.

Variants of Risk–Reward Bubble Diagrams

3M's Ellipses

3M's method is unique in that it visually portrays uncertainty and probabilities, which must be a key parameter in any portfolio decision. One problem with the standard risk–reward bubble diagrams shown so far (for example, Company T's in Exhibit 3.1) is that they require a point estimate of the reward, namely, the likely or probable NPV. In reality, there is a distribution or range of probable rewards or NPVs. Technical risks are captured by the vertical axis, namely, probability of technical success, but not so for the commercial risks. Even the estimate of technical success probabilities is problematic, because it may involve a range of estimates as well (for example, "the probability of technical success is in the 50 to 70% range").

Some business units at 3M use a variant of the bubble diagram that *portrays uncertainties via the size and shape of the bubbles.* In calculating the NPV, high and low estimates are made for uncertain variables. This leads to high- and low-case NPV estimates for each project. Similarly, high/low estimates are made for the probability of technical success. The result is shown in Exhibit 3.2. The size and shape of the bubbles or balloons on the portfolio map thus capture uncertainty or fuzziness of projects. Here, very small bubbles mean highly certain—very tight—estimates on each dimension. In contrast, large bubbles or ellipses mean fuzzy or loose projects with considerable uncertainty—a high spread between worst case and best case for that project.[3] Note: The size of the ellipse is such that there is an 80% probability that the value of the project falls within the ellipse.

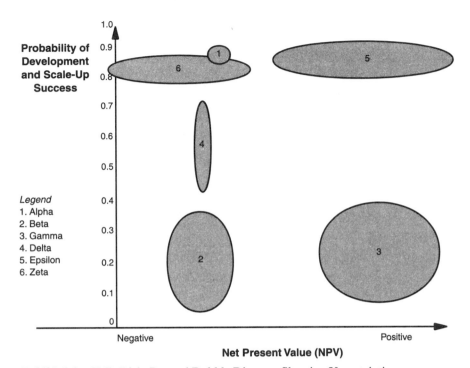

Exhibit 3.2   3M's Risk–Reward Bubble Diagram Showing Uncertainties

Note: Larger circles and ellipses denote more uncertain estimates.

Source: Adapted from "New Product Investment Portfolio" by Dr. Gary L. Tritle.[3]

Proctor & Gamble's Three-Dimensional Portfolio Model

Procter & Gamble is experimenting with a novel three-dimensional plot, made possible via computer-aided design (CAD) software. Our Exhibit 3.3, on two-dimensional paper, does not do the model justice! Here, time to market, NPV, and probability of commercial success are the three axes. The model can be rotated in three-dimensional space to provide various views. Considerable information is displayed in this type of model:

▶ The horizontal or *x*-axis is the *time to market,* with long times being less fa-vorable (here, time is viewed as a proxy for both uncertainty as well as for more distant economic returns).

▶ The vertical or *y*-axis is the *NPV.* This is calculated using a Monte Carlo probability model called "At Risk" (more on this later in the chapter). The I-beams in the vertical direction show the range of NPV values per project.

▶ The *z*-axis (into the page) is the *probability of commercial success.* This is derived from the NewProd model, tailored for P&G's use (described in Chapter 2).

▶ There are four possible shapes to each project, which capture the *degree of fit* the project has with the company's strengths: spheres are the best-fit projects; cubes are the worst-fit; cylinders and cones are somewhere in between.

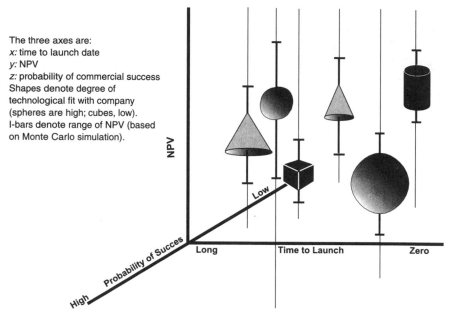

Exhibit 3.3 Procter & Gamble's Three-Dimensional Risk–Reward Bubble Diagram Using Nonfinancial Axes

Source: Developed by Tom Chorman, formerly Finance Manager, CNV, P&G.

The model also shows the ROI of each project (by clicking one's mouse on each shape); the color of the shapes shows what stage the project is in according the Product Launch Road Map (P&G's Stage-Gate model); and tracking of projects over time can be displayed via a "comet's tail" for each project (optional). Finally, because this is CAD software, any view from any direction, as well as zooming in or out, is possible. For example, the model can be rotated in three-dimensional space to give the decision-making audience different perspectives of their portfolio.

From a visual standpoint, this is the most sophisticated bubble diagram we encountered. It was also relatively inexpensive to develop via off-the-shelf CAD software. P&G's model demonstrates what a creative mind can do in terms of the elegance of the visuals and the ability to display more than the usual amount of information in a user-friendly fashion.

Capturing Reward via Nonfinancial Metrics

Some pundits argue that strict reliance on financial estimates can do considerable damage; that low-risk, simple, "low-hanging fruit" projects will be favored while strategically important or potential breakthrough projects will fare less well. Sometimes strategic issues and the quest for significant projects must take precedence over strictly financial and short-term return. Moreover, financial data are very often highly unreliable, especially in the predevelopment stages, where the portfolio is being decided. And portfolio models, where one axis is the NPV, assume a level of precision of financial data far beyond what most project teams can provide.

Arthur D. Little Inc.'s proposed alternative is to use a nonfinancial measure of reward: this is a subjective estimate ranging from "modest" to "excellent" and depends not only on the financial prospects for the project, but also its strategic importance and impact on the company. Conveniently, both probabilities—commercial success and technical success—are incorporated into the vertical axis, as shown in Exhibit 3.4.[1]

A Simpler Risk–Reward Portfolio Map

A somewhat simpler illustration of the risk–reward diagram is provided by Reckitt & Colman, as one of the many visual charts that comprise their portfolio model.

Example: Reckitt & Colman (R&C) is a major multinational producer of frequently purchased household consumer goods and pharmaceutical products.

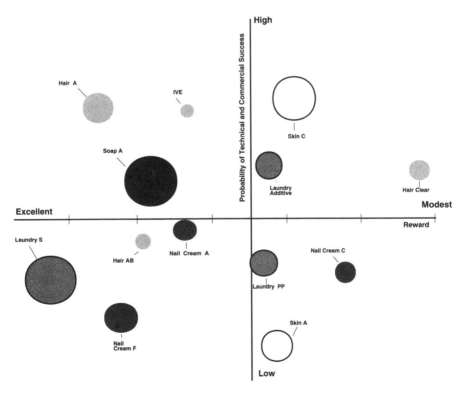

Exhibit 3.4   Risk–Reward Bubble Diagram Using Nonfinancial Axes

Note: Circle size = resources (annual); color = timing (not shown); shading = product line.

Source: Based on Arthur D. Little Inc. model.[1]

Headquartered in London, England, the firm distributes its products in most countries worldwide under a variety of brand names. In North America, familiar brands sold by R&C include Easy-Off oven cleaner, Air Wick air freshener, Lysol disinfectant cleaners, and Woolite fabric wash. R&C's worldwide sales revenues are in excess of $4 billion (U.S.).

Reckitt & Colman portrays the portfolio of projects on a less complex portfolio map diagram than Company T. Here the NPV is plotted against the overall probability of success, as shown in Exhibit 3.5. The various types of projects are also shown on the diagram: new business (new products in a new category), new products, and product improvements. Thus, two elements of balance are revealed in a single diagram: risk–reward and project type.

Here, the probability of overall success (horizontal axis) is simply the two probabilities—technical and commercial success—multiplied together. And the NPV considers only incremental sales (that is, cannibalized sales are subtracted).

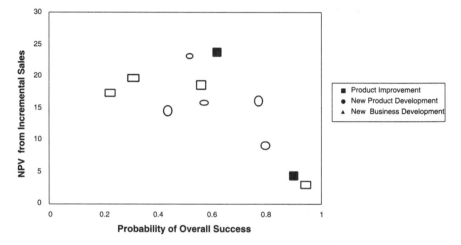

Exhibit 3.5   Reckitt & Colman—Probability of Success versus NPV

Note: This chart is an illustration of the type of additional information available at Portfolio Reviews at R&C. Probability of overall success = probability of technical success × probability of commercial success.

POINTS FOR MANAGEMENT TO PONDER

Do you consciously consider the *risk profile* of your business's new product portfolio via any of the popular bubble diagrams outlined above? If not, begin with one of the easier diagrams (Exhibit 3.1 or 3.5., for example); or, if you are more comfortable with a less financially driven approach, try using a qualitative assessment of reward (Exhibit 3.4), or better yet, a scoring approach (described below). The point is that these bubble diagrams are proving to be very useful, with the risk–reward diagram emerging as the most popular, and for good reason!

Portfolio Maps with Axes Derived from Scoring Models

Some companies combine the *benefits of a scoring model* with the *visual appeal of a bubble diagram.* Here the axes of the bubble diagram are computed or derived from scores on scaled questions (a scoring model); in some cases, the scoring results from the gate meetings are used as direct input into the portfolio model. Three firms we encountered use variants of this approach: Reckitt & Colman (above); the Royal Bank of Canada (Chapter 2); and Specialty Minerals, a spin-off company from Pfizer.

Specialty Minerals' Risk–Reward Scoring Method

A combined scoring model and bubble diagram is used by Specialty Minerals, and merits attention because it solves several problems encountered in bubble diagrams. Management at Specialty Minerals is very aware that overuse of financial criteria—for example, using NPV as one of the axes of the bubble diagram as in Exhibit 3.1—is problematic. They argue that reliable financial data are simply not available at the very point in a project's life when prioritization decisions are required. Similarly, arriving at quantitative estimates of probabilities of success was also proving difficult. Finally, management wanted a way to link the portfolio model to the gate decisions. Note that Specialty Minerals employs a Stage-Gate new product process, which relies on a scoring model at gates.

The solution adopted is to combine the gate scoring model with the portfolio bubble diagram. Here's how. Specialty Minerals' gate scoring model considers seven factors:

- management interest[*]
- customer interest
- sustainability of competitive advantage
- technical feasibility
- business case strength
- fit with core competencies
- profitability and impact.

These factors are scored at gates on 1–5 scales in order to make Go/Kill decisions on individual projects. Five of the seven factors are also used to construct a bubble diagram, with probability of success and reward as the two axes (see Exhibit 3.6): both axes are derived from the scores on the seven factors as follows:

Vertical axis: probability of success, consisting of a weighted combination of

- customer interest (0.25)
- technical feasibility (0.50)
- fit with core competencies (0.25).

Horizontal axis: value to the company, consisting of a weighted combination of

---

[*]Modified slightly from Specialty Minerals' exact list.

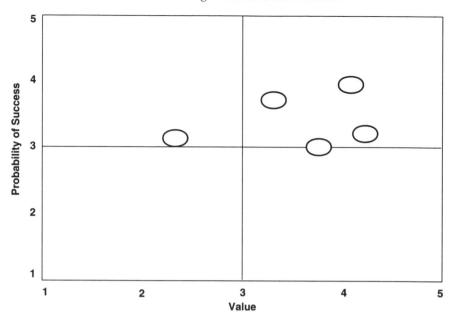

Exhibit 3.6 Specialty Minerals' Risk–Reward Bubble Diagram Using Scored Axes

Note: Based on gate 3 scoring results. Value = 0.66 (Profitability) + 0.34 (Competitive Advantage); Probability of Success = 0.25 (Customer Interest) + 0.5 (Technical Feasibility) + 0.25 (Fit).

- profitability (0.66)
- competitive advantage (0.34).

The numbers in parentheses are the weights used.

This company's seven-factor scoring model does double duty: it is the basis for Go/Kill decisions at gate reviews; it also provides five factors (and data) to construct the two axes of the portfolio bubble diagram. The gate decisions are thus closely linked to portfolio reviews. In adopting this hybrid method, and using the scores obtained at gate reviews to provide inputs to the bubble diagram, Specialty Minerals achieves two goals of portfolio management in one approach, namely, maximization of the portfolio (the gate scoring model) and appropriate balance in terms of risk and reward (the bubble diagram in Exhibit 3.6). The model has only been recently implemented, and time will tell whether it proves effective.

Ease versus Attractiveness

A very useful portfolio map at Reckitt & Colman, in management's view, is their ease versus attractiveness chart. As in Specialty Minerals' method, this bubble diagram also eliminates the heavy reliance on precise financial data yet incorporates factors that R&C management considers vital to project selection and portfolio balance.

Here the axes are market/concept attractiveness and ease of implementation (see Exhibit 3.7). Both axes in Exhibit 3.7 are constructed from a scoring model, namely, multi-item 1–5 scales, which are added in a weighted fashion.

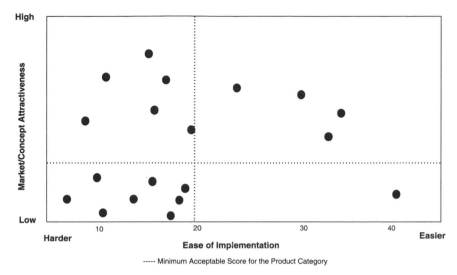

Exhibit 3.7   Reckitt & Colman—Market/Concept Attractiveness versus Ease of Implementation

Note: Both axes are based on a weighted addition of multiple items (much like a scoring model)—see Exhibit 3.8. Black circles represent new product projects.

Concept attractiveness is made up of scores on six items, including, for example, purchase intent, product advantage, sustainability of advantage, and international scope. Similarly, *ease of implementation,* the second axis, is comprised of scored items, such as the firm's technological strengths and the expected absence of problems in terms of development, registration, packaging, manufacturing, and distribution (see Exhibit 3.8 for the details of the scoring questions). Thus R&C uses a scoring model, but in this case to construct the axes of the two-dimensional portfolio bubble diagram.

A second and parallel bubble diagram plots market/concept attractiveness (defined in Exhibit 3.8) versus financial attractiveness (see bubble diagram in Exhibit 3.9). The latter axis is based on a NPV calculation.

Using the Ease versus Attractiveness Portfolio Map

R&C's portfolio maps are used much the same way that Company T uses its bubble diagram. Managers look for projects in favorable quadrants (toward the upper right of the diagram in Exhibit 3.7), scrutinize those in the "unattractive and hard-to-do" quadrant, and look for balance between ease and attractiveness. For example, in Exhibit 3.7:

- There is a surprising shortage of easy-to-do projects. This is a departure from the plethora of "low-hanging fruit" projects the company typically focused on only a few years ago. Perhaps the pendulum has swung too far the other way and a better balance should be sought between easy and challenging projects. Therefore, management should be looking for ways to increase the number of easier projects.

Items Comprising Market/Concept Attractiveness Score (Vertical Axis)		
Factor	**Weighting**	**Scale (1–5)**
Purchase Intent	5	1. Significantly below average. 2. Slightly below average. 3. Equal to average. 4. Slightly above average. 5. Significantly above average.
Advantage over What's Available	5	1. Significantly below average. 2. Slightly below average. 3. Equal to average. 4. Slightly above average. 5. Significantly above average.
Performance in Use	5	1. Little prospect of performance advantage. 2. Uncertain prospect of performance advantage. 3. Some prospects for slight advantage. 4. Some prospects for important product advantage. 5. Good prospects for important product advantage.
Competitive Position Improvement	2.5	1. Helps modernize brand, but doesn't enhance franchise long term. 2. Contributes to brand's strategic plan and helps make franchise contemporary. 3. Contributes to brand's strategic plan and keeps franchise contemporary. 4. Builds brand and franchise long-term. 5. Significantly builds brand and franchise long term.
Sustainability of Competitive Advantage	2.5	1. < 6 months 2. 6–12 months 3. 1–2 years 4. 2–5 years 5. > 6 years
Geographic Scope*	2.5	1. Local project—developed market. 2. Local project—developing market. 3. Regional project—developed market. 4. Regional project—developing market. 5. Multiregional project.

Note: The market attractiveness of a project is the weighted summation of scores on the items above.

*R&C divided the world into regions: Europe, North America, Central/South America, Pacific, and so on. A "regional project" accommodates multiple countries (for example, Europe). A "local" project is one country.

Exhibit 3.8   Reckitt & Colman—Definitions of Market/Concept Attractiveness and Ease of Implementation

Items Comprising Ease of Implementation Score (Horizontal Axis)		
Factor	**Weighting**	**Scale (1–5)**
Technical Competitive Strength	4.5	1. Weak 2. Tenable 3. Favorable 4. Strong 5. Dominant
Technical Maturity	9	1. Embryonic 2. Growth 3. Mature 4. Aging
Registration/Clinical Trial	4.5	1. Major problems are anticipated in most markets. 2. Major problems are anticipated in some markets. 3. Minor problems are anticipated. 4. No problems are anticipated. 5. No registration or clinical trial required.
Packaging Components	3	1. Needs basic advances in packaging technology. 2. Several new components need development. 3. A new component needs development. 4. Needs modifications to existing components. 5. Uses existing components.
Manufacture	3	1. Needs basic advances in manufacturing technology. 2. Needs new manufacturing equipment (> £100,000). 3. Needs major modifications (< £100,000) or use of co-packer. 4. Needs minor modifications (< £25,000) 5. Uses existing manufacturing equipment.
Sales and Distribution	3	1. New sales/buyer skills needed in new distribution channel. 2. Existing sales skills in new distribution channel. 3. New skills required by both salespeople and buyers. 4. Some new skills required. 5. No change necessary to exist-ing sales effort.

Note: The ease of implementation of a project is the weighted summation of scores on the items above.

Exhibit 3.8　　(*continued*)

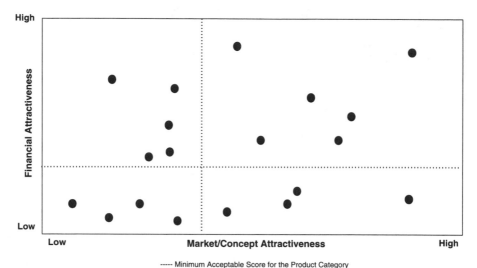

----- Minimum Acceptable Score for the Product Category

Exhibit 3.9 Reckitt & Colman—Financial Attractiveness versus Market/Concept Attractiveness

- There are clearly too few projects in the desirable upper right quadrant. One outcome of this analysis is recognition of the need for increased focus on idea/concept generation and the need to move more concepts through the early phase screening. Further, while resource allocations are not shown on the diagram, clearly resource commitments for the three potential stars is an issue.
- With eight projects out of 19 in the lower left quadrant (more difficult and less attractive), management must ask some very tough questions: Why are there so many projects here? Which ones should be cancelled? What is the rationale for each? (Perhaps there are strategic, competitive, or defensive reasons for doing these.) How much are we spending this year on projects in this quadrant? (Perhaps management can postpone a few to reduce resource commitment here.) Can some of the better ones be made more attractive or easier to do by changing the definition, scope, resource commitment, or plan of action?
- Six projects are in the attractive but hard-to-do quadrant. Again, vital questions about these six must focus on ways to improve their ease of implementation. For example, by increasing resource commitments, can some of the technical, manufacturing, and packaging barriers be overcome?

Importance versus Ease

The Royal Bank of Canada uses a variation of the ease versus attractiveness bubble diagram witnessed at Reckitt & Colman. Indeed, RBC's portfolio method has seen considerable evolution over the past four years as the bank has gained experience with it.

Initially, a standard financially based bubble diagram was used, whereby NPV and probability of success were plotted (much like Exhibit 3.1). Project teams provided the data necessary to do the NPV calculation, and the probability of commercial success was derived from a tailored version of the NewProd model (Chapter 2), with the project teams again providing the input data. Unfortunately, the method led to self-serving data inputs from the team: teams soon realized what the data were being used for, and started to slant the input data to favor their own projects.

The current bubble diagram features two dimensions or factors, which are comprised of six scored scales (see Exhibit 2.9). The resulting bubble diagram is very similar to R&C's in Exhibit 3.7, except that circle sizes represent the current year funding for each project (see Exhibit 3.10).

RBC has also developed decision rules for projects in each of the four quadrants in Exhibit 3.10. For example, for the "easy and important" projects (upper left quadrant), the resources are budgeted for full development; for "less important and hard" projects, the decision rule is "NO GO—do not resource." Exhibit 3.11 shows these rules.

A subtle but important difference between Royal Bank's method and the methods used at both R&C and Specialty Minerals is that RBC management *rescores all projects* at the portfolio review meeting to generate the risk–reward bubble diagram. Note that both R&C and Specialty Minerals use the gate scores (updated as needed) as input to their portfolio bubble diagrams. By contrast, even though RBC does use a detailed scoring model at gate decision points, management nonetheless reevaluates all projects on the six scales at the portfolio review. The reasons for this are as follows:

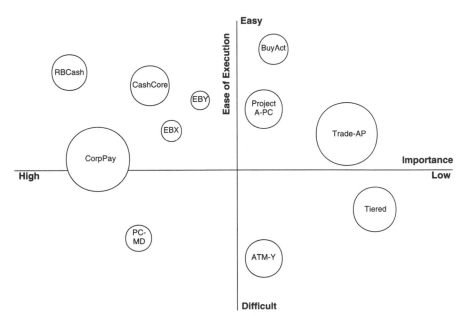

Exhibit 3.10   Royal Bank's Portfolio Map of Ease versus Project Importance

Note: Ease and importance are scored axes—see Exhibit 2.9 for criteria. Circle sizes show current annual funding per project.

	10	
Easy and Important GATE 1 "GO" (Budget resources for full development)		**Important But Difficult** GATE 1 "GO" (Use full resources and budget a research team)

0 Difficulty ➡   10

Easy But Less Important GATE 1 "HOLD" (Do not budget resources, but "cherry pick" from list of projects to fill holes in actual resource usage)		**Less Important and Hard** GATE 1 "NO GO" (Do not resource)

0 Importance

Exhibit 3.11   Royal Bank's Decision Rules

▶ At gate meetings, projects are scored independently of each other and by different groups of gatekeepers; at portfolio reviews, there is a single group of decision-makers and also the opportunity for comparative scoring— viewing projects against each other. Thus the scoring is a little more discriminating and potentially more consistent.

▶ It may have been several months since the previous gate meeting, and hence new information is available on a given project. Further, there are some totally new project proposals—ideas—which have not yet been scored at a gate.

The disadvantage, of course, is that relatively little time can be spent discussing and rating each project at the portfolio review (100 projects in one day!) and the process is quite time-consuming.

POINTS FOR MANAGEMENT TO PONDER

If too heavy a reliance on financial data and financial metrics is a concern, or if multiple objectives beyond strictly financial ones is the goal, consider building a risk–reward bubble diagram whose axes are based on scored criteria, as in the three companies above. If feasible, you might even use some of the same scoring criteria here that you use in your gate scoring model; in fact, we'd suggest that you even *use project scores from gates directly as inputs* to your risk–reward bubble diagram.

Factoring Risk and Uncertainty into the Reward Calculation

Frequently, in the companies we studied, the *reward of the project* is captured on the portfolio map or bubble diagram by the NPV. In the examples above, P&G,

Company T, 3M, and Reckitt & Colman all use NPV in their bubble diagrams, as was the case in many other firms we visited. The issue of how to calculate the NPV, given uncertain estimates, is a common concern, however. Different models and different firms treat risk in a variety of ways in this NPV calculation:

- *Build probabilities into the NPV calculation:* Company G, which uses the Dynamic Rank Ordered-List in Chapter 2, also displays portfolio maps similar to those in this chapter. This company simply factors down all uncertain estimates in the NPV calculation by their probability of occurring. For example, if projected revenues are uncertain, the finance department multiplies these by a probability of 0.80, or perhaps 0.60, to account for that uncertainty. Mathematically, this procedure is not strictly correct, but it does serve to dramatically scale back wildly optimistic financial projections.
- *Use risk-adjusted discount rates:* Company T uses variable discount rates when it calculates the NPV. In effect, these are risk-adjusted discount rates. For example, new product projects whose commercial projections are highly uncertain use a discount rate of *double the risk-free hurdle rate.* Low-risk projects, such as product modifications and renewals or process improvements, use a discount rate of 1.5 times the risk-free hurdle rate, and so on. What this procedure does is penalize higher-risk projects—their NPV is scaled back accordingly.
- *Use Monte Carlo simulation:* Company M, a medical products firm, uses a portfolio model similar to Company T's in Exhibit 3.1. The probability of technical success is taken into account on the vertical axis, but the probability of commercial success is not. To account for commercial uncertainty, every variable requires three estimates: high, low, and likely.* So, revenue, costs, launch timing, and so on each have three estimates provided by the project team. From these three estimates, a *probability distribution curve* is determined for each variable. Next, random scenarios are generated for the project using these probability curves as variable inputs. Thousands of scenarios are computer-generated (hence the name Monte Carlo—thousands of spins of the wheel), and the result is a distribution of financial outcomes. From this, the expected NPV is determined—an NPV figure with all commercial outcomes and their probabilities figured in. This is an interesting technique, and a mathematically elegant one. Management at Company M strongly endorses the rigorous method, but it is proving to be a significant burden to the project teams, who are asked to supply an endless stream of data! Moreover, private conversations with team members revealed that they simply did not have the data required, and that they were providing the "model owner" with nonsense data—largely invented numbers. Even with this fault, however, a number of other companies find the Monte Carlo approach useful (for example, Procter & Gamble, which employs a version of Monte Carlo simulation called "At Risk"; and Nova Chemicals in Canada).
- *Build a decision tree:* The Expected Commercial Value (ECV) method, used by ECC International, is based on a simple decision tree (see Chapter 2). It

---

*The 10%, 50%, and 90% points on the probability distribution curve.

appropriately incorporates the future stream of earnings, various capital and development costs incurred throughout the project, and the probabilities of technical and commercial success. The computation is relatively straightforward, and the ECV certainly can be used here in various bubble diagrams. Based on its success at ECC, we recommend considering the ECV method as one way to build risk into the NPV calculation.

- *Use high case/low case:* This method, used at 3M and described earlier in this chapter, captures uncertainties on both risk and reward dimensions of the bubble diagram by using "high" and "low" case scenarios. The size and shape of the bubbles or ellipses denote the uncertainty associated with each project (see Exhibit 3.2).
- *Employ nonfinancial measures of reward:* Recall that the ADL bubble diagram model (shown in Exhibit 3.4) relies on a nonfinancial measure of reward and hence does not use an NPV calculation per se. Realistically, however, the NPV is hard to ignore when assessing a project's potential reward to the company. The ADL method has one major advantage: the approach eliminates the need to build probabilities or uncertainties into the NPV reward calculation: the metric here is a simple "modest" to "excellent" scale. Note that both probabilities (commercial and technical success) are captured outside the reward metric: they are conveniently combined into an overall probability of success on the vertical axis of the bubble diagram (see Exhibit 3.4).
- *Use scoring methods of arriving at reward:* Using a scoring model to determine the reward metric also eliminates the need to handle uncertainty and probabilities in a financial calculation. Specialty Minerals' approach to deriving a reward measure from their gate scoring model was outlined earlier in this chapter. This method is that firm's way of coping with the uncertainty of financial estimates. You might also wish to review Hoechst-U.S.'s scoring method in Chapter 2: recall that this company uses a three-scale scoring model to determine reward (one of five factors considered).

POINTS FOR MANAGEMENT TO PONDER

How are *uncertainty* and *probabilities* built into your financial analysis calculations? Or perhaps you've chosen to use a nonfinancial metric to capture project reward. Whether you're determining an NPV or a reward estimate for use in a bubble diagram (above), or in a value maximization method (previous chapter), or simply calculating an NPV, IRR, or ROI for a project gate review, probabilities and uncertainty must be considered. The previous chapter showed how to apply rigor to the estimates of probabilities of success; in the section above, various options were presented on how to incorporate these probabilities into your financial analysis. The point is that you cannot ignore the *uncertainty aspect* of the determination of the expected reward. Review the methods cited above and decide on one!

Other Bubble Diagrams

There are numerous parameters, dimensions, or variables across which one might wish to seek a balance of projects. As a result, an endless variety of *x–y* plots or bubble diagrams is possible.

Market and Technology Risk

Should all projects be low-risk ones for the company? Exhibit 3.12 portrays projects in terms of both technology risk and market risk (used at Reckitt & Colman). Once again, a balance is sought.

A similar risk–risk bubble chart is generated and used at Rohm and Haas. Here the probability of technical success is plotted against the commercial probability (not shown). The bubble sizes denote the total cost of projects, so that resource allocation can be seen. Recall from Chapter 2 that Rohm and Haas uses a matrix approach to determining probabilities of success.

Market Segment versus Strategic Intent

One attempt to view the portfolio balance in terms of strategy was witnessed at Rohm and Haas. The next chapter deals with *strategic link* in detail, but because this chart is in the form of a bubble diagram, we show it here.

Projects are displayed on a bubble diagram (Exhibit 3.13) that has two dimensions:

- strategic intent: the purpose and type of project (defend, grow, new application, new business, fundamental research)
- market segment served

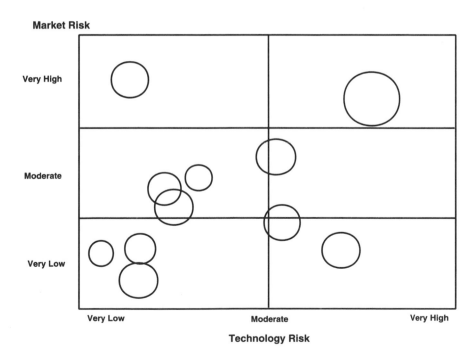

Exhibit 3.12   Market and Technology Risk Bubble Diagram

Note: Circle size = R&D resources to each project.

Market Segments

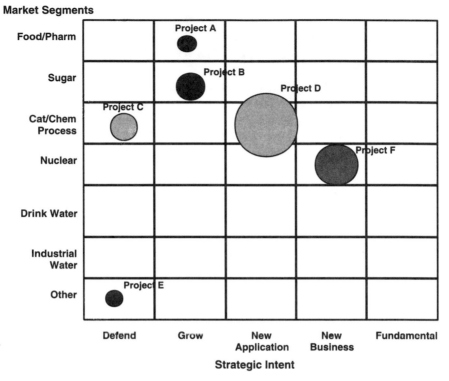

Exhibit 3.13   Rohm and Haas—Strategic Intent Bubble Diagram

Note: Circle size = total cost; different circle shading represents different product lines.

The bubble size is the total cost of the project.

Rohm and Haas has done much work to develop custom software for portfolio management. Each business has a portfolio manager, who is also the manager of the business's new product Stage-Gate process. Using this software, these portfolio managers are able to display virtually any plot of any variable they wish in bubble diagram format.

Traditional Charts for Portfolio Management

Our investigation also uncovered a countless array of traditional histograms, bar charts, and pie charts, which help portray portfolio balance. Indeed, there are many parameters and characteristics across which you might wish to consider portfolio balance. Some examples follow.

Capacity Utilization

What proportion of allocated or budgeted resources are projects actually using? Often there are gaps between actual and proposed spending. The bar chart in

Exhibit 3.14 shows an example. This is a useful chart when discussing the resource allocation issue in a portfolio review.

Project Timing

Timing is a key issue in the quest for portfolio balance. One does not wish to invest strictly in short-term or long-term projects. Another timing goal is for a steady stream of new product launches spread out over the years—constant "new news" with no sudden logjam of product launches all in one year. The histogram in Exhibit 3.15 captures the issue of timing and portrays the distribution of resources to specific projects according to years of launch. For example, for Company T, 35% of resources are allocated to four projects—all due to be launched within the year (year 1). Another 30% of resources are being spent on four projects whose projected launch date is the following year (year 2), and so on.

Another timing issue is cash flow. Here the desire is to balance projects in such a way that cash inflows are reasonably balanced with cash outflows. For example, one might wish to avoid the situation where, when all projects are considered together, there are huge cash outflows in one year and huge cash inflows several years later. Reckitt & Colman thus produces a histogram that captures the total cash flow per year for all projects in the portfolio (Exhibit 3.16). This histogram also reveals cash flows by project type.

Project Types

Project types is yet another vital concern. What is the spending on genuine new products versus updates versus fundamental research? And what should it be? Pie

Project Name

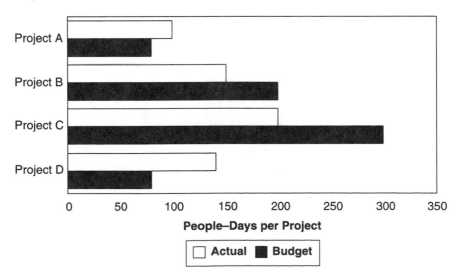

Exhibit 3.14 Capacity Utilization

% of Resources (this year)

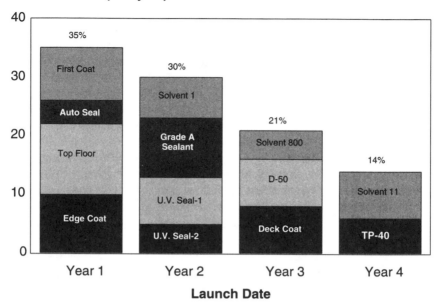

Exhibit 3.15   Timing of Product Launches

Note: Shading = product line.

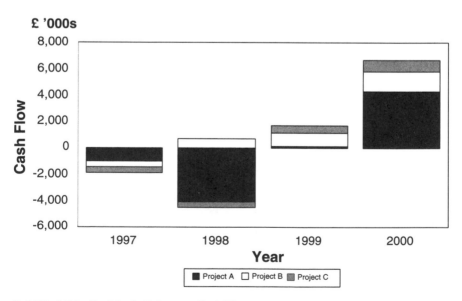

Exhibit 3.16   Reckitt & Colman—Cash Flow versus Time

Note: This chart is an illustration of the type of additional information available. Numbers have been disguised for each year.

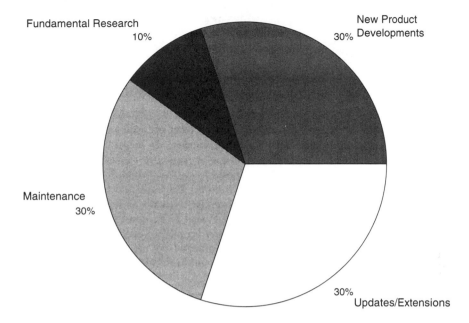

Exhibit 3.17 Spending Allocation across Project Types

or similar type charts, which capture the spending split across project types, were found in just about every company we studied. Exhibit 3.17 provides an illustration.

Markets, Products, and Technologies

Another set of dimensions across which managers seek balance is product, market, and technology type. Exhibit 3.18 provides a sample visual breakdown using pie charts that demonstrates how a specialty chemical company allocates funding across product lines and markets. The question is: Do you have the appropriate

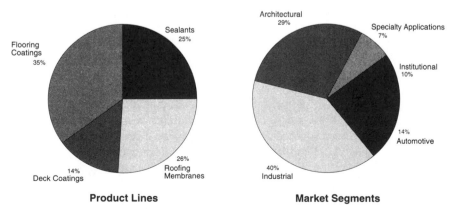

Exhibit 3.18 Breakdown of Resources by Product Lines and Markets

split in R&D spending across your various product lines? Or across the markets or market segments in which you compete? Or across the technologies you possess? Pie charts are an excellent approach for capturing and displaying this type of data.

POINTS FOR MANAGEMENT TO PONDER

Some of the pie and bar charts and histograms presented above (Exhibits 3.14–3.18) are commonsense ways of viewing a portfolio and the types of breakdowns one ought to consider. Does your business produce these charts and review them? If not, start with a few simple breakdowns. We suggest breakdowns by market or market segment and by product line (as shown in Exhibit 3.18); by project type (see Exhibit 3.17); and perhaps by timing (as in Exhibit 3.15). Gather data from project teams in order to develop a *breakdown of current annual spending*. This exercise is usually an eye-opener, and you may receive some unpleasant surprises! Then arrive at a consensus with the leadership team of your business on what the ideal or *target breakdown* ought to be. Remember: resource allocation for new products is a fundamental business issue; therefore, the leadership team of the business, at minimum, ought to decide appropriate targets for spending breakdowns.

Balance: Some Critical Comments

There is more to life than simply striving for a high-value portfolio; balance is also a critical issue. The trouble is that achieving balance—or selecting an appropriate tool to help achieve balance—is easier conceptually than in practice.

What impressed us was how many intricate and ingenious methods and diagrams companies had invented to deal with this balance issue. We could have filled an entire book with the maps, bubble diagrams, and pie charts we discovered in our study. However, there remain problems with the quest for balance:

1. First, some of the more popular bubble diagrams suffer the same fate as the maximization models outlined in Chapter 2: they rely on substantial financial data, which are often unavailable or, at best, highly uncertain. Witness the popular risk–reward bubble diagrams (Exhibits 3.1, 3.2, 3.3, and 3.5) where NPV is one of the axes.
2. Second, there is the issue of information overload. "Maps, endless maps!" was the complaint of one exasperated executive, as he leafed through more than a dozen maps plotting everything versus everything in his firm's portfolio model. Note that very few companies had even attempted to use all the maps and charts recommended by the various pundits. Further, many firms had begun portfolio management with a number of maps, which over the months, had been whittled down to the two or three deemed most important.
3. Third, these visual and balance models are information display, not decision models per se. Unlike the value maximization methods of Chapter 2, the result is not a convenient rank-ordered list of preferred projects. Rather, these charts and maps are a starting point for discussion only. Management still has to translate these data into actionable decisions. Some had failed here. Too many maps, or the wrong maps, may have contributed.

4. Next, it wasn't clear in all cases how the charts and maps are actually used. At Reckitt & Colman, the initial inclination was to make these part of gate meetings. After a few attempts, this practice was halted because it added to the confusion. The company has since worked out a better method of integrating portfolio and gate decisions, which we will see in Chapter 5. At the Royal Bank of Canada, electronic portfolio maps were also used at gate meetings, but only a few times before they, too, gave up. Company G used the maps as an after-the-fact course correction—"to make sure we have the right balance." But it was never clear what would happen if the "wrong balance" ever occurred: would management immediately start cancelling projects, and approving others in the hold tank?

5. Finally, the "right balance" of projects was rarely defined. Management could stare all they wanted at various charts, but unless a portfolio is obviously and extremely out-of-balance (as in Company T's Exhibit 3.1), how does a manager know whether the right balance is there? If one lacks an idea of what the right balance is in the first place—the *what should be*— then all these balance maps and charts—the *what is*—are meaningless. What is the existing balance being compared against? A portfolio manager at Hewlett-Packard speculated about the optimal balance of projects— about whether there might be any "rules of thumb" about the best split in long-term versus short-term projects, high-risk versus low-risk, and so on—much like rules of thumb exist in stock market investment portfolios.

The fact that portfolio balance methods are far from perfect does not mean we suggest they be dismissed outright. *Certainly not!* But such methods should be used with care; the choice of maps (which axes to use in the plots, for example) and charts (which parameters to show) must be well thought out. One must avoid the temptation to portray too many maps and charts, and one must be sure to test the maps in portfolio or gate meetings before adopting them.

One added benefit of the various balancing charts and maps is that they connect very well with the methods used to achieve the other two goals in portfolio management. Portfolio maps, for example, provide inputs into maximizing the portfolio value against goals (Chapter 2). In one firm, projects that scored high on the risk and reward matrix were flagged for priority. These projects, if successful, would help the company achieve its goals of increasing the average margin of its portfolio of products on the market.

Portfolio maps can also be used as an effective aid in monitoring a firm's portfolio versus its strategy. In other words, maps can serve as a tool for monitoring to ensure that the portfolio is in line with the strategy. If not, then course corrections can be made periodically during the year. The next chapter explores this third goal of portfolio management—the strategy link—in more depth.

CHAPTER 4

Portfolio Management Methods: A Strong Link to Strategy

Goal 3: The Need to Build Strategy into the Portfolio

Strategy and resource allocation must be intimately connected. Strategy begins when you start spending money! Until you begin allocating resources to specific activities—for example, to specific development projects—strategy is just words in a strategy document. These are the views shared by enlightened management of the companies we investigated. In some firms the prime focus is to ensure that:

- active projects are on-strategy
- resource allocations truly reflect the desired strategic direction of the business.

The mission, vision, and strategy of the business must be operationalized in terms of where the business spends money. Well-meaning words are worthless without the resource commitments to back them up. For example, if a business's strategic mission is to "grow via leading-edge product development," then this mission must be reflected in the number of new product projects underway—projects that will lead to growth (rather than simply defend the status quo) and projects that really are innovative. Similarly, if the strategy is to focus on certain markets, products, or technology types, then the majority of R&D spending must be focused on such markets, products, or technologies. After all, isn't this what strategy is all about: to guide the actions and efforts of the business?

Not every company we studied has achieved proficiency here. For example, a midsize company's dedication to product development was stated in its annual report as "growth through industry leadership in product development." The magnitude of the effort did not quite match this strategic intent, however, with this firm's R&D spending at *half of its industry average* as a percentage of sales! In another company, one business unit's senior executive claimed that "my SBU's strategy is to achieve rapid growth through aggressive new product development"; yet when we examined his SBU's breakdown of R&D spending, the great majority of resources was going to maintenance projects, product modifications, and extensions—not very aggressive at all! Clearly, both examples are cases of serious disconnects between *stated strategy* and *where the money is spent.* And these companies were not alone!

Linking Strategy to the Portfolio: Approaches

Two broad objectives arise in the desire to build in strategy and to achieve *strategic alignment* in portfolio management:

- *Strategic fit* is the first and addresses this question: Do all your projects fit strategically; that is, are they consistent with your business's strategy? For example, if you have defined certain technologies or markets as key areas to focus on, do your projects fit into these areas—are they in bounds or out of bounds?
- *Strategic priorities* is more difficult, and addresses this question: Does the breakdown of your spending reflect your strategic priorities? That is, if you say you are a growth business, then the majority of your R&D spending ought to be in projects that are designed to grow the business. In short, when you add up the areas where you are spending money, are these totals consistent with your stated strategy? Often the answer is no, so there are serious disconnects.

Companies studied use three general approaches to deal with strategic alignment:

Top-down approach: This method begins with the business's vision and strategy, and then moves to setting aside funds—envelopes or *buckets of money*—destined for different types of projects. We label this the Strategic Buckets approach.

Bottom-up approach: This approach begins with a review of specific projects and focuses on selecting the best. Strategic criteria are built into the project selection tools: thus, strategic fit is achieved simply by incorporating numerous strategic criteria into the Go/Kill and prioritization methods.

Top-down, bottom-up approach: This combination of the two methods above has merit because it overcomes deficiencies in both. It begins both at the top, with strategy development and definition of strategic buckets of money. It also proceeds from the bottom with a review and selection of the best projects. And the two sets of decisions—top-down and bottom-up—are reconciled via multiple iterations.

Note that the top-down, bottom-up approaches are fundamentally quite different in terms of philosophy, in how they are operationalized, and finally in terms of the list of projects that results.

Top-Down Approach: Strategic Buckets Model

The top-down approach is the one method we observed that is specifically designed to ensure that the eventual portfolio of projects truly reflects the stated (or desired) strategy for each business unit: that *where the money is spent mirrors the business's strategy.*

New Product Strategy

The word "strategy" is derived from Greek, where it means "the art of the general." Until recently, even in the English language, strategy was a *military term*. It has only been since the 60s that the business world has adopted the word.

Since there exists such a long tradition of military strategy and thinking, perhaps one should begin here. What is "the art of the general"? And what does the general concern himself with? Consider recent military initiatives, such as Desert Storm. Generals usually have goals—for example, to win the war or to eliminate or render an enemy harmless. But goals are not enough. Generals also make decisions about which battlefield they will fight or meet the enemy on—they have choices about which *strategic arenas* they elect. Generals also make decisions on deployment of troops and equipment—about *how many resources they will commit* to each battlefield or strategic arena. And, finally, they make choices about *how they will attack in order to win*.

A business's new product strategy flows from (or is a component of) the total business strategy. This new product strategy has much in common with military strategy, and contains or consists of:

- the business's new product goals (for example, percent of sales from new products)
- how these new product goals mesh with the business goals (for example, the role of new products or how much new products will contribute to the total business goals)
- arenas or strategic areas of focus and their priorities (for example, which markets, technologies, product lines, or platforms are areas of focus, and the relative priorities of each)
- the split or breakdown in spending and resources across arenas (for example, how much R&D and new product marketing effort to spend in each market or across each product line)
- how to attack each arena with new products (for example, leader versus fast follower; differentiator versus low-price competitor; and emphasis on or leverage of certain product advantages or core competencies)

This method operates from the simple principle that *implementing strategy equates to spending money on specific projects* (or, put another way, "strategy is not real until it translates into spending money on specific activities or projects"). Thus, setting portfolio requirements really means "setting spending targets." A number of firms we studied use parts or all of this approach. What we describe below is a composite of several companies' methods.

The Strategic Buckets Model operates this way:

- The vision and strategy for the business are developed first.
- Then decisions are made about where management wishes to spend its R&D and new product resources: which types of projects, across which markets and product lines, and so on.
- Envelopes of money—buckets with ideal spending levels—are defined: for example, $x\%$ to be spent on platform developments; $y\%$ on new products; $z\%$ on product enhancements and improvements; and so on.
- Projects are then prioritized within buckets (via the maximization approaches presented in Chapter 2).

▶ The results:

- There are multiple portfolios or multiple prioritized lists of projects, one portfolio per bucket.
- Dissimilar projects do not compete against each other (for example, product extensions do not compete with genuine new products for priority or resources).
- Resource spending, at the end of the year, is consistent with the desired or target breakdown: new product spending reflects the business's strategy!

Strategic Buckets: The Details

First comes the development of the business strategy and the new product strategy. The leadership team of the business are the *generals of the business*. Like military generals, they must have clear business and new product goals—but that's not enough! They must make decisions about which battlefields or *strategic arenas* they wish to attack—that is, which markets, product types, platforms, or technology arenas they wish to focus on; how they will attack these arenas; and finally how much they want to spend in each arena (see box insert, "New Product Strategy").

Example: Recall the Modified Plastics business from Chapter 1 and the general manager who faced so many problems with his new products. One problem was a *lack of strategic focus and direction* to projects in the pipeline. A more thorough analysis revealed there wasn't really much of a new product strategy in the business at all! The first task for the leadership team of the business was to develop a *new product strategy.* Here's how they progressed over a three-day strategy retreat:

▶ First, a set of new product goals was discussed and developed—a fairly tentative list initially.
▶ Next, possible strategic arenas were identified. At first, it was difficult to define these. After discussion, however, strategic arenas were defined on a two-dimensional matrix of *market segments* and *product performance characteristics:*
  - Various *market segments* in which the business operated (or had projects in) were identified: packaging, construction, automotive, agricultural equipment, and so on.
  - Then, various *product performance categories* were identified: fire resistance, high temperature, stiff/tough, high through-put, electrical conductivity, and so on.
▶ The various cells in this market segment/product performance matrix where there might be opportunities were delineated (*possible strategic arenas*). In this instance, there were about 20 strategic arenas identified.
▶ Next, a *set of criteria* was developed so that management could rate and prioritize the various arenas. These criteria captured elements of *segment attractiveness* to the business's *relative technological and marketing strengths* in each arena.

▶ Considerable homework had been done in advance, so that data were available for at least some of the segments and product performance categories. At this point, management began to discuss and *rate the various arenas* on the defined criteria.

▶ At the end of the exercise, *five key arenas were defined:* stiff/tough materials for automotive; stiff/tough materials for agricultural equipment; high through-put for packaging, fire-resistant materials for construction; and stiff, tough materials for construction. These became the *arenas of focus.* These arenas were next prioritized: number 1, number 2, and so on.

▶ Then, *resource splits* were made across the five arenas—a percentage split in R&D funding.

By this point, the leadership team had gone a long way toward defining a new product strategy: they had defined goals; they had identified possible strategic arenas; they had made decisions on arenas of focus and had prioritized these; and they even had decided on a split of resources across arenas. The only task they *failed to address* was how to attack each arena. Nonetheless, much progress had been made on their new product strategy, which eventually led to more effective portfolio management.

The role of the Strategic Buckets Model is to translate the business's strategy into clearly defined arenas (buckets) and to decide resource allocation to each. To summarize, the approach begins with the business's strategy and requires senior management to make forced choices along each of several dimensions—choices about how they wish to allocate their limited money resources. This enables the creation of "envelopes of money" or "buckets." Existing projects are sorted into buckets; then, one determines whether actual spending is consistent with desired spending. Finally, projects are prioritized within buckets to arrive at the ultimate portfolios of projects: ones that mirror management's desired strategy. Several companies are using variants of this method.

Here are the key steps in more detail:

1. A vision and strategy for the business are first developed. This includes defining strategic goals and the general plan of attack to achieve these goals—a fairly standard business strategy exercise.
2. Forced choices are made across *key strategic dimensions.* That is, based on this strategy, the management of the business allocates R&D and other resources (either in dollars or as a percent) across categories on each dimension. (In some businesses, this allocation is for R&D funds only; in others, it includes R&D, capital and marketing resources for new products.) Seven important dimensions that companies consider include:

   ▶ *Strategic goals:* Management splits resources across the specified strategic goals. For example, what percent (or how many dollars) should be spent on defending the base; on diversifying; on extending the base; and so on.

   ▶ *Product lines:* Resources are split across product lines. For example, how much to spend on product line A? On product line B? On product line C? The stage of the product life cycle of each line's market should influence this split. Other factors include the product line's strength in the market, the importance of the product line to the business, its technological strength, and so on.

▸ *Market segments:* The business may operate in several different market segments, with varying degrees of attractiveness and potential for the future. Thus, management splits resources across market segments. How much R&D to spend on segment A? On segment B? and so on.

▸ *Technology types:* The business may rely on several types of technologies or technology platforms. Technologies might be categorized as base, key, pacing, and embryonic technologies. Management may wish to split resources across technologies, technology types, or platforms.

▸ *Project types:* What percent of resources should go to new product development? To platform development? To fundamental research? To maintenance-type projects? To process improvements? and so on.

One business within Exxon Chemical uses the product/market newness diagram illustrated in Exhibit 4.1 to visualize this split across project types. Here, each of the six types of projects receives a certain percentage of the total budget.

A somewhat simpler breakdown is used at Allied Signal, Engineered Materials Division. The chief technology officer explains: "We have our 'Mercedes-Benz star' method of allocating resources. We [the leadership team of the business] begin with the business's strategy and use the Mercedes star emblem [a three-point star] to help divide up the resources. There are three categories: fundamental research and platform development projects which promise to yield major breakthroughs and new technology platforms; new product development; and maintenance—technical support, product improvements and enhancements, and so on [Exhibit

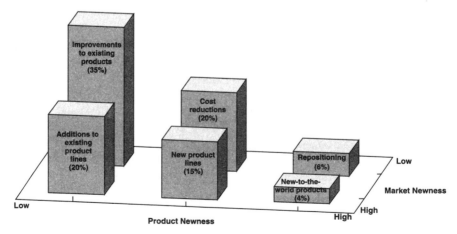

Exhibit 4.1   Six Project Categories (used in an SBU in Exxon Chemical)

Note: Each type of project is represented by a box on the chart.

4.2]. We divide up the R&D funds into these three categories, and then rate and rank projects against each other within a category. This way, we ensure that we end up spending money according to our strategy."

▶ Familiarity matrix: What should be the split of resources to different types of markets and to different technology types in terms of their familiarity to the business? Some firms use the "familiarity matrix" proposed by Roberts, where both markets and technologies are categorized into three types (see Exhibit 4.3*):

1. existing markets (or technologies) for the company
2. extensions of current markets (or technologies)
3. new markets (or technologies) for the company.

Eastman Chemical uses a four-cell version of this matrix to allocate resources into buckets; Dow Corning uses a nine-cell matrix.

▶ Geography: What proportion of resources should be spent on projects aimed largely at North America? At Latin America? At Europe? At the Pacific? Or aimed globally?

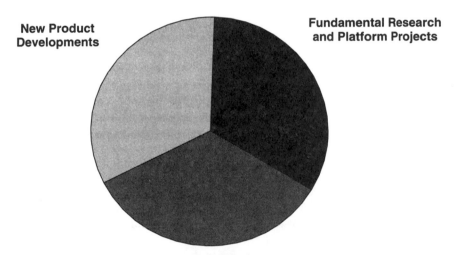

New Product Developments

Fundamental Research and Platform Projects

Maintenance: Technical Support, Product Improvements and Enhancements, and the Like

Exhibit 4.2   The Mercedes-Benz Star Method of Allocating Resources across Project Types

---

*See Roberts.[1] Note that the Roberts familiarity matrix (Exhibit 4.3) is somewhat different than the one used by Exxon in Exhibit 4.1. In the Roberts matrix, both dimensions are "newness to the company"; whereas, in the categories of new products matrix, originally proposed by Booz-Allen and Hamilton, one dimension captures newness to the company, the other newness to the market. These are subtle but very important differences, and they lead to quite different definitions of projects within each cell.

Technology Newness	Market Newness	
	Existing/Base	**New**
New Step-Out	Step-Out Product Development	New Businesses and New Ventures
New But Familiar	New Items (existing lines)	Market Development
Base	Defend or Penetrate	Market Expansion (customer application projects)

Exhibit 4.3   Familiarity Matrix—Technology and Market Newness

---

Seven Possible Dimensions on Which to Split Resources

1. Strategic goals
2. Product lines
3. Market segments
4. Technology types or platforms
5. Project types
6. Familiarity matrix
7. Geographic regions

---

3. Strategic buckets are defined. Here the various strategic dimensions (above) are collapsed into a convenient handful of buckets (see Exhibit 4.4). For example:

   ◗ product development projects for product lines A and B
   ◗ cost reduction projects for all products
   ◗ product renewal projects for product lines C and D.

   The number of buckets varies, but typically ranges from four to a dozen. Exhibit 4.4 shows only four buckets or columns (due to space constraints) but there were actually 10 buckets in this case.

4. Current spending in each bucket is determined. This is a relatively simple accounting exercise of categorizing current or existing projects by bucket, and adding up annual spending on each project within a given bucket.

5. Desired spending by bucket is determined. This involves a consolidation of the "what is" information from item 4 above with the "what should be" from the strategic allocation exercise in items 2 and 3 above.

6. Gaps are identified. This step compares the actual spending per bucket (item 4 above) with the desired spending (item 5). Differences between the two levels are identified as gaps.

7. Projects within each bucket are rank-ordered. Companies use either scoring models or financial criteria here (see Exhibit 4.4). Further, it is possible to use *different criteria* within each bucket: for example, in Exhibit 4.4, the cost reduction projects in the far right column might be rated on a simple cost–benefit financial ratio, whereas the new product projects in column 1 might be rated and prioritized via a scoring model that takes into account a number of qualitative and strategic criteria.

   Note that the result in Exhibit 4.4 is four distinct portfolios of projects— four lists. Note further that the projects in column 1, the first bucket, are not

New Products: Product Line A Target Spend: $8.7M	New Products: Product Line B Target Spend: $18.5M	Maintenance of Business: Product Lines A & B Target Spend: $10.8M	Cost Reductions: All Products Target Spend: $7.8M
Project A 4.1	Project B 2.2	Project E 1.2	Project I 1.9
Project C 2.1	Project D 4.5	Project G 0.8	Project M 2.4
Project F 1.7	Project K 2.3	Project H 0.7	Project N 0.7
Project L 0.5	Project T 3.7	Project J 1.5	Project P 1.4
Project X 1.7	**Gap = 5.8**	Project Q 4.8	Project S 1.6
Project Y 2.9		Project R 1.5	Project U 1.0
Project Z 4.5		Project V 2.5	Project AA 1.2
Project BB 2.6		Project W 2.1	

Exhibit 4.4　Projects Prioritized within Strategic Buckets

Note: Projects rank-ordered within columns according to a financial criterion: NPV × Probability of Success; or ECV; or a scoring model (Chapter 2).

ranked against the projects in column 2 (that is, do not compete for resources) nor with projects in other buckets. Projects only compete against each other within the same column!

8. Adjustments are made. Where overspending occurs within a bucket—for example, too many maintenance projects—projects can be pruned; or, as most companies do, management gives proportionately fewer approvals for upcoming projects of this type. Conversely, where underspending is occurring—for example, not enough genuine new product projects for product line B in Exhibit 4.3—then management encourages more such projects, and may even relax some of the Go/Kill gating criteria.

Over time, the portfolio of projects, and the actual spending across buckets, will eventually equal management's desired spending levels across buckets. At this point, the portfolio of projects truly mirrors the business's strategy.

How to Make Forced Choices

How does management make forced choices in resource splits across goals, or across product lines, or across markets? The Strategic Buckets approach requires that such choices be made, but often firms were unclear about the management decision process. Here are three resource-splitting approaches we saw:

1. *Discussions and consensus:* Each member of the leadership team proposes his or her split, the views are discussed, and a consensus is reached.
2. *Scoring method:* Criteria are developed for scoring a market, product line, or strategic arena; managers then rate each product line, market, or arena on

these criteria and prioritize accordingly. The Modified Plastics example (described earlier in this chapter) and the StratPlan exercise (outlined later in this chapter) are examples of this quantitative scoring method.

3. *Directional decision rules:* Some companies have developed powerful rules to guide the breakdown of resources across product lines, product categories, or even businesses.

Example: One major U.S. consumer goods firm relies on a very simple three-part rule to allocate new product R&D and marketing resources to different product categories:

- Feed the strong.
- Focus the weak.
- Build the new.

In practice, this means that product managers who are successful at new products (for example, many successful and profitable launches) receive proportionately more resources each year; those who are less successful are instructed to do less product development and to focus their business (for example, focus on a certain market segment or on fewer products). This decision rule is thus a heuristic which, over time, directs more resources to more fertile areas—to those areas where there are more opportunities for winning new products, or where management in the area is more successful at developing winners.

Strategic Buckets: Strengths and Weaknesses

Of all the attempts to build strategy into the portfolio selection process, top-down approaches, such as the Strategic Buckets Model, are perhaps the most impressive and comprehensive. These methods are certainly the most holistic and all-encompassing, extending from *top to bottom of the organization* and *across all possible types of projects.* They begin with the strategic goals of the business and end with a list of projects to be undertaken. The process thus scores top marks for trying to link *projects undertaken* (that is, where the money is spent) to the *goals* of the business.

This comprehensiveness, however, may also be the Achilles' heel of the process. This is a huge model and framework to implement and use:

- ◗ It requires a business to develop a business strategy and a new product strategy.
- ◗ It means management must make some very tough choices about how it wants to operationalize that strategy. Vague statements about strategic direction, which we find in so many firms, are not good enough!
- ◗ It means management must become very specific about where it wants to spend money—again, more tough choices.

The method is also sophisticated and somewhat difficult to fully comprehend; it requires much data; and it has many steps, each involving hard work (especially from the senior management of the business). Whether management will stay the course is an issue. By contrast, bottom-up approaches—which build strategic criteria into project selection methods and are described next in this chapter—are much simpler and less ambitious in scope. Implementation is rather straightforward by comparison.

One complaint about the Strategic Buckets approach is that there are just too many dimensions and too many resource splits required. One firm we interviewed is using five of the seven splits we outlined above: there the leadership team breaks down resources by strategic goals, by markets, by product lines, by project types, and via the familiarity matrix. Assuming four choices on each of these five dimensions, that works out to 5^4 or 625 buckets! This is unworkable. We still aren't sure how they are able to reduce this number of buckets to a more manageable size. One way to avoid this problem is *to focus on only a few of the most relevant dimensions,* as defined by your strategy (and these will vary by business, even within the same corporation).

Example: The view expressed by the head of strategic planning for R&D at Rohm and Haas is *not* to split spending along every possible dimension, as expressed in the Strategic Buckets Model; rather, the secret is *selective breakdowns:* "The key is to define the areas of *strategic thrust* of the business. That is, a business must have its strategy clearly defined, whether it be in terms of markets, or product lines, or technology areas. For example, if an area of strategic thrust is to 'grow via product development of products aimed at China,' then that's the definition of areas of strategic thrust. Then the leadership team must define how much effort [or money] it wishes to spend against each area of strategic thrust. That's the essence of portfolio management!"

Other than the physical challenge of implementing the Strategic Buckets approach, we hear four specific complaints:

1. Strategy should not always drive the portfolio in a top-down fashion. There are times when new product projects *should create the strategy!* That is, getting into a specific new product project that might even be "off strategy" could open up all kinds of windows of opportunity, and thereby change the strategy of the business. A strictly top-down approach prevents such opportunities and strategic changes from occurring.

   Was 3M's decision to enter the Post-it Notes business a strategic decision? Or was this a serendipitous discovery and project, which caused the company to change strategic direction? Most companies have their Post-it Notes examples.

2. How can one split the resources across buckets—for example, by project types—without first considering the projects within each bucket and how good they are? Some managers claim that this top-down dividing of resources into buckets is a very theoretical exercise and that it is *impossible to do* without first looking at the relative attractiveness of potential projects in each bucket—more of a bottom-up approach. As one executive exclaimed, "Surely the choice of buckets, and how much to spend in each, depends in part on *what opportunities are available in each*—on what projects are

underway. You can't do this splitting exercise without looking inside each bucket!"

3. A parallel concern focuses on suboptimization. Note that in Exhibit 4.4, the first bucket or column has too many projects, with projects X, Y, Z, and BB as excess. The Strategic Buckets Model suggests that they should be cut and that resources should be diverted to the second bucket, where there is a gap. But suppose projects X, Y, Z, and BB—the four bottom projects in Bucket 1—*are better projects* than the top four in Bucket 2, namely, projects B, D, K, and T? Now would you still divert resources away from Bucket 1?

   The quick rebuttal argument, of course, is that the strategic allocation of resources was wrong in the first place—that Bucket 2 should never have received so much money, given the limited value or number of identified opportunities there, and that Bucket 1 should have received more money.

   Be careful of this knee-jerk conclusion, however. Another reasoned argument is that one should not let a shortage of good projects (or good opportunities) thwart an otherwise well-founded strategy: the problem might not be that the targeted heavy allocation to Bucket 2 is wrong, but rather the lack of effort (and people) to identify the good opportunities within Bucket 2. Thus, the solution is to devote *more effort*—people and energy—in this arena so that Bucket 2 will be filled with excellent projects. As one general manager of a division put it: "If we decide to enter a totally new arena— say, a new market for us—we might also decide to allocate a certain percentage of our R&D budget there. The fact that we have no active projects or identified opportunities should not be the reason to say no to this arena!"

4. The final concern is what action should be taken. For example, faced with the situation outlined in Exhibit 4.4, *would you really kill* projects X, Y, Z, and BB simply because there are too many in Bucket 1? Suppose you know that all four are excellent projects, and that they are three-quarters completed! Of course, you wouldn't kill them. That wouldn't make sense. So what action does the model suggest now? Pundits claim that, while immediate action to kill projects would not be taken, signals would be sent that no more Bucket 1 projects should be approved for the foreseeable future; additionally, there would be a great initiative to generate quality projects for Bucket 2. Another possible action is to simply change the strategy and deprioritize Bucket 2 in the future, allocating fewer resources to it.

In spite of these concerns, the Strategic Buckets Model has many positive features. The obvious one is that it links *strategy and strategic priorities* very clearly to the *choice and prioritization of projects*. Further, when one strips away the complexities of the Strategic Buckets Model, the model is not as complex as it first appears: the method really boils down to two major elements:

1. a strategic exercise whereby desired spending levels are established for each project type (the buckets that specify levels of spending)
2. a rank-ordering of projects within each bucket, using one of the traditional maximization methods (for example, via a scoring model; or a financial criterion such as NPV, PI, or ECV—see Chapter 2)

Additionally, we witnessed examples of firms using only *some elements* of the Strategic Buckets approach, rather than the full model, and achieving positive results. For example, Allied Signal does not consider all seven dimensions we outlined above, but only "project types" in its three-sector Mercedes star method (Exhibit 4.2); and the Exxon Chemical business unit cited above did much the same thing (project types, as in Exhibit 4.1).

Another positive facet of the Strategic Buckets Model is the recognition that *all development projects that compete for the same resources can and should be considered in the portfolio approach.* Conceptually, this is correct. For example, product development projects must be considered along with cost reduction projects, because both utilize R&D resources. Note that, while varied types of projects are considered, they do not directly compete with each other: separate buckets are established, and separate project portfolios—one portfolio per bucket—are developed.

Example: The analogous situation is that of running a financial portfolio. The portfolio manager makes strategic choices about how she wishes to split her investments: what percent to bonds, what percent to blue chip stocks, what percent to more speculative stocks. Next, from the amount allocated to bonds, she prioritizes the available bonds and picks the best ones; she does the same with blue chip stocks; and so on. Note, however, that specific bonds are not compared to specific stocks.

Another feature of the Strategic Buckets Model is that different criteria can be used for different types of projects, as previously mentioned. Therefore one is not faced with comparing and ranking very different types of projects against each other, an apples versus oranges situation. Because this is a two-step approach (first allocate money to buckets, then prioritize like projects within a bucket), it is not necessary to arrive at a universal list of scoring or ranking criteria that fits all projects. Similar types of projects are only compared against each other. So, one is comparing all apples against each other within one bucket, and all oranges against each other in another bucket.

Example: One company, which divides resources according to strategic buckets, uses somewhat different criteria for trying to rank-order projects within buckets. For example, for the bucket "product developments," one set of scoring model criteria is used—criteria that emphasize strategic fit, market attractiveness, and competitive advantage. For other buckets—namely, cost reductions and process improvements—the ranking criteria change to cost–benefit and financial ones.[*]

In this way the company is able to handle all projects competing for the same resources yet recognize the differences between projects and that selection criteria for different types of projects ought to be different.

---

[*]The argument here is that the characteristics of a successful new product are somewhat different than those for a successful process improvement; hence different selection criteria ought to be used. Further, since cost reductions or process improvements are internal projects, usually the financial outlook (or cost–benefit) is much more predictable; hence it ought to be a principal selection criterion for such projects. By contrast, for new products, the financial outlook is very often a highly uncertain estimate.

A Variant on Strategic Buckets: Target Spending Levels

Some companies use an approach similar to Strategic Buckets, but arrive at a resource allocation guide or Target Spending Levels instead of buckets. After developing the business's strategy, spending splits are agreed across relevant dimensions. For example: "Our target spending split for R&D is 40% for market A and 60% for market B." Thus far, the method is identical to the Strategic Buckets approach.

The major difference is that there is only a *single portfolio list of projects,* a list that covers all markets, product lines, project types, and so on (unlike Strategic Buckets, which has multiple portfolios, one portfolio list per bucket). A running count or tally of the breakdown of spending is kept during the year, so that actual spending along dimensions (for example, by product line or project type) can be compared to the Target Spending Level, and adjustments made as the year progresses. The pie charts in the previous chapter, which portray balance along various dimensions, are useful display methods here (see Exhibits 3.17 and 3.18), but with spending targets added—the *what should be* versus the *what is* (Exhibit 4.5).

Example: One SBU in Exxon Chemical uses a similar but after-the-fact strategic check. Management begins with a good understanding of the SBU's strategy and strategic priorities; tentative spending splits or target spending are then decided according to a *project newness matrix* (Exhibit 4.1). As the year progresses, all projects are prioritized using a scoring model, both at gate decision points and during periodic portfolio review meetings. The split in actual spending is then displayed using the same newness matrix. Imbalances become evident, and adjustments are made for the upcoming year—decisions to emphasize certain types of projects or to rethink the target spending splits.

Although seemingly similar, the two methods—Strategic Buckets and Target Spending—are somewhat different in operation:

▶ In Strategic Buckets, the walls of each bucket or compartment are quite firm: money and projects do not slide between buckets. By contrast, the Target Spending method yields just that: guides or targets, which are somewhat flexible (porous buckets).

▶ With Strategic Buckets, the result is *multiple portfolios* or multiple lists of projects, one for each bucket. With a Target Spending approach, there is only one portfolio or one prioritized list of projects.

▶ With the Target Spending approach, *all types* of projects compete against each other; using the Buckets method, only projects within one bucket compete (for example, projects within a single column in Exhibit 4.4).

▶ The Target Spending approach means the *same criteria* must be used to rate all projects; with Buckets, different criteria and different ranking methods can be used to rank projects for each bucket.

▶ The Target Spending approach enables splits across many dimensions: markets, product lines, project types, technologies, and so on, without encountering the problem of too many individual cells or too many separate buckets. It is not necessary to create buckets, only desired splits.

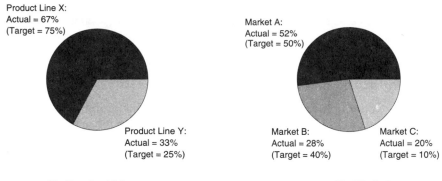

Product Line X:
Actual = 67%
(Target = 75%)

Product Line Y:
Actual = 33%
(Target = 25%)

Market A:
Actual = 52%
(Target = 50%)

Market B:
Actual = 28%
(Target = 40%)

Market C:
Actual = 20%
(Target = 10%)

By Product Line   **By Market**

Exhibit 4.5   Target Spending Levels—Guides to Spending across Key Dimensions

A viable compromise is to use Strategic Buckets for very important dimensions (as does Allied Signal with its Mercedes star method, which creates buckets across project types), and then a series of Target Spending Levels—guides, not buckets—on other dimensions, such as markets, technologies, product lines, and so on.

POINTS FOR MANAGEMENT TO PONDER

The Strategic Buckets Model has much to commend it. Senior management in many firms seems to be intrigued by the opportunity to better link the business's strategy to portfolio management. If your business is like many—the link to strategy is missing and there are too many of the wrong types of projects in your portfolio—then consider this Strategic Buckets Model. Even if you only consider a *few simple splits*—for example, by project type (recall Allied Signal's "Mercedes star" approach or Exxon's in Exhibit 4.1) or by product line or market area—at least you will be bringing your portfolio closer to the strategic direction of your business. Finally, you can use Strategic Buckets across one or a few dimensions and then Target Spending Levels on the other dimensions.

Bottom-Up Approach: Strategic Criteria Built into Project Selection Tools

"If you pick good projects, and build strategic criteria into your project selection method, then the portfolio will take care of itself!" This is the view expressed by a senior executive in a major firm with considerable experience in the portfolio management field. His point is that the emphasis ought to be on project selection—namely, at the bottom—and that in the process of selecting excellent projects, the portfolio will evolve and spending breakdowns will emerge. He also was quick to point out that strategic criteria ought to be built into the project selection tool so that the resulting portfolio of projects will be both *on strategy* and *strategically important*. We witnessed other businesses adhering to the same philosophy, either explicitly or implicitly.

The most popular and appropriate project selection method to achieve these multiple goals is the scoring model (introduced in Chapter 2). Scoring models can help achieve two key portfolio goals: ensuring the strategic fit and importance of projects, as well as maximizing the value of the portfolio (as seen in Chapter 2). One of the multiple objectives considered in a scoring model—along with profitability or likelihood of success—can be to *maximize strategic fit and importance.* The way to achieve this is to build into the scoring model a number of strategic questions.

Example: Hoechst is one of the firms that has adopted this bottom-up approach. In the scoring model used by Hoechst (Exhibit 2.8), 40% of the major factors—two major factors out of five—are strategic. Of the 19 criteria used to prioritize projects, six (or almost one-third) deal with strategic issues. Thus, projects that fit the firm's strategy and boast strategic leverage are likely to rise to the top of the list. Indeed, it is inconceivable how off-strategy projects could make the active list at all; the scoring model naturally weeds them out.

Note that the use of a bottom-up approach at Hoechst does not suggest that the business lacks a business or new product strategy; quite the contrary. For without a clearly defined new product strategy, there are *no answers to the strategic fit questions* in Hoechst's scoring model!

Example: Reckitt & Colman subjects all projects to a list of must-meet criteria at gates before any prioritization consideration is given. At the top of this list is *strategic fit.* Projects that fail to meet this criterion are knocked out immediately. Next a set of should-meet criteria is used via a scoring model. Unless the project scores a certain minimum point count, again it is knocked out. Embedded within this scoring model are several strategic direction criteria. For example, Reckitt & Colman's strategy calls for more international products (and fewer domestically oriented developments); hence this international criterion is one of the scoring criteria, so that projects that are international receive more points. In this way, the portfolio over time will be deliberately biased toward international projects. Finally, in Reckitt & Colman's bubble diagram (where attractiveness is plotted versus ease—see Exhibit 3.7), of the six parameters that make up attractiveness, two capture important strategic directions:

- competitive position improvement (ability to build the brand and franchise in the long term)
- geographic scope (international projects favored).

Thus Reckitt & Colman builds in strategic fit and direction throughout its scoring and bubble diagram portfolio approaches.

Note that in both companies the result is a single portfolio or rank-ordered list of projects, with all projects competing against each other (unlike the Strategic Buckets Model, which yields multiple buckets and lists).

The scoring model approach is recommended for three reasons:

- First, it is simple to use and understand.
- Second, it kills two birds with one stone. Scoring models are appropriate techniques to achieve maximization of key variables (including financial), and at the same time can be used to ensure strategic fit.

♦ Finally, scoring models are suitable for both gate project review meetings as well as portfolio review meetings (recall that in Chapter 2, Hoechst uses its scoring model at gates [Exhibit 2.8]; and Royal Bank uses its scoring model at the portfolio review, where all projects are considered [Exhibits 2.9 and 2.10]).

This bottom-up approach—using project selection methods that build in strategic criteria—overcomes a critical concern with top-down approaches. Remember that one very tough criticism aimed at the Strategic Buckets Model is that undertaking the resource split based only on a top-down strategic view, and without first considering what projects are available, is theoretical and difficult to do; indeed, it may even be conceptually wrong. By contrast, the bottom-up approach *begins with projects* and their relative attractiveness, and by incorporating strategic criteria, attempts to yield a "strategically correct" portfolio.

The weakness is that *only one-half of the strategic goal is achieved,* namely, ensuring that all projects are on-strategy. What scoring models do not do is ensure that the spending breakdown in the portfolio (where the money is spent) reflects the strategic priorities of the business. In short, all projects may be on-strategy, but the balance or *split of resource spending* may be wrong. For example, there may be too many projects in one strategic market and not enough in another. This shortfall leads logically to the third strategic method, which combines Strategic Buckets with this bottom-up approach.

POINTS FOR MANAGEMENT TO PONDER

This bottom-up approach allows the specific projects to shape the portfolio, and even shape the business's strategy. On the positive side, the fact that the gates are tough and rigorous means only the better projects survive; so the method eliminates one deficiency in many companies' approaches, namely, that projects are never killed. Thus, if value maximization and on-strategy projects is your main goal, then this might be the approach for you. But the bottom-up approach won't necessarily lead to the right mix or balance of projects, nor to a spending breakdown that mirrors your business's strategy. So you might want to add an element or two from the top-down approach into your thinking. That's what the next method does (below).

Top-Down, Bottom-Up Approach

In an attempt to overcome the deficiencies of the two methods outlined above, some firms adopt a hybrid approach, a top-down, bottom-up method. This method is similar to the Strategic Buckets Model (more specifically, to its variant, the Target Spending Levels approach):

♦ The top-down, bottom-up method begins with the business's strategy: mission, strategic arenas, and priorities.

▶ Next, flowing from this strategy, tentative target breakdowns of spending across different categories are developed (for example, tentative splits across product lines, or markets, or technologies, or project types, or across some or all of these).

So far the method closely resembles a top-down approach, namely, Target Spending Levels.

Now the method moves to a bottom-up approach:

▶ All existing or active projects and all on-hold projects (potential projects) are rated and ranked. This ranking is achieved via a maximization method, for example, a scoring model or some other criterion or method outlined in Chapter 2. Some firms use the scores, ratings, or data from most recent gate meetings to do this; others rescore all projects. In this respect, the method is similar to that employed by Hoechst.

▶ This exercise yields a single prioritized list: a ranking of all projects and potential projects that are in the pipeline. Those projects near the top of the list are obvious "Go" projects; those near the bottom (or below the cutoff line) are obvious kills, at least, on this first iteration.

The final step is to merge top-down and bottom-up outcomes. Note that frequently the list of projects generated by the bottom-up ranking yields splits in resources that are quite inconsistent with the top-down tentative spending splits—the two methods do not coincide on the first iteration:

▶ The breakdown of proposed spending on projects is computed, using the rank-ordered list of projects above (bottom-up exercise); this breakdown is done along the same dimensions as the top-down method employed (across product lines, markets, technologies, or project types).

▶ These bottom-up spending breakdowns are next checked against the desired tentative spending splits derived from the top-down approach.

▶ Where gaps are identified, action may be taken: for example, reprioritizing some active projects (fewer resources); activating projects on hold; and so on.

Several iterations may be required to reconcile the top-down and bottom-up decisions. Here the prioritized list of projects may be shuffled somewhat, with projects from overrepresented categories being removed from the active list; also, the strategic priorities of the business are revisited, and tentative spending splits might be modified in light of available project opportunities. After these several iterations, the top-down and bottom-up decisions are in sync.

This top-down, bottom-up method thus checks that the resulting list of projects (and their spending breakdowns) is indeed consistent with the business's strategy and with the tentative desired spending breakdowns; at the same time, the method fully considers what projects—active and on-hold—are available as well as their relative attractiveness.

In some respects, one might argue that the method tends to be more of an "after-the-fact" model—a check or correction method designed to bring the portfolio closer to the strategic ideal. Thus, instead of deliberately setting up firm buckets of resources, as in the Strategic Buckets Model, tentative spending targets per bucket are agreed to (more like the target spending approach); but these splits are modified as a result of the project prioritization exercise—that is, according to what projects are available in each bucket.

Example: The strategic planning exercise used at the Royal Bank of Canada is fairly typical. Recall that the bank uses a scoring model to rate and rank projects (see Exhibits 2.9 and 2.10). This is Royal Bank's bottom-up approach. The end result is a listing of projects, rank-ordered, with the tentative "Go" projects above the line.

The StratPlan exercise is one check that the business has built into its portfolio method to ensure that project spending is linked to strategy, and is Royal Bank's way of tentatively allocating resources across product lines. StratPlan is essentially a *strategic planning exercise* whereby the 12 product groups in Royal Bank are analyzed via a high-level portfolio exercise. (Product groups are major product lines.)

This StratPlan exercise results in missions and macrostrategies for each of the product groups, as well a rough idea (directional) of what each product group ought to receive in R&D funding. In this example, the tentative buckets are thus product lines; that is, this rough allocation of resources is across product groups or product lines. However, as in the Strategic Buckets Model, buckets could just as easily have been market segments, product/market arenas, or even project types.

This *macrostrategic exercise* is a fairly traditional one, but worth mentioning because of the way it is tied to new product spending and Royal Bank's scoring model. The process is this:

▶ First, the 12 product groups (product lines) are scored on each of 18 rating scales (0–10 ratings) that capture three main factors: market attractiveness, business position, and strategic importance. The evaluators are from the product groups as well as other units and functions (operations, sales, systems, and so on). Scoring takes place in an electronic meeting room, using a computer-based scoring technique along with a large-screen computer display of results. Several rounds of scoring are necessary to arrive at consensus. The computer display highlights areas of inconsistencies and uncertainties requiring further discussion. Animated exchanges are usually part of this meeting. Note that evaluators, invited from other units and functions (outside the product line), keep the discussion and scoring objective and "honest."

▶ Three product line portfolio maps or bubble diagrams are constructed from the scores, showing the locations of the 12 product groups on all three factors or axes: market attractiveness, business position, and strategic importance.

▶ Based on their respective locations, each of the 12 product groups is then classed as a diamond (star product lines), strong box (cash generator), wildcat, or cross-roads product line. A mission and vision are developed contingent on this classification, along with a strategy for each product group. Virtually all groups are either diamonds (which means a "growth" mission) or strong boxes (which translates into a "hold and maintain the course" mission and strategy). A few newer and smaller ones are wildcats. Rarely is a product line classed as a cross-roads—these product groups have either been weeded out or merged with a unit in another part of the corporation.

▶ Spending breakdowns (very tentative and directional) are decided across product groups. For example, diamond product lines receive a higher percentage of their revenues for product development than would strong box product lines, while cross-roads product groups receive a fairly low percentage of their revenue for product development.

So far, the exercise resembles a fairly standard top-down strategic planning portfolio exercise, except perhaps for the use of electronic scoring. It is *the use of the classifications* as an input to the new product portfolio exercise that is noteworthy. Recall that Royal Bank uses a scoring model that yields a single prioritized list of projects from all 12 product groups (see Exhibits 2.9 and 2.10)—a bottom-up approach. But this list *is only the first cut.* The list of projects "above the line" (that is, judged as "Go") is quickly broken down by product group, and the total expenditures by group are determined. Exhibit 4.6 shows the outcome of this process: a rank-ordered list of projects, with expenditure breakdowns by product line.

These totals by group, as a percentage of revenue, are then compared across groups for inconsistencies. As noted above, the normal rule is that diamond product groups should receive far more than their "fair share" of project spending—as much as double the norm. Conversely, strong box product groups receive proportionately less. Gaps are identified among spending levels per business, based on the first-cut list, versus the desired spending.

A second round of project prioritization ensues, with some projects originally "above the cutoff line" now being removed, while those below the line move up. This usually moves the project portfolio closer to desired spending splits dictated by the StratPlan exercise. Several rounds or iterations are required before the final list of projects "above the line" is agreed to. At this point, the prioritized list contains very good projects, according to the scoring model, and the spending allocations correctly reflect the various strategies and missions of each product group.

To summarize, this top-down, bottom-up method, and the example presented, resemble the Strategic Buckets Model (or the Target Spending Levels approach) in that desired spending levels per strategic arena are decided, in this example, by product group. Then, projects are rated and ranked, spending per arena or category is determined, gaps are identified, and adjustments are made: either the portfolio of projects is adjusted as needed in order to close the gaps, or desired spending splits are modified.

POINTS FOR MANAGEMENT TO PONDER

The top-down, bottom-up approach is one attempt to overcome the weaknesses of a strictly top-down approach, namely, artificially splitting resources into buckets without considering specific projects and opportunities. It also deals with the major deficiency of the bottom-up method, namely, the failure to provide for strategic alignment and the right spending breakdowns. As in all hybrid or combined approaches, however, the end result—in this case, the portfolio management method—isn't quite as simple and tidy: the model becomes complex and cumbersome.

RBC's First-Cut Prioritized List of Projects

Rank Order	Project Name	Product Group	Score (%)	Development Cost (S&T dollars $000)	Cumulative Development Cost ($000)
1.	RBCash	Cash Management	83	2,400	2,400
2.	CashCore	Cash Management	76	1,920	4,320
3.	EBX	EDI	76	1,800	6,120
4.	EBY	EDI	73	500	6,620
5.	BuyAct	Deposits	73	6,000	12,620
6.	CorpPay	Payroll	70	2,000	14,620
7.	Project A-PC	Loans	70	1,600	16,220
8.	PC-MD	Loans	68	7,500	23,720
-	-	-	-	-	-
<u>26</u>	Tiered/Interest Accounts	Deposits	55	930	<u>90,150</u>
27	Tiered	Loans	52	1,000	
28	Trade-AP	Trade	52	1,200	
29	ATM-Y	Deposits	50	500	
.	.	.	.	.	.

Split in Total Expenditure by Product Group

Target	Actual	Product Group
10%	18%	Cash Management
25%	30%	Deposits
5%	4%	Payroll
25%	15%	Loans
20%	13%	Disbursements
10%	11%	EDI
.	.	.

Exhibit 4.6   Royal Bank of Canada—Prioritized List of Projects by Product Group

The main advantage of the top-down, bottom-up approach over a strictly bottom-up method is that spending priorities are decided strategically, and these splits then direct the choice of projects. By contrast, in the bottom-up method, project choices dictate the spending splits and priorities. The top-down, bottom-up method's principal advantage over strictly top-down approaches (for example, Strategic Buckets or Target Spending methods) is that the method is also bottom-up as opposed to just a theoretical top-down approach; that is, the method incorporates project attractiveness into decisions on spending splits (projects are concurrently prioritized, and spending breakdowns subsequently checked for consistency with strategy).

But How Much Should We Spend?

One portfolio issue that all strategic portfolio methods largely avoid is the issue of *magnitude of spending*. They have much to say about how the resource pie should be allocated across projects and project categories, but are silent regarding the *size of the pie* in the first place. That is, what is the optimal spending level on development for our business? The assumption always seems to be that the resources available are always a "given," and that portfolio management is about allocation of these "given" resources. Yet magnitude of spending on development is clearly a strategic issue, and the size of the portfolio is surely one element of portfolio management.

Some methods businesses use to decide how much to spend on development (R&D, marketing and capital expenditures) are:

- *Competitive parity:* spend on your business roughly what the rest of the industry does (usually this means R&D spending as a percent of sales).
- *Objectives and task:* begin with your objectives (for example, sales from new products, next five years); translate these into numbers of successful launches per year; then break these into numbers of projects at each stage of the process; assign an approximate dollar cost (or person-days) to do each stage; and multiply numbers of projects per stage times the cost per stage. This yields the total cost or expenditure (dollars or full-time equivalent people) required to achieve the objectives.
- *History:* take last year's budgeted amount, and add or subtract a little.
- *Opportunistic rules:* spend enough to finance the solid projects—those that clear a minimum financial hurdle (that is, don't operate with a preconceived upper spending limit each year; many "good" projects will be put on hold, thereby reducing the total return of the company). An added rule we saw was: never spend more than the cash inflow of the business (that is, do not borrow to finance projects).
- *Based on results:* recall the "feed the strong, focus the weak" rule; this also applies across businesses. Each year, pour more development money into businesses that are successful at product development and take away from those that are less successful.
- *Corporate planning models:* classify businesses according to the quadrants in the BCG or GE/McKinsey models (stars, cash cows, dogs, and so on), and allocate money accordingly (more about these in Chapter 7). For example, Rhode & Schwarz[*] has developed scoring criteria against which each business is rated. Criteria include: technological strength, market growth,

---

[*]Rhode & Schwarz is an electronics company located in Germany.

business strength, and so on. R&D funds are allocated across businesses according to their overall scores.

Few of the above methods are particularly well developed, and there remains suspicion about others (for example, mechanistic corporate planning models have many detractors).

Summary

This chapter concludes our discussion on the three portfolio management goals—maximization of value, balance, and strategic alignment. In the next chapter, we begin to look at the actual design and implementation of a Portfolio Management Process for your company. Chapter 5 starts by highlighting our conclusions and then by identifying the various problems and pitfalls that other companies have experienced and that you might have to deal with. This, in turn, will permit you to preempt much of the learning curve that other organizations have undergone the hard way. Chapters 6, 7, and 8 outline how to design and implement a Portfolio Management Process tailored to the needs of your own organization.

CHAPTER 5

Challenges and Unresolved Issues

Thirty years of development of portfolio management methods, and are we any further ahead? The answer is clearly yes! At worst, we've discovered *what does not work* in portfolio management. More positively, some companies are very close to a solution that works for them. But there remain many unresolved issues and barriers yet to be overcome. This chapter highlights our major conclusions, identifies the problem areas, and leads up to our recommendations in the final three chapters.

In this chapter, we depart from our normal "points for management to ponder" because virtually *every conclusion and challenge* we present is food for thought.

General Conclusions

Portfolio Management Is a Vital Issue

The portfolio management question is a *very important one*—perhaps more important than we had previously judged. If the amount of time and money that firms are spending on the problem is any indication, then portfolio management and project selection is likely the *number one issue in new product development* and technology management for the next decade. It may even be in the top three or four strategic issues faced by today's corporations.

Portfolio management is critical for at least three reasons, according to companies we interviewed:

1. First, a successful new product effort is *fundamental to corporate success* as we move into the next century. More so than ever, senior management recognizes the need for new products, especially the right new products. This logically translates into portfolio management: the ability to select today's projects that will become tomorrow's new product winners.

2. Second, new product development is the *manifestation of the business's strategy*. That is, one important way a company operationalizes strategy is

through the new products that it develops. If its new product initiatives are wrong, then the company fails at implementing its business strategy. The new product choices one makes today define the business tomorrow.

3. Third, portfolio management is about *resource allocation.* In a business world preoccupied with value to the shareholder and doing more with less, technology and marketing resources are simply too scarce to allocate to the wrong projects. The consequences of poor portfolio management are evident: the firm squanders scarce resources on the wrong projects. As a result, the truly meritorious projects are starved.

No Magic Solution

There is no magic answer or *black box model* to solve the portfolio management challenge. Indeed the firms we studied—in spite of expensive and extensive attempts to develop such portfolio models—were quick to admit that there was no single "right" answer here. Management said they were still actively seeking solutions and making improvements to their own approaches.

Not only is there no magic answer; there is not even a *dominant approach!* In spite of the fact that many of these executives had read the same reports, articles, and books, had benchmarked against the same firms, and had even hired many of the same consultants, the approaches they arrived at for their own companies are quite different from each other. There is no universal method, dominant theme, or generic model here; rather, the models and approaches employed are quite company-specific.

A great variety of concepts, tools, and approaches is employed by these leading firms. The most popular are sophisticated variants on *scoring models* and *financial indexes,* and also various *portfolio mapping* approaches, such as bubble diagrams. Some progressive firms employ a hybrid approach: a combination that looked at the issues of *balancing the portfolio* as well as *maximizing the value of the portfolio against certain objectives.*

There is no evidence at all of use of, or interest in, mathematical programming and optimization techniques, according to our study. Ironically, such models are very common in the literature, but have rarely been implemented or tested in industry. Indeed, the notion of a "black box decision model" that would yield a prioritized list of projects has been rejected by all firms studied. Instead, a *decision tool* or *decision support system* designed to help managers make the decision is preferred.

No "Flavor of the Month" Solutions

The problem is far from solved. Many of the models we observed in companies, although elegant and comprehensive, are as yet relatively untested. These are largely new approaches being implemented only now in these firms. No doubt it will be years before well-accepted portfolio models and methods are commonplace in industry.

In spite of the lack of quick and easy solutions, virtually all of the firms in our study had arrived at moderately satisfactory approaches. No solution was easy to come by, however. Developing a portfolio approach proved much more difficult, time-consuming, and expensive than initially expected.* Nonetheless, the progress made by some companies is encouraging. In the next three chapters, we offer a glimpse into the solutions to managing the portfolio of projects. These insights are based on the varied experiences of the firms in our study.

But first, let's have a closer look at specific conclusions of our study of firms' practices, and also at the challenges and issues that were encountered by the companies we investigated—challenges that we hope to resolve in Chapters 6, 7, and 8.

Specific Conclusions and Challenges Identified in Effective Portfolio Management

Our investigation revealed eight specific conclusions or findings regarding effective portfolio management; these are highlighted below. In addition, another eight key issues and challenges were identified: questions, pitfalls, problems, and concerns that management must address if they are to develop effective portfolio management approaches. These conclusions and challenges are summarized in Exhibit 5.1 and explained in more detail below.

Findings and Conclusions
1. There are three main goals in portfolio management:
   Goal 1 is maximizing the value of the portfolio against objectives.
   Goal 2 is seeking the right balance or mix of projects.
   Goal 3 is the link to your business's strategy.
2. Gate decisions must be integrated with portfolio decisions.
3. Imaginary precision exist: the quality of information inputs is lacking.
4. Portfolio management must consider all types of projects that compete for resources.
5. There is information overload in portfolio management.

Challenges and Issues
1. Are Portfolio Reviews monitoring reviews or project selection meetings?
2. When should the Portfolio Management Process kick in?
3. How firm are resource commitments?
4. What should be done with too many on-hold projects?
5. Why have a prioritized or rank-ordered list at all?
6. Should portfolio models provide information display or be decision models?
7. How should needed information on projects be acquired?
8. What problems do financial analysis methods pose?

Exhibit 5.1   Findings, Conclusions, Challenges, and Issues in Designing an Effective Portfolio Management Process

---

*We estimate two of the firms that we investigated in depth had probably spent close to $500,000 each on outside consultants to resolve the portfolio management problem. Two other firms had likely spent almost this amount in staff time and consultants combined.

Our Specific Findings and Conclusions

1. Three Main Goals

Three goals provide the underpinnings of portfolio approaches. These are:

- *Maximizing the value of the portfolio:* A prime goal is to maximize the value of the portfolio against objectives, such as profitability or strategic importance. Here financially based methods (such as the ECV or the Productivity Index) and scoring models (which build the desired objectives into the criteria) are most effective.
- *Balance in the portfolio:* Portfolios can be balanced in terms of numerous dimensions. The most popular are risk versus reward; ease versus attractiveness; and breakdown by project type, market, and product line. Visual models, especially bubble diagrams, are thought to be most appropriate way to portray balance.
- *Link to strategy:* Strategic alignment—strategic fit and resource allocation reflecting the business's strategy—are the issues here. Top-down methods (strategic buckets or target spending levels), bottom-up methods (building strategic criteria into scoring models), and combinations of the two are appropriate techniques.

Of the three, no one goal seems to dominate; moreover, no one portfolio model or approach appears capable of delivering on all three goals.

2. Goal 1: Maximizing the Value of the Portfolio against Objectives

Maximizing value is an obvious goal for portfolio management. Yet some of the techniques, notably the visual maps, are not particularly effective here. For example, mapping techniques do not logically lead to the highest-value portfolio of projects.

The maximization goal is more challenging when multiple objectives, such as NPV, IRR, and strategic importance, are sought concurrently. The four methods that work best for maximization of the portfolio's value include the following:

- The ECV, a financial model based on a *decision tree,* as practiced at English China Clay, incorporates probabilities and recognizes that total project costs are not incurred if the project is aborted. The method is consistent with options theory, which allows the investor to opt out of a project, thereby reducing the overall risk of the project.
- The productivity index, a *financial index,* considers the ratio of payoffs (risk-adjusted NPV) to the R&D expenditures. Various methods for computing the risk-adjusted NPV are proposed.
- The dynamic rank-ordered list, as found at Company G, is again *largely financial* and has the advantage of considering several objectives concurrently, including nonfinancial criteria.
- The scoring model, which is the least financial of the four and captures *multiple objectives* or desired characteristics of projects, is used by Hoechst, the

Royal Bank, Specialty Minerals, Reckitt & Colman, and many others. Hoechst has developed an excellent list of scoring criteria; Royal Bank uses a novel method of obtaining scoring data from senior management; and Specialty Minerals, Royal Bank, and Reckitt & Colman all combine scoring models with bubble diagrams (hybrid models).

3. Goal 2: Seeking Portfolio Balance

Maximizing the value against an objective is *not the only decision rule* in selecting a portfolio of projects. There is also a need to achieve the right balance of projects on a number of dimensions. For example, companies should look for the right mix of long-term versus short-term projects; or high-risk versus low-risk projects; or offensive versus defensive projects; or step-out versus close-to-home products; or across markets and product lines; and so on. For these dimensions, *more is not necessarily better;* rather, the goal is to achieve the *right mix, balance,* or *distribution of projects.* Scoring models are clearly inappropriate here, as they tend to rank projects in terms of maximization against an objective—the more, the better. Thus, various mapping approaches are more useful, such as bubble diagram risk–reward maps, or pie charts and histograms, which portray the split in resources by timing or across project types, markets, and product lines. In particular, bubble diagrams or portfolio maps provide a visual portrayal of the portfolio, where balance or distribution of projects can be seen and debated.

Some visual maps also have the advantage of being able to hint at the appropriate portfolio. For example, in risk–reward maps, certain quadrants denote projects that are clearly better than others. One quadrant contains "White Elephant" projects, suggesting that pruning is needed. Thus, although mapping and chart models are information display methods and effectively portray balance, they are also important inputs to the maximization of the portfolio's value.

4. Goal 3: Link to Strategy

Portfolio management—the selection and prioritization of specific R&D projects—must be *very closely tied to the business's strategy.* Strategic alignment has two meanings, with subtle but important differences:

- First, portfolio management must ensure *strategic fit*—that all projects are on-strategy and consistent with the strategic direction of the business. For example, senior management defines the arenas of focus or areas of strategic thrust—the product, market, and technology areas on which to focus—and then selects projects only within these boundaries.
- Second, and most important, portfolio management must *allocate spending* across projects so as to *mirror the strategy* of the business. For example, if the business's strategy is very much a growth one, then the majority of spending on new product projects should be on business and market development projects rather than on "maintain the business" projects. Or if management has defined certain areas of strategic thrust—for example a certain market or technology—then a heavy percentage of spending ought to be on projects in these areas.

Traditional portfolio models, such as mathematical programming models, have failed to account for this strategic link. And many of the financial models, such as the Productivity Index and ECV, are weak here as well (although English China Clay was ingenious in building a strategic factor into their financial ECV calculations; see Chapter 2). The three best methods we witnessed in which the portfolio-strategy link is well handled are:

- Top-down approaches, namely, the Strategic Buckets Model. This is a comprehensive method that begins with the business unit's strategy and culminates in the designation of envelopes, or buckets, of money for different types of projects. Within these buckets, projects are rank-ordered and prioritized. In this way, the spending allocation mirrors the strategic direction and desired spending patterns of the business. A variant of Strategic Buckets is the Target Spending Levels approach, where spending split guides are established and the breakdown of spending on projects tallied against these guides.
- Bottom-up approaches, namely, scoring models that build in strategic criteria. These are comprised of multiple scoring scales, some of which capture strategic direction and importance, as illustrated by the Hoechst method. By using a large number of scoring criteria that rate projects in terms of strategic fit, strategic impact, and strategic leverage, this company ensures that the right projects—from a strategic perspective—rise to the top of the pile.
- Top-down, bottom-up approaches, which combine the two methods above. The Royal Bank's StratPlan exercise classes product groups (product lines) and defines strategic missions for each, which then become major inputs to the allocation of resources in the portfolio selection exercise—this is the top-down part (see Exhibit 4.4). Concurrently projects are also prioritized using a scoring model—bottom-up. Results from the two methods are reconciled via several iterations. There are also simpler variants of this approach. At Exxon Chemical, some SBUs use rigorous scoring models (bottom-up, like Hoechst) and also check for spending breakdowns after-the-fact (Exhibit 4.1), which leads to adjustments for the upcoming year.

5. Integration between Gate Decisions and Portfolio Decisions

Almost all the companies we studied rely on some type of new product process model, such as Stage-Gate, to drive new product projects from idea to market. Embedded within these processes are *gates* or *Go/Kill decision points*. The gates are, in effect, resource allocation decisions, where the senior decision-makers or "gatekeepers" make Go/Kill and prioritization decisions on individual projects.

A potential for conflict exists between this gating decision process and portfolio reviews, namely:

- real-time decisions are made on individual projects at gates
- portfolio decisions are made periodically, but on all projects together

These are two different decision processes (and in some firms, even involve different people and somewhat different criteria!), yet both purport to select projects and allocate resources—hence the potential for conflict. Consider some of the strengths and weaknesses of each decision process:

▶ Portfolio reviews consider *all projects together*—a comparison of one against another. This holistic view is healthy, but it does limit the amount of time decision-makers can spend on any one project. Witness Royal Bank's portfolio meeting, where 100 projects are scored in one day! By contrast, gate meetings tend to *focus on only one project.* That single project receives a thorough management review—there is much debate and time to reflect on the project's merits—but the evaluation is done in relative isolation from the other projects.

▶ Gate decisions occur in *real time* as the project moves from one stage to the next. By contrast, portfolio review meetings are held in *calendar time,* perhaps annually, semiannually, or quarterly.

Given these two decision processes, the questions become: Which process should dominate? And how should the two processes be integrated?

Some firms, particularly those whose portfolio methods have been in place for some time, have developed rules or conflict resolution methods. These rules tend to let one or the other decision model dominate.

• *The portfolio model dominates.* Royal Bank has developed a set of decision rules to integrate the portfolio model with gate decisions. Here, the annual portfolio meeting earmarks funds for certain projects for the next year (there are quarterly updates, so the portfolio list is relatively current). But merely being "in the portfolio" does not guarantee funding or "Go" decisions. Each project still has to pass through each gate. In short, the gate decisions can override the portfolio decisions. In practice, however, it is rare that a project, once approved at a portfolio meeting, is rejected at a gate meeting (unless the project is in serious trouble). In effect, the portfolio meeting takes precedence.

• *The gates dominate.* Hoechst management is adamant that the gate decisions take precedence. Here, the portfolio review is viewed only as a *course correction.* The view is: "Make sound decisions at the gates, and the portfolio will take care of itself." The argument is that one might not achieve the optimal balance or mix of projects, but if the gates have been rigorous, at least all the projects in the portfolio will be good ones.

We conclude that both decision approaches—gate decisions and portfolio reviews—have their merits:

• As noted above, decisions made at gates are focused on single projects. Gate reviews can last hours, they are in-depth, they utilize many criteria, and they have access to current information. Thus, the decision is likely to be a more thoughtful one for that particular project. But the decision is made in relative isolation (all projects are not considered together), and the project may not be prioritized against either all other active or on-hold projects (although many companies do build in project prioritization for the project under review right at the gate meeting).

- Portfolio reviews are holistic; they consider all projects together and take into account the ideal balance of projects, strategic alignment, and the desire to maximize against an objective. But with all projects considered in one meeting, the discussion on any one project is likely to be limited and superficial. Moreover, the data may not be the most current. For example, the data used to develop portfolio maps or lists are often retrieved from a databank whose input comes from the most recent gate meeting for each project, which may have been months ago for some projects.

Neither decision approach is robust enough to eliminate the need for the other; thus, both methods—gate decisions and portfolio reviews—must be married to yield the best portfolio and project selection decisions.

Further, letting one decision process make all the decisions is dangerous: for example, in some firms, the gating process is noticeably weak (no projects are ever killed at gates!), so that management is forced to rely totally on the semi-annual portfolio reviews to make all the Go/Kill decisions. The problem is that these reviews are often not timely ones; nor is enough time allowed for a thorough discussion on all projects. Equally, having excellent and tough gate meetings may yield a high-quality portfolio containing many high-value projects, but because a holistic portfolio review is missing, the mix of projects may be all wrong and the total portfolio may not support the business's strategic direction.

Example: Reckitt & Colman has developed a useful approach to link gate decisions with its portfolio model. Recall that Reckitt & Colman's portfolio model features a number of maps: ease versus attractiveness; probability of success versus NPV; and so on. Reckitt & Colman also boasts a Stage-Gate new product process. Here's how the two are linked.

Reckitt & Colman's portfolio model kicks in at gate 3, the "Go to Development" decision point. That is, before a project is considered in the portfolio analysis, it must first clear the gate 3 Go/Kill criteria:

- First, the project must pass a set of Yes/No must-meet criteria—a set of knockout hurdles or questions.
- Next the project is scored at gate 3 on rating criteria via a scoring model. The project's scores are then compared with standard hurdles preset for the product category.

Thus, at gate 3, for Go/Kill decisions, individual new projects are not compared to the whole portfolio, but to hurdle scores that ensure that the minimum standards of the portfolio are met. These hurdles are adjusted periodically to *favor certain types of projects desired in the portfolio.* Exhibit 5.2 provides a flowchart to illustrate the decision process.

Quite separately, portfolio reviews are conducted periodically. Here management reviews the balance and mix of active projects. Reckitt & Colman utilizes a number of the bubble diagrams and charts displayed in Chapter 3 to check for bal-

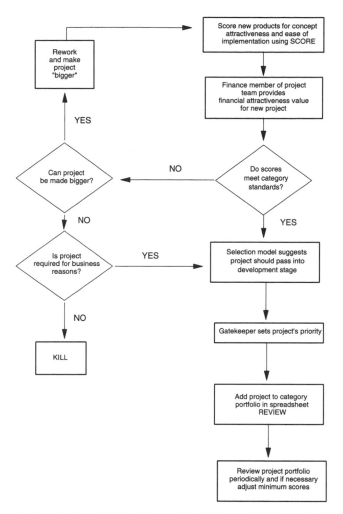

Exhibit 5.2 Reckitt & Colman's Logic Flowchart of Selection Model

Note: SCORE and REVIEW are Lotus 123 spreadsheets provided for use with the selection model.

ance and strategic alignment. If imbalances are spotted, or if there are gaps between target and actual spending in given arenas, then adjustments are made. For example, the minimum hurdles for the gate scoring model are adjusted accordingly—hurdles are raised for some types of projects and lowered for others—in order to correct portfolio imbalances.

Additional concerns regarding integrating gate decisions with portfolio reviews focus on the criteria used at each. In a handful of firms, we were surprised that management was using different sets of criteria at gate meetings versus portfolio reviews! For example, in one major consumer goods firm, projects were rated at gates on a comprehensive set of scoring criteria via a scoring model and then were rescored at portfolio reviews (also via a scoring model), with fewer and different criteria. In another consumer goods firm, a scoring model was used to make gate decisions, while the Productivity Index was used at portfolio reviews to rank projects. The potential for conflict and confusion is clear.

Suggestion: In order to minimize confusion and conflict between gate meetings and portfolio reviews, we suggest the following:

- Define clearly the role of each decision process and meeting: *gate meetings* focus on Go/Kill decisions on individual projects; by contrast, *portfolio reviews* consider the entire set of projects and deal with issues such as portfolio value, balance, and strategic alignment.
- Use the same criteria at both the gate and the portfolio review (or at least an abbreviated version of the gate criteria at portfolio reviews).
- Why not even use the same scores? Use the scores or ratings from the most recent gate meeting as input to the portfolio review (updated if needed).
- Finally, life is much simpler if the same people—the leadership team of the business, for example—are at both reviews (that is, they are the gatekeepers at the critical gate meetings; and they also conduct the portfolio reviews).

6. Imaginary Precision: The Quality of Information Inputs Is Lacking

A universal weakness is that virtually every model we studied implies a *degree of precision far beyond people's ability to provide reliable data.* That is, the model's sophistication far exceeds the quality of the data. Recall the criticism that using a scoring model imputed a degree of precision that simply did not exist: "They're trying to measure a [soft] banana with a micrometer!" The same concern was voiced for other models as well.

While useful, portfolio models should not be overused nor their results blindly accepted. Ironically, management sometimes confessed to being mesmerized by their models into believing that the data were accurate. The financial models, rank-ordered lists, or bubble diagrams appear so elegant that one sometimes forgets how imprecise the data are upon which these diagrams or charts are constructed.

Clearly, before one proceeds to develop even more sophisticated portfolio approaches, there is a great need to bring the quality of the data up to the levels required by the current models. We identified three key areas where data are consistently weak:

- Poor market information, including estimates of market size, expected revenue, and pricing plagues many projects. Not only are inadequate market analysis and poor market research cited as major reasons for new product failure, but they are major causes of difficulties in portfolio management and project selection. If revenue and pricing estimates are inaccurate, how can one believe portfolio models that rely heavily on NPVs?

  The dilemma was summed up by one frustrated executive: "If we had spent as much money on improving the quality of market information in projects as we have on developing the perfect portfolio model, we'd be further ahead!"

- Technical success estimates (probabilities of technical success) prove elusive for many managers, especially in the predevelopment stages. Various consensus, Delphi, scoring model, and matrix scoring methods are employed (see Chapter 2), but the fact remains that predicting the probability of technical success remains problematic for some types of projects.
- Manufacturing and capital cost estimates are also difficult to obtain, especially during the earlier phases of a project. Note that many firms require a financial analysis prior to the beginning of development, and these financial data (such as NPV) become inputs to the portfolio model. The problem is that the product is not even developed yet. Still, manufacturing (including material) costs and capital equipment needs are estimated.

Much better information—market, technical, and manufacturing—fairly early in the project—is essential if effective portfolio decisions are the goal. This means much better up-front homework is required in projects. The effectiveness of the portfolio model is severely limited by the quality of the data in too many firms!

7. Portfolio Management Must Consider All Types of Projects

All projects that compete for the same resources ought to be considered in the portfolio approach! "All projects" includes new product projects as well as process improvements, cost reductions, fundamental research, platform developments, and perhaps even customer request projects and maintenance items. Conceptually this is quite correct, but it does increase the magnitude of the portfolio problem. Rather than simply comparing one new product project to another, management must deal with a myriad of different types of projects—a much more complex decision situation.

This issue of whether all projects should be compared against each other has proponents on both sides of the argument. Some firms studied simply set aside envelopes or buckets of money for different types of projects. Within each envelope, projects are rated and ranked against each other. The Strategic Buckets Model outlined in Chapter 4 is an example of this route; so is Allied Signal's Mercedes star method. Using Strategic Buckets solves two thorny problems:

- First, the Strategic Buckets Model removes the task of comparing and ranking unlike projects against each other. Ranking dissimilar projects against each other is a very difficult task, for these reasons:
  - The nature and quality of information differ greatly between project types. For example, a process improvement project is likely to have fairly certain cost and benefit estimates, while a new product project does not, especially early in the project.
  - The criteria for comparison are likely different. The most important criterion for a cost reduction project may be cost–benefit; for a new product project, it may be strategic importance and sustainable competitive advantage.

    So how does one compare two projects when even the criteria for a good project differ? Via the Strategic Buckets Model, the task is simplified: one uses different rating or scoring models and quite different criteria for evaluating projects in different buckets.

▶ Second, by setting aside buckets of money or resources, one is assured that spending and resource allocation across different types of projects mirror the business's strategy—that the right balance among project types is the result. Recall that this is the major strength of the Strategic Buckets Model: it forces resources to be allocated into buckets a priori.

The opposing viewpoint is the Darwinian theory of portfolio management: *survival of the fittest*. That is, all projects should compete against each other, and there should be no pool of money or resources set aside for any particular type of project. For example, if all the cost reduction projects are superior to all the product development projects, then all the resources ought to go to the cost reduction projects. This is survival of the fittest, where the merits of each project should decide the total split of resources, rather than having some artificial and a priori split in resources. The decision rule may be applauded by financial people as yielding efficient allocation of resources and hence maximizing shareholder value, but the strategist might have problems with this lopsided portfolio that features no new product projects.

8. Information Overload in Portfolio Management

One deficiency with certain visual methods—maps, charts, and bubble diagrams—is the large number of possible displays and exhibits. Admittedly, portfolio selection is a complex problem, and one is tempted to plot everything against everything. As noted in Chapter 3, there are many possible parameters to consider. Indeed the possible permutations of x–y plots, histograms, and pie charts are almost endless.

Are managers simply overwhelmed with all the information and plots? Experience in some firms suggests they are. In one company, the illness that management was suffering from was labeled "bubble-itis"—exposure to too many bubble diagrams. Further, when first conceived, Reckitt & Colman's portfolio approach contained far more maps and charts than the final version now in use. Managers quickly realized that they needed to simplify the problem and boil the decision down to a few key parameters and a few important charts.

In Chapter 3, we illustrated some of the more useful maps and charts from among the many we saw in companies:

▶ the various reward versus probability-of-success bubble diagrams
▶ the concept attractiveness versus ease-of-implementation bubble diagram
▶ the timing histogram (resources being spent and projects by year of launch)
▶ various pie chart breakdowns: project types, markets, and product lines.

Challenges and Issues

So much for the conclusions about successful portfolio management. Many challenges and issues remain to be dealt with, however, before effective portfolio management is realized. Here are the more critical issues and unanswered questions we identified.

1. Portfolio Reviews: Are They Monitoring Reviews or Project Selection Meetings?

Some firms view portfolio reviews (and the portfolio models used at them) as monitoring meetings—a check on the portfolio and its mix. Others think that portfolio reviews are active project selection meetings. Here are the different points of view, and reasons for them:

View 1—Monitoring: Some businesses view a portfolio review as a simple "monitoring and review exercise," enabling senior management to gain a better view of the current portfolio. The portfolio review is expected to provide *minor course corrections* only—5 degree course shifts—but not result in numerous project Go/Kill decisions or a total realignment of resources—a 90 degree shift! Witness the Reckitt & Colman example cited earlier in this chapter (conclusion 5), where portfolio reviews signal shifts needed in gating hurdles. The argument here is that the gating process should be making fairly sound Go/Kill and allocation decisions on projects on an ongoing basis; assuming this is true, the portfolio review should be largely a *sanity check* that the gating process is indeed working and that the resulting gate decisions are yielding the right balance of projects, high-value projects, and projects with strategic alignment.

Example: This monitoring view, in its extreme, was expressed by the manager of research planning for a major U.S. chemical firm, who had been implementing portfolio management across the corporation for the past five years: "The Portfolio Review *should not look at individual projects* (except for a few very large ones that dramatically impact the business strategy). Rather, at Portfolio Reviews, we look at projects *in aggregate*—at where we are spending our money, and where we should be; and that the portfolio of projects is consistent with the business's strategy. We don't confuse the portfolio review with project selection! Project selection takes place at gates."

View 2—Selection: The position in other firms is that portfolio reviews are very much project selection meetings. Indeed, in one major firm, virtually *all project selection* is done at the portfolio reviews, with the gate meetings on individual projects reduced to a project progress report—in effect, a rubber stamp. We witnessed two sets of circumstances where the Portfolio Review involved numerous project selection decisions:

‣ First, where the business's gating process was broken. By default, project selection had to be done at the periodic Portfolio Review meetings.
‣ Second, where portfolio management began very early in the life of projects, even before gate 1, the idea screen. That is, the Portfolio Review becomes a substitute for the first few gate decision points in the business's new product process.

Example: Telenor's business communications division had set up RAT* teams to undertake portfolio reviews. Projects considered at these reviews included new product ideas, which had not even entered their new product process (that is, had not even cleared gate 1, the idea screen). Thus, this division is using portfolio reviews not only to monitor the portfolio's balance and composition, but also to make the first few gate decisions—project selection.

Example: Other companies, such as some businesses at Rohm and Haas, have a definite policy: a project must go through at least one gate and be defined before it can be considered in the portfolio review.

Opinion: We tend to favor view 1, the monitoring approach: ensure that the gating process is working and use the portfolio reviews to monitor the mix and composition of the portfolio, but *not* as the principal project selection venue.

The problem at both major firms, who were the strongest proponents of view 2, where portfolio reviews are selection exercises, is that *projects tend never to be killed once the initial "Go" decision is made* at the portfolio review. In short, there is only one review point in the process, namely, the entrance gate. Thus, even as new—and possibly negative—information becomes available, the project continues along. Coincidentally both these firms are in the services sector and are heavily reliant on software and electronics for their new products. We speculate that perhaps the risks of their projects are reasonably low (technical success is all but guaranteed for their projects, unlike in some industries; and both firms have enormous market power in their respective markets), so that subsequent rigorous reviews at later stages of the project are not perceived to be required. We disagree!

2. When Should the Portfolio Management Process Kick In?
Again, there are widely differing views here; some of these coincide with whether the portfolio review is a monitoring effort or a selection process (issue 1 above).

View 1—Projects Enter Very Early: Projects should enter the portfolio management process at the idea stage. That is, not only should the portfolio review consider projects already underway, but it should include *brand-new proposals* or *ideas* and make decisions based on these. Royal Bank takes this position: indeed, their portfolio review meetings have evolved to become a substitute for their idea screen (gate 1), as well as the next two gates in their new product process. Ironically, once past gate 3 (the "Go to Development" gate), projects are not reprioritized—they are simply "in the portfolio," unless they turn sour.

The arguments we heard at this and other firms are convincing:

▶ The initial decisions to start projects (the idea screen) are important ones, and therefore should involve the senior people. Therefore, ideas should be on the table at the portfolio review (where the senior people are).
▶ "Ideas are future projects; we want to see early on what the impact on the portfolio will be if certain ideas are approved. Why even begin a project if it's wrong for the portfolio?"

*RAT: resource allocation teams.

View 2—Projects Enter at Later Stages: Projects should pass at least one or two gates in the new product process before they are seriously considered in the portfolio management process. The majority of firms took this position. The argument is pragmatic:

‣ For the first few stages, projects are too ill-defined to consider in the portfolio. For example, many of the portfolio models require estimates of NPVs and probabilities of commercial or technical success. These data are simply not available at the idea stage.

‣ Resource commitments in the early stages of a project are minimal; and portfolio management is about resource allocation. If the resources committed are so small, then such projects shouldn't be on the portfolio maps or on the rank-ordered lists.

‣ One should not confuse portfolio reviews with idea screening (gate 1 decisions)! There still can be an effective idea screening decision point quite separate from the portfolio review. Here, ideas are screened, and strategic issues, rather than financial and technical feasibility, are the main screening criteria.

Even an executive at Royal Bank (view 1) expressed concerns about entering projects so early into their portfolio model: "Some of the projects we considered that day [at the portfolio review meeting] were little more than a gleam in people's eyes—it was very difficult to score and rate them against projects already underway."

There were some words of caution about not considering embryonic projects in the portfolio review (view 2), however. For example, at Rohm and Haas, although projects do not enter the portfolio model until they have passed a gate or two in their new product process, there is concern that "there is the right number and balance of early-stage [pre-portfolio] projects coming down the pipeline." Thus some businesses in Rohm and Haas do monitor these early-stage projects, but in aggregate, and they do not appear on the business's portfolio maps.

Example: Company G's portfolio management method kicks in at gate 2 in their new product process, after some technical and market investigation has been undertaken. Recall that Company G uses the financially based Dynamic Rank-Ordered List (Chapter 2); hence management argues that it must have at least first-cut estimates of NPV and IRR in order to undertake a ranking of projects. And before gate 2, these data are not available at all.

However, to ensure the right number and balance of projects in the early stages of their pipeline, management sets aside a bucket of money for all early-stage projects (projects prior to gate 2). This bucket or fund of money—the VP of marketing calls it the "seed corn money"—is allocated to projects in stage 1 (investigation) and stage 0 (ideation); there is some attempt to look at the balance of projects in these early stages; and the senior people are informed of gate 1 decisions (idea screening)—no surprises coming down the pipe. Thus, although the formal portfolio management process does not kick in until later in the process, there are techniques in place to oversee, at least informally, the *portfolio of early-stage projects.*

3. How Firm Are Resource Commitments?

Should viable and active projects be killed or put on hold, just because a better one comes along? Here, too, we encountered very different philosophies:

View 1—Very Flexible: Resource commitments to projects *are not firm.* Resources should be moved at will from one active project to another. For example, even though one project has been given a "Go" decision and resources have been committed, and even if it remains a positive one, when a better project comes along, resources can be stripped from the first project to feed the second (for example, Rhode & Schwarz's new portfolio approach uses an adaptation of this method). The argument here is that management must have the flexibility to optimally allocate resources, regardless of commitments previously made to project teams.

One implication is that the portfolio is a *very dynamic one,* constantly changing (no project has a firm "Go" commitment); and the portfolio of projects must constantly be reviewed. A dynamic portfolio management method is essential here.

View 2—Fairly Firm Commitments: Resource commitments *are quite firm.* That is, resource commitments made to project teams must be kept—for the sake of continuity and team morale—even if a more attractive project comes along. While it may be desirable to have resource flexibility to allocate resources optimally, team morale and the negative implications of "jerking around" project teams and leaders are more important. Further, if projects are "on again, off again," there is a great waste of resources and time. Shifting resources from one project to the next is not seamless. Project start-ups and shutdowns cost time and money. Finally, newer projects always look better than ones that are partway through development (warts always seem to appear as time passes!), so that the inevitable outcome is that resources are stripped from projects in their later phases to support new ones. Taken to an extreme, no project ever is completed!

One implication of this second philosophy is that the portfolio of projects has some stability. As a consequence, the portfolio of projects does not need to be reviewed so frequently, nor does the portfolio management method need to be quite so dynamic.

Generally companies with a longer-term perspective and considerable experience in major new product projects embrace the more stable view that resource commitments are firm (for example, some of the chemical companies we interviewed). Firms in shorter-term projects and in very dynamic markets lean more toward the flexible resource model (for example, some of the nondurable consumer goods firms in the study).

Even among companies that embraced the "committed resources" (view 2), there are differences regarding just *how long or firm the commitment is.* All agreed that if the project "shot itself"—that is, ran into serious problems such as delays, negative changes in the business case, or technical barriers—it must be reviewed immediately. This review or immediate gate meeting could change the resource commitment and even kill the project. Some companies had even developed a list of red flags that signaled problems and required the project leader to call for an immediate project review. Exhibit 5.3 provides a sample list of red flags from Company G; one business within Motorola uses a similar flagging approach.

Assuming the project avoids red flags and remains in good shape—met milestones, continues to look financially attractive, and so on—then how firm is the commitment?

At Exxon Chemical, the commitment is firm until the next gate. That is, "once resources are committed, they are not expected to be changed until the next gate review, barring an extraordinary development in the project."[1] In short, at each gate in Exxon's process, the project "is up for grabs." The implication is that the project can be reprioritized at each gate. The portfolio model is applied at each gate decision point, and the portfolio of projects—including where this project fits in—is discussed at each gate meeting.

Rohm and Haas's management suggests that they cannot guarantee resource commitments once they are approved and that project leaders must recognize the realities of business: circumstances change—for example, better opportunities do come along—and the corporation must be able to respond. At one SBU within Mobil Oil, management makes the commitment to project teams that resources are firm between gates (much like Exxon Chemical above), but that if circumstances do change, management will call an "emergency gate meeting" to re-review an active project and possibly strip away committed resources.

At other firms, the commitment is made *right through to the end of the project.* That is, barring negative results or red flags, commitments made at the "Go to

---

New product projects sometimes encounter problems. Often original estimates are revised and render the project less attractive. When a red flag situation occurs, the project leader must inform gatekeepers at once, who may call for an immediate gate review. Here are some red flags:

Project Schedule: if the project falls behind schedule by more than 30 days, according to the agreed-on time line.

Project Budget: if the project goes over budget by more than 5% at a point defined in the plan approved at the previous gate (for example, versus milestone projections).

Resources: if any major functional area is unable to meet ongoing resource commitments according to the agreed-on time line.

Product Cost: if any change in the expected product cost occurs (for example, manufacturing cost) that is greater than 5% above cost estimates provided at the previous gate.

Sales Forecast: if any change greater than 10% occurs in the number of forecast sales units; or if any change occurs in the configuration ratios (product mix) that affects margin by more than 3%.

Business Case: if any change occurs that affects significantly (more than 5% impact) the business case and financial outlook for the project.

Product Specs: whenever the product design or product requirements are revised and affect negatively meeting a customer need or the product specs.

Service: whenever a change in the service and support planned for the product occurs, which affects negatively a customer need or requirement.

Quality: if product quality metrics fall outside 0.3 sigma value.

Exhibit 5.3 Red Flags for Projects

Development" decision point are firm through to launch. The project still has to pass all gates and reviews, and could still be killed in the event of negative information. Royal Bank employs this practice.

The implication of the latter commitment model is that really there is *only one major decision point* in the new product process, and as long as the project remains in good shape, it continues to obtain needed resources. Thus, the role of gates is to provide a critical review to ensure that the project remains sound. The portfolio model applies to *one key decision point only,* where the proposed project is compared to all ongoing active projects and to those in the queue (on hold).

4. What Should Be Done with Too Many On-Hold Projects?

When more projects pass the gate criteria than there are resources to fund them, this places even greater pressure on the prioritization process. In some firms interviewed, the list of projects "on hold" was far longer than the list of active projects!

The problem here is that no one—especially senior managers—wants to kill potentially good projects, even when it is recognized that:

- there are likely a number of other projects better than this one
- prioritization decisions are essential to achieving focus—this means killing projects.

So it becomes much more convenient to start a "hold tank" and to dump good projects into this tank. The implicit argument is this. A kill decision is averted and no one's feelings are hurt. Besides, someday there may be resources available to do some of the projects in the "hold tank" (often wishful thinking on the part of the senior gatekeepers).

When it first implemented its Stage-Gate new product process, ECC encountered this hold problem. Quickly, a logjam of projects awaiting entry to development occurred. By the time the hold list exceeded the active project list by a factor of two, managers knew they were in difficulty. A new decision rule was instituted: a project can remain on hold for no longer than three months. After that, it's "up or out"—either it becomes an active and resourced project, or it's killed. A tough rule perhaps, but at least it forces the gate decision-makers (gatekeepers) to be more discriminating and to make the needed decisions. Further, it has encouraged gatekeepers to search for additional funding and resources for meritorious projects that are in danger of being killed (for example, new people, joint ventures or partnering arrangements, outside help, and so on).

5. Why Have a Prioritized or Rank-Ordered List at All?

This is a philosophical question. According to management in one leading firm, there are only three classes of projects:

- funded and active projects with assigned people
- good projects with no one working on them (currently unfunded)—these are the on-hold projects
- dead projects.

If there are only three types, why the need for rank-ordered lists? In this instance, management believed there was no great need for a prioritization or scoring model (as outlined in Chapter 2) or any other model that led to a rank-ordered list. All that was needed was a *triage approach:* active, hold, or dead!

A contrary opinion expressed at many other firms is that a rank-ordered list is not only important; it is necessary. For example, even though a project is "Go," there are *varying degrees of "Go,"* depending on the project's importance, pay-offs, and priority. For example, management at Hoechst regularly selects a subset of active projects and performs a *full court press* on these; that is, they resource these chosen projects to the maximum, ensuring that they are done as quickly as possible. Given that different levels of resource commitments can be made to any project, logic dictates that not only must projects be separated into "Go" and "Hold" categories, but that "Go" projects themselves must be prioritized. These top-priority projects receive maximum resources for a timely completion.

6. Should Portfolio Models Provide Information Display or Be Decision Models?

Should the portfolio method merely *display information to managers* in a useful way (as bubble diagrams do), or should it produce a *prioritized list of projects* (as a scoring model or Dynamic Rank-Ordered List does)? The *display approach* means that management must review the various maps and charts, integrate and assess the information, and then arrive at prioritized lists themselves. By contrast, the *prioritized list* approach provides management with a first-cut list of projects, prioritized according to certain criteria. Management then reviews and adjusts the list as needed.

Managers interviewed are divided on this issue:

- A common view is that the portfolio model ought to be an input to the port-folio meeting, discussion, and decision. However, the ranking of projects into a final prioritized list must be a nonmechanistic process. There are sim-ply too many factors, many of them "soft," which are far beyond the capa-bility of any decision-making model to capture. Managers are the decision-makers, not a decision model.
- An opposite view is that mangers are not necessarily makers of consistent and good decisions. If a model can be developed that captures most of the considerations that should enter the portfolio decision, then at least part of the managerial decision process can be replaced by this model. Moreover, these models, such as a financially based ranked list or a scoring model, only provide a first cut at the list of projects. Management retains the final say on the exact prioritization. They adjust the list to capture factors not considered by the portfolio model.

7. How Should Needed Information on Projects Be Acquired?

Often portfolio management must deal with dozens of projects, both new and ex-isting. One problem is acquiring and presenting the data (or profile information) on these many projects.

Example: In one health care products company, project leaders claimed they were being "driven to distraction" by the amount and detail of information required by the portfolio manager and the consulting firm he had hired. Very detailed financial information, uncertainty estimates, and resource requirement data were required for every project—data far beyond that normally required for regular gate meetings. Project leaders complained bitterly about how much time this "make work" task was taking, when often their projects were suffering from lack of time and attention. Others had simply given up, and had resorted to providing nonsense data.

Portfolio models invariably require at least some data on all the projects in the pipeline. This means that a pipeline database must be established. It also means that methods for routinely collecting and inputting the vital data must be established.

Example: When Company T first implemented the bubble diagram approach to portfolio management, the data collection task was thought to be relatively easy. "Data on NPV, likelihoods of success, resources being spent, and a few other pieces of information for every project seemed like a straightforward information request I made of each project leader," the portfolio manager explained. But it took more than three months to gather this "readily available" data, often after considerable arm-twisting.

One solution is that only existing projects that have passed at least some gate reviews—for example, the "Go to Development" decision point—should be considered in the portfolio model (see issue 2 above). This greatly reduces the number of projects under consideration, with a corresponding decrease in the amount of data required. This approach also means that the results of the "Go to Development" gate review—for example, financial data, resource requirements, probabilities, and ratings on the scoring model—can be collected at the gate meeting and be used as input data to the database and the portfolio model.

8. What Problems Do Financial Analysis Methods Pose?

For most firms, strict reliance on financial methods and criteria in order to prioritize projects is considered inappropriate. Financial data are simply too unreliable during the course of a project, especially in the earlier phases when prioritization decisions are most needed. Post-project reviews suggested that estimates on key variables, such as expected revenues and profits at the "Go to Development" decision point, are highly inaccurate. Yet this is the point at which serious resource commitments are made and the project enters the portfolio model.

A second problem is that sophisticated financial models and spreadsheets often imply a level of reliability beyond the facts on which the data are based. Computer spreadsheets in some firms have become quite complex, and produce best- and worst-case scenarios, sensitivity analysis, and so on. Managers are often mesmerized by these in a gate or portfolio meeting. They begin to believe the financial projections (due in part to the elegance of the financial model and the dazzling output it produced) and lose sight of the fact that the data inputs are highly unreliable.

Even when valid financial data are available and reasonably reliable, there are still problems. Here are some examples:

▶ Traditional NPV (discounted cash flow) *incorrectly penalizes some types of projects,* because it does not consider the options facet of new product decisions. Recall from Chapter 2 that NPV assumes an *all or nothing* investment situation. Reality suggests that in most new product projects, companies invest a small amount, seek additional information, and, assuming positive information, invest more in the project: that is, there are *investment options* along the way. NPV's failure to recognize these options portrays certain kinds of higher-risk projects—high-cost ones with low probability of success—much more negatively than they should be. A more appropriate route is to use a decision tree approach (much like the ECV method in Chapter 2), which unfortunately can make the computation considerably more complex, but yields the more correct economic value of the project.

▶ How does one deal with the possible *cannibalization of other products* already in the product line? Often negative interrelationships among products—especially between new and existing ones—are complex. Hence quantitative estimates are difficult to arrive at. For example, a new product might be expected to cannibalize the sales of an old product in the company's lineup. But at how fast a rate? Reliable estimates are very difficult to make. And this argument was often heard: "If we don't cannibalize our own products, a competitor surely will; thus, no cannibalization costs effects should be borne by the new product." The issue is difficult to resolve.

▶ The treatment of *capital cost requirements* is another complex issue, especially in the case of *shared facilities* or *idle facilities.* For example, one capital-intensive product developer always faces the problem of determining the cost of spare production capacity on capital equipment. How much of this cost should the new product project bear? Some pundits in the company argue "none." They reason that, after all, the equipment is idle and that there is no opportunity or incremental capital cost. Others in that company make a case that the new product should bear a "fair share" of the equipment capital costs, even when equipment is otherwise idle. Finally, the argument often is that the equipment may be idle this year, but may not be next year, so there really is an opportunity cost.

▶ How does one deal with *terminal values* of projects? That is, what is the project "worth" at the end of the five- or 10-year projection considered in the cash flow analysis. An assumption that the project is worth nothing after, say, 10 years could penalize a project severely, especially in the case of projects where the IRR is relatively low and close to the hurdle rate.*

---

*Note that when the IRR (or discount rate) is quite high in a 10-year cash flow analysis, the value of income earned in year 11 is almost negligible. For example, suppose you undertook a 10-year cash flow analysis of a project, which had profits of $1 million in year 10. One might logically argue that the project is still worth something in year 11, say, 10 times the earnings of the previous year. So you value the project at $10 million in year 11. If this is discounted at 15%, then this adds $2.1 million to the NPV of the project, which might make the difference between a Go and Kill decision. If discounted at 35%, however, this $10 million amounts to only $350,000, likely a negligible amount to the total value of the project.

The Royal Bank had developed a standardized, compiled spreadsheet analysis for use in all business cases from their "Go to Development" gate on. This standard 10-year cash flow model provides three assumptions, or treatments, of the terminal value:

- the project has no terminal value in year 11
- the project is worth 5 times of year 10 earnings in year 11
- the project is worth 10 times of year 10 earnings in year 11.

For each assumption, both the NPV and IRR are calculated. Management can then view the effects of the three different terminal value treatments, and judge accordingly. Interestingly, the three different treatments often yield quite different IRR or NPV results.

Summing Up

This list of 16 findings, conclusions, issues, and challenges (above) are the points that you and your leadership team must consider as you move toward effective portfolio management. All 16 may not apply to you, but do read over this list a second time and envision how you and your business might handle each problem or challenge. Finally, there is one more conclusion to consider: don't rely too much on portfolio management for all the answers! This final conclusion is explained below.

Portfolio Management Is Not the Complete Answer

Some managements we interviewed have taken the case for portfolio management to an extreme. The view seems to be that portfolio management will solve all that ails their new product efforts. Perhaps the fact that portfolio management appears, at first glance, to be such a *tangible and immediate solution* is attractive; additionally, the notion of *optimizing resource allocation* has a certain theoretical appeal to some; next, portfolio management has been pitched at *senior management,* so senior people see this as an avenue for them to become more directly involved; and finally the fact that a number of pundits are *popularizing the topic* and proposing elegant solutions has generated much interest.

Viewing portfolio management as a total solution, however, is a very dangerous and simplistic view. Portfolio management is a very important piece of the new product puzzle, but it is by no means the single answer.

Years of investigation into the critical success factors that underlie new product performance have revealed myriad performance drivers. Many of these drivers are directly connected to portfolio management and project selection, but others are not.[2] These important success factors are listed in Exhibit 5.4; two types of factors are identified:

1. *Controllable:* First, there are those success factors that are readily controllable, and hence against which action can be taken. Examples are:

> **New Product Process Factors—Largely Controllable by Project Team:**
> - Product advantage (partly controllable)
> - Proficiency of technological activities
> - Proficiency of marketing activities
> - Voice of the customer built in
> - Proficiency of up-front (homework) activities
> - Getting sharp, early product definition
> - Top management support
> - Speed to market
> - Proficiency of financial/business analysis
> - The new product's strategy
> - Internal/external relations (of the team)
> - How the project team was organized
>
> **Noncontrollable Factors (Given):**
> - Market potential and size
> - Market growth rate
> - Market competitiveness
> - External environment (hostile/friendly)
> - Product advantage (partly a given)
> - Marketing synergy (ability to leverage competencies)
> - Technological/manufacturing synergy (ability to leverage competencies)
> - Project familiarity (familiar markets, technologies)
> - Availability of resources

Exhibit 5.4 Factors That Drive New Product Success at the Project Level

Source: Refer to reference note 2.

- building the voice of the customer into the new product process
- achieving sharp, early product definition prior to the beginning of development
- undertaking solid up-front homework prior to moving ahead with a full project
- utilizing a true cross-functional team, with empowerment, accountability, and a defined leader
- developing a unique, superior product: one that is differentiated, offers unique benefits to users, and provides superior value for money to customers
- quality of execution of key activities from idea to launch.

An understanding of these critical success factors is important, because management and project teams can take immediate action to ensure that they are built into your new product process and into specific projects. For example, a well-designed Stage-Gate new product process incorporates these success factors into the game plan in a deliberate fashion.

2. *Givens:* Next, there are success factors that are more situationally defined, and not quite as controllable by the project team. These are characteristics that are more or less "givens" for a specific project. Examples are:

- how large and growing the market is
- how tough and entrenched the competition is
- whether the project leverages the business's core competencies in marketing, technology, or production
- whether the project fits the business's strategy
- whether the product is unique and differentiated (this factor fits into both categories—partly controllable; partly not)
- whether the competitive advantage is sustainable.

> Often these characteristics are difficult to control: for example, the project team cannot suddenly make the market grow, or wish the competition away, or develop instant business core competencies that the project might leverage. Where these characteristics see their greatest benefit is in *project selection.* That is, an understanding of the profile of a winning new product helps define the selection criteria.

A thorny and provocative question is this: Which is more important in the success equation:

- doing the *right* projects? Or
- doing projects *right*—in a quality fashion?

That is, are success factors under item 1, namely, controllable factors (what the project team does) most important? Or are situational factors (list 2 above) the most vital—factors that characterize the types of projects undertaken and hence are more useful as project selection criteria? Today we have some answers. An analysis of the various success factors and their impacts shows that success depends on *both* doing the right projects and doing projects right. The point is that there is more to new product success than project selection. Project selection and portfolio management are not panaceas—don't forget quality of execution, doing projects right!

On the other hand, there are other positive outcomes of effective portfolio management that go beyond simply picking the right projects and indeed affect quality of execution and hence new product success:

- One outcome of effective portfolio management is picking the *right number of projects.* One reason why projects are so poorly executed—poor up-front homework, deficient product definition and moving targets, weak voice of customer, and so on—is that there are too many projects in the pipeline, project team members are spread too thin, and too many corners are cut. By having the right number and balance of projects, quality of execution decidedly improves.
- A second outcome is *management commitment.* That is, effective portfolio management leads to alignment among the functions in the company, together with senior management commitment to specific projects and common priorities across projects. This, too, impacts positively on quality of execution and ultimately on new product success.

In spite of the later arguments, we still urge senior management *not to place too much emphasis on portfolio management as the total answer.* Remember: quality of execution, having a solid new product process, building best practices into projects, and practicing discipline in projects still account for much new product success.

The Path Forward

Overcoming the challenge of developing an effective portfolio approach for your company is no small task. In today's business environment, there is no question that portfolio management is a vital issue. Our investigation points to several fundamental truths, however. Do not expect a "magic solution" here! And the "flavor of the month" solution probably will not work long term. We also identified a number of conclusions regarding effective portfolio management, and uncovered numerous issues that must be addressed by management (summarized in Exhibit 5.1). Our eight conclusions and eight issues and challenges naturally lead to the next question: Now that we know the different approaches and have identified a number of challenges, how do we do it? In the next three chapters we present our recommendations on an effective Portfolio Management Process for your company.

CHAPTER 6

Managing Your Portfolio

The Right Portfolio Method

Which portfolio management method is right for you? In Chapters 2 through 4, we examined the portfolio approaches used by leading firms. We had a glimpse into the strengths and weaknesses of these methods, and into some of the thorny issues faced. Now the key question: *Which approach is best?*

This is not an easy question, because there is no single best answer. In Chapters 6 and 7, we map out the preferred portfolio approaches and indicate which ones are most appropriate for different situations. Our recommendations are based, in part, on what managers told us worked and what did not. They are also based on our own efforts to implement portfolio methods within firms, as well as on our benchmarking studies of business's new product performance.[1]

Let's now provide a road map for this chapter and the next. In this chapter, we

- consider briefly the top-level decision regarding *allocation of resources* across business units
- provide a *strategy-process matrix* that helps in deciding which Portfolio Management Process (PMP) is right for your company and business unit
- define what is meant by *business strategy* and *new product strategy* (see also Chapter 4)
- provide an overview of the components of an appropriate Portfolio Management Process for each of four situations or quadrants in the strategy-process matrix.

And in the next chapter,

- for the best, yet most complex of these situations—where your business has both a well-defined new product strategy and an effective new product process or Stage-Gate system in place—we provide a detailed description of the components of a PMP.

The Portfolio Management Process (PMP) is illustrated throughout these discussions via a real but disguised example of a business unit in a large corporation. We will call this business the Agro division.

Top-Level Resource Allocation across Business Units

Portfolio management for new products is about resource allocation; namely, how to allocate limited human and financial resources across various projects and potential projects. In medium and larger firms, however, we cannot escape the macro-allocation question: What about total resource allocation across entire business units (BUs)?

Resource allocation across BUs is a top-level issue. It deals with corporate strategy and corporate planning at the highest level, and a detailed treatment here is certainly beyond the scope of this chapter. While methods vary by firm, Exhibit 6.1 provides a typical framework:

▶ Here, the corporation decides strategy and direction (top of Exhibit 6.1). Resources are then allocated to individual BUs (downward arrow in Exhibit 6.1).

▶ Concurrently, each BU develops its own business and new product strategy. In this way, opportunities and resource needs are identified and fed upward as input to the corporate strategy (upward arrow in Exhibit 6.1), which in turn impacts the resource allocations.

This resource allocation exercise across BUs should be a fairly iterative process, with corporate strategy and goals helping decide the allocations across

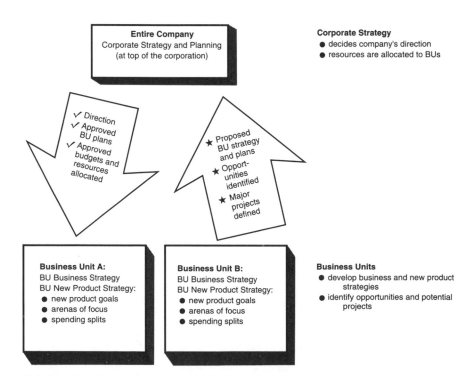

Exhibit 6.1   Corporate Strategy Linkage to Business Unit Strategy

---

Suboptimizing at the BU Level

Should R&D resources be allocated to BUs, which then decide which projects to do? Or should all projects from all BUs be prioritized against each other in a centralized fashion?

The argument against BUs managing their own portfolios is this. Suppose your corporation has three BUs; further, suppose each BU is given enough resources to do two major new product projects each. So six projects in total are selected. However, what if business unit A's first six projects are better than the four projects selected by the two other BUs? Shouldn't business unit A's six projects be done (that is, A receives *all* the money)? Not so, according to a decentralized approach. Each BU does its two projects, which is subopti-

mization! The counterargument is that a solid corporate planning and resource allocation model, like the BCG or GE/McKinsey models, will recognize that business unit A has much better opportunities and allocate more money here in the first place. This allocation decision, however, is a corporate planning, high-level one, not a project selection decision.

A major reason for a decentralized project portfolio approach is that the BU senior management is much closer to the market and technology. Thus, they're in a better knowledge position to make the Go/Kill and prioritization decisions needed on projects—certainly in a far better position than a group of corporate executives at the top!

BUs; and at the same time, the performance, strengths, opportunities, and plans of the BU provide upward input into the decision. If your firm has deficiencies here, note that there have been many methods proposed over the years for deciding resource allocations across BUs. Some typical approaches we witnessed were outlined in Chapter 4:

- ▶ *Objectives and task:* Each BU begins with its business and new product objectives (for example, annual growth; and thus, sales from new products, next five years); and then computes how many product launches, how many projects per stage, and hence amount of resources that will be required to achieve the objectives.
- ▶ *Competitive parity:* R&D resources are allocated across BUs so that each business spends roughly what the rest of its industry does (R&D spending as a percent of sales).
- ▶ *History:* Some companies base the allocation largely on history: take last year's budgeted amount, and add or subtract a little.
- ▶ *Opportunistic:* Spend all you can afford in each business, as long as the projects are good ones (for example, profitability exceeds the risk-adjusted cost of capital).
- ▶ *Based on results:* This approach is not strategic at all (that is, it does not begin with either the corporate or the BU's strategy), but simply *focuses on results.* Allocate more development money to businesses that are successful at product development, and take away from those that are less successful; that is, feed the strong, focus the weak. Before you dismiss this method, recall that this decision rule tends to allocate money to those business units with excellent new product opportunities or to those with considerable

product development expertise—which is exactly where the money *should* be allocated!

♦ *Corporate planning models:* Perhaps the best known models for resource allocation across businesses are the traditional "stars, cash cows, dogs" models, specifically the BCG and GE/McKinsey models.[2] In these corporate strategy and planning models, each BU is scored or rated on various factors, which are then combined into several major dimensions. Depending on the model, the axes or main dimensions usually boil down to market attractiveness and business position. That is: Is the BU facing an attractive market? And is the BU a strong one—well poised to attack the market? A two-by-two or three-by-three cell matrix is constructed and BUs are located on this two-dimensional matrix (see Exhibit 6.2).

Each BU develops a strategic mission, which depends in part on its location on the matrix. For example, the BCG model classifies BUs as cash cows, stars, dogs, and problem children, and provides suggested strategies or a mission for each. Resource allocation then ensues. The matrix location (which cell the BU is in according to Exhibit 6.2), together with the strategic mission for the BU, helps determine how much funding the business unit receives. Both R&D monies and people are part of this resource allocation decision.

Example: Agro is a smaller BU within a large corporation. Annually, Agro's management develops its business plan, largely financial, for the BU. Plans from all BUs are reviewed and discussed annually in a meeting of the unit general managers and corporate executives. Here, resource allocations are made. Via this process, Agro's financial projections are accepted and Agro receives its capital

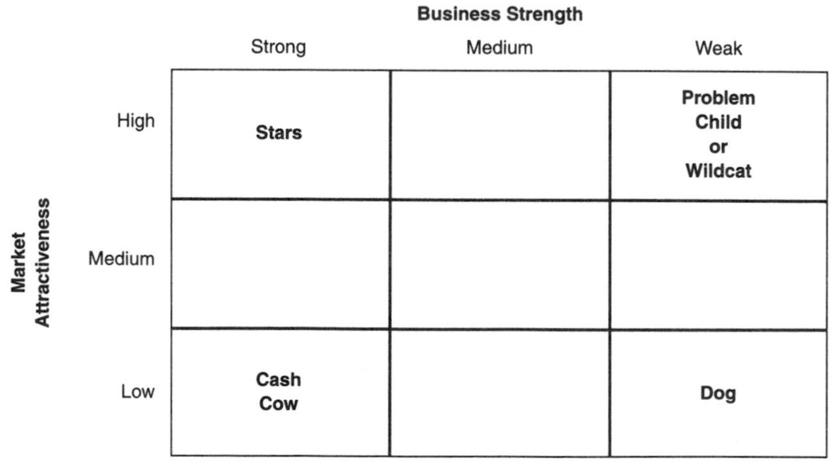

Business Strength

	Strong	Medium	Weak
High	**Stars**		**Problem Child or Wildcat**
Medium			
Low	**Cash Cow**		**Dog**

(Market Attractiveness)

Exhibit 6.2   Typical Corporate Allocation Model

Note: Business units are classed into one of the 9 cells. A mission and strategy are decided; resources are allocated.

Source: Adaptation of the General Electric (GE) model.

A Centralized Project Portfolio

Although many major firms are decentralized and leave new product and R&D spending decisions to the BU level, there are several notable exceptions where projects from the BUs might be considered centrally:

- *Large projects:* In some firms, the magnitude of certain projects demands that they be reviewed at a higher level than the BU senior management. Such approvals go right to the top of the organization. An example is a new product project involving a major capital expenditure.

The result is that the BU manages a portfolio of projects, most of which are likely within its spending and approval levels. Portfolio management is thus self-contained within the BU. But there is also a portfolio of major projects, which is the domain of the senior executives in the corporation. Thus there is a project portfolio management process at the top of the corporation, one that focuses on a few major projects, is centralized, and includes projects from all BUs.

- *Cross-BU projects:* Some projects involve several BUs and might be dealt with centrally. For example, platform projects could cut across BU boundaries. In some firms, these multi-BU projects are simply part of each participating BU's portfolio. In other firms, however, there may be a desire to deal with such projects centrally, thus requiring a centralized portfolio management approach, much like that described above for large projects.

Although such projects are limited to the few largest platform projects, or the ones that involve several BUs, the point still must be made that project portfolio management *also occurs centrally,* even in decentralized firms. This chapter deals with portfolio management at the BU level. But recognize that these *same approaches* can be used *at the top* of the corporation as well in centralized portfolio management.

- *Inability to let go:* Some senior corporate executives still want the ultimate say on all new product projects in their corporation. The paradigm is this: the BUs rate and rank their own projects and develop their own project portfolio. This prioritized list then goes to a central or corporate office for approval. The corporate executives put their blessing on certain projects, and in so doing, assign the new product budget to that BU. We did not see much evidence of this procedure in North America, but it was common in Europe (for example, in certain German firms we interviewed). The net result is that each BU requires its own portfolio management process—but so does the corporate management, in order to oversee all projects.

---

and operating budgets. The operating budget includes R&D and marketing budgets, both of which are used to develop and launch new products.

Allocation of resources across businesses is, strictly speaking, not portfolio management of new product or R&D projects. Nonetheless, these allocation decisions across BUs are intimately connected to project portfolio decisions, so much so that they cannot be dismissed. We recommend that you address the BU allocation decision and consider some of the more useful methods described above as useful tools here: objectives and task; competitive parity; results-based; or corporate planning models.

The premise in Chapters 6 and 7 is that if you are a decentralized company and there are defined business units in your company, then you likely already have in place a resource allocation method across BUs. That is, each BU has a budget, including R&D, marketing, and capital monies and people. Thus, the question facing you is not, "How much money and people should our BU be allotted to undertake development projects?" but "How do we spend the money and people we have been allocated?" (see Exhibit 6.1). For the smaller firm—a single BU—the question is moot: the R&D, marketing, and capital budget and people resources for the company are by default the resources and money that the BU owns.

The Strategy-Process Matrix: An Introduction

Assume we begin from a position where top-level resource allocation has occurred across BUs, using perhaps one of the corporate strategy and planning tools outlined (such as the BCG, McKinsey, or GE models). At this point, the question becomes: How should the BU allocate its limited product development resources? Note that the methods outlined below also apply both to smaller firms, where the BU is the entire company, and to larger firms using centralized portfolio management.

Now to the question: What type of PMP is right for you and your business? Not surprisingly, as we discovered, there is no single answer. The "right PMP" depends on the nature of your business and on what decision processes you already have in place for charting your new product direction and project selection.

The Strategy-Process Matrix

The two dimensions of the strategy-process matrix owe their legitimacy to a major benchmarking study of new product performance.[3] This study of 161 businesses sought to investigate new product performance across business units, and to determine what causes some BUs to perform better than others. The study identified many performance drivers, including climate and culture, the role of top management, a strong market and customer orientation, and so on. *Three cornerstones of performance* stood out, however, and are shown in Exhibit 6.3—our "three-legged stool." They include:

1. Having a *high-quality new product process* in place: one that features tough Go/Kill decision points or gates; builds in solid up-front homework and the voice of the customer; ensures sharp, early product defini-

tion; and focuses on quality of execution. This is the number one driver of performance, with strong positive impacts on new success rates and the business unit's ability to achieve its new product sales and profit performance objectives.

2. Having a *new product strategy for the business:* one with clear new product goals; which is linked to the business's overall strategy and goals; which identifies strategic arenas and their priorities; and which has a long-term thrust.

3. Having the *necessary resources* in place: adequate R&D spending and the appropriate numbers of people allocated to product development, in light of the business's goals. In short, there is no free lunch here: magnitude of spending very much affects performance!

Exhibit 6.3   The Three Cornerstones of Performance

We use a two-by-two strategy-process matrix to define the appropriate Portfolio Management Process (see Exhibit 6.4). The two key dimensions of this matrix are the first two drivers of performance from the benchmarking study outlined in the box, namely,

▶ whether the BU has a systematic *Stage-Gate or new product process,* with clearly defined *gates and criteria* in place and working
▶ whether there exists a clear and specific *new product strategy* for the BU.

The third cornerstone of performance, *resources,* is precisely what we are trying to determine how to allocate.

Your business's location in the four-quadrant figure in Exhibit 6.4 helps to decide the appropriate Portfolio Management Process. For example, if you have both a well-defined and proficient new product process (complete with gates or Go/Kill decision points that really work), along with a defined new product strategy for your business, then you are in quadrant IV in Exhibit 6.4. That means that you require the most sophisticated of Portfolio Management Processes: one driven by strategy that totally integrates your real-time gating process (where individual project decisions are made) with a periodic portfolio review mechanism (which adjusts the portfolio). Other quadrants demand other types of PMP.

	No New Product Strategy	New Product Strategy with Defined Goals and Arenas
No New Product Process: No Stage-Gate Process with Tough Gates	**I: No Process, No NP Strategy** - A budgeting exercise: - projects selected annually based on financial merits.	**II: NP Strategy Exists, but No Stage-Gate Process** - The portfolio review decides the portfolio at annual or semiannual meetings; project selection based on strategy. - No gates, but occasional project reviews, which are largely information updates.
Systematic, Defined New Product Stage-Gate Process with Go/Kill Gates	**III: No NP Strategy, but Stage-Gate Process in Place** - The portfolio is decided at the gates. - The gates must be rigorous. - The portfolio review is little more than an update of gate decisions already made.	**IV: Both Stage-Gate Process and NP Strategy in Place** - An integrated portfolio management process (PMP). - The strategy drives the portfolio. - The gates operationalize the portfolio method. - The portfolio review makes course corrections.

Exhibit 6.4   The Strategy-Process Matrix

POINTS FOR MANAGEMENT TO PONDER

Where is your business in the strategy-process matrix of Exhibit 6.4? Note that the highest new product performance is achieved in quadrant IV: the business has both an effective gating process (a new product process with Go/Kill decision points that work!) and a new product strategy for the entire business. If you lack either or both, the next section provides some insight into developing a new product strategy for your business, while Appendix A provides details on a new product process with gates.

What Is New Product Strategy?

Business strategy in our context refers to the business unit's strategy, and new product strategy is a component of business strategy. By *business and new product strategy,* we do not mean a vaguely worded statement of intent, like a vision or mission statement. Rather, we mean operational, action-specific strategies as defined in Chapter 4. Recall that strategy is about where you spend money, and that a business's new product strategy includes:

1. new product goals for the business
2. how new products tie into the business's overall goals
3. arenas of strategic focus, including priorities
4. spending splits across these arenas (R&D funds, possibly marketing and capital funds for developments)
5. how to attack each arena.

The concept of *strategic arenas* is at the heart of a new product strategy. A business and new product strategy, at minimum, specifies clearly defined *strategic arenas* for the BU to focus on, including how it will focus its product development efforts. These strategic arenas can be defined in terms of dimensions such as:

◗ markets
◗ product types, product lines, or product categories
◗ technologies
◗ technology platforms.

Strategy definition goes further, however: it indicates the relative emphasis—or strategic priorities—accorded each arena of strategic focus. For example, if markets A, B, and C are identified as "strategic arenas," the *relative priorities* of these markets should be part of the strategy. This means that the strategy must be translated into spending decisions: the relative spending priorities or splits (allocation of resources across arenas: how much to spend in each of markets A, B, and C).

The issue of *how to attack* each strategic arena should also be part of the business's new product strategy. For example, for one arena, the strategy may be to be the industry innovator (the first to the market with new products); in another arena, the attack plan may be to be a "fast follower," rapidly copying and improving upon competitive entries. Other strategies might focus on being low-cost versus the differentiator versus a niche player; or on emphasizing certain strengths, core competencies, or product attributes or advantages. The attack plans logically lead to decisions regarding how much to spend on different types of projects (spending split by project types such as platform developments versus new products versus maintenance and renewal projects).

Define Spending Splits

Decisions on spending splits must be made in order to translate strategy into reality. Strategic priority decisions should be considered on a *variety of dimensions* other than just markets A, B, and C. Some options you have (from Chapter 4) are:

- *Types of projects:* Decisions or splits can be made in terms of the *types of projects.* For example: "Given our aggressive strategic stance, we target 30% of R&D spending to genuine new products and another 20% to fundamental research and platform development (technology development for the future); 30% will go to product modifications and improvements, only 10% to cost reductions, with another 10% to product maintenance and fixes." (There are various ways to define "project types"; see examples in Exhibits 3.17, 4.1, 4.2, and 6.5.)
- *Project newness:* Decisions or splits can be made in terms of project newness, using the "newness matrix." Recall from Chapter 4 the six-cell matrix with technology and market newness as the key dimensions. Projects might be classed as "defend or penetrate" projects through to "new businesses/new ventures" (see Exhibit 4.3).
- *Technologies or technology platforms:* Spending splits can be made across technology types (for example, base, key, pacing, and embryonic technologies) or across specific platforms (platforms X, Y, Z, and so on).

- *By stage or phase of development:* Some firms distinguish between early-stage projects and projects into development and beyond: two buckets are created, one for development projects, the other for early-stage projects. Recall Company G in Chapter 5, where management allocated *seed corn money* to a separate bucket for early-stage projects.
- *Markets:* Markets or segments are key arenas, and an obvious way to split development resources. For example, "Market A is top priority. We will aim 50% of R&D spending at Market A."
- *Product lines:* Similar spending splits may be made across product lines in your business. Alternately, consider using a *product-market matrix* to identify cells or strategic arenas, and split money across these, much as Telenor did in Chapter 1.

Note that these spending splits across arenas can be expressed in terms of dollars or percentages; additionally, priorities can be translated into numbers of projects or numbers of launches expected in each strategic arena.

POINTS FOR MANAGEMENT TO PONDER

1. Recall from Chapter 4 that you have many options in the way that this splitting of resources is done. These spending splits can be along selective dimensions (pick your most important strategic dimension, as suggested in Chapter 4 by Rohm and Haas); or along a single but vital dimension, such as project types (the Mercedes star method at Allied Signal), or along multiple dimensions as listed above (and as done at other firms—see Strategic Buckets, Exhibit 4.4).
2. Additionally, note that you can establish Strategic Buckets, with *solid walls* and each bucket with *its own portfolio* of projects (multiple portfolios); or Target Spending Levels, with *more porous walls* and a *single portfolio* of projects; or some mixture of both.
3. Finally, note that establishing these buckets or spending splits logically proceeds via a top-down and strategic planning exercise; but don't forget a bottom-up view as well: that is, the realities of the situation, namely, the opportunities available (ongoing projects, projects on hold, and new proposals) must also influence the resource splits across arenas. This splitting exercise should not be a strictly top-down and theoretical effort!

Example: Senior management at Agro spent an exhausting session mapping out the BU's strategy. This involved reviewing the strategic mission and vision for the BU—this had already been developed in previous years and remained valid (see Exhibit 6.5). Next a thorough SWOT (strengths, weaknesses, opportunities, threats) analysis was undertaken. A market-by-market analysis and core competency assessment yielded a set of product line and market segment priorities. These were markets that Agro management really wanted to focus on and the product lines that management wanted to target these markets with. For the majority of markets, the BU already had a presence and the majority of product types were familiar ones—existing product lines for Agro. Different technology types as possible arenas of focus were briefly discussed, but the BU was focused largely on one very successful biological technology where it had considerable strengths. Other technologies as arenas of focus were ruled out.

These selected markets and product lines were next prioritized. Then management moved to the issue of *new product strategy* for the BU, which logically evolved from the business's strategy. Management went through a difficult exercise of splitting the development budget across these prioritized markets and product lines for the BU—in effect, making forced choices, much like the top-down approach outlined in Chapter 4. Target Spending Levels were established across markets and product lines (Exhibit 6.5). The "attack plan" across arenas was fairly uniform: leading-edge product development, first to market with innovative new products.

Perhaps the most important dimension to management was *project types,* however. Thus, management created Strategic Buckets here, and made some idealized splits in development resources by project type: that is, how much money for genuine new products, product improvements and modifications, product maintenance and fixes, fundamental research projects, and cost reductions (for example, process improvements). The two latter categories—fundamental research and cost reductions—are not new product projects, but these projects do compete for the same pool of resources and must be considered in the split.

The result of this new product strategy session is summarized in Exhibit 6.5, where Target Spending Levels across product lines and markets are shown (top two pie charts) and Strategic Buckets across project types are also displayed (bottom pie chart).

There are several positive points to note in Agro's strategic exercise:

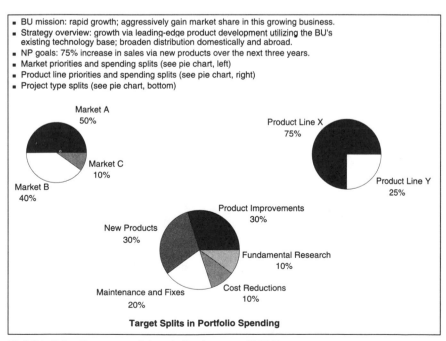

Exhibit 6.5   Summary of Agro's Business and NP Strategy

1. First, senior management leads the way: it is the senior people of the business who took up the challenge and decided the business's strategy.
2. Next, this business strategy is translated into a new product strategy, complete with arenas (markets, product lines, and project types). In management's eyes, the most important of these was project types; hence buckets were created here.
3. The split in resources across arenas, although top-down and strategically driven, also considers opportunities within each arena. This is not a sterile strategic exercise, but rather an *iterative one* between a top-down, strategic approach and a bottom-up approach which takes into account active as well as proposed projects and opportunities.
4. Finally, note that this split in resources across key dimensions at Agro took two forms:
   • Target Spending Levels: For example, the proposed splits in resources by markets and product lines (target amounts in top two pie charts in Exhibit 6.5) were established as guides or targets.
   • Strategic Buckets: The split by project type is a much more concrete split; five buckets were established for Agro. The difference here is that, in the case of buckets, Agro ends up with five portfolios or lists of projects rather than a single list; that projects do not compete with each other across buckets; and that different criteria can be used to rate and rank projects in different buckets.

POINTS FOR MANAGEMENT TO PONDER

The place to begin portfolio management is with the *strategy of your business*—both your business strategy, and flowing from it, *your new product strategy*. Strategy development is the job of the leadership team of the business: the senior people must lead here. Indeed this is how the senior people become very involved in your Portfolio Management Process—by charting the business's strategy.

After defining goals for the business, map the battlefield: that is, identify arenas of strategic focus (markets, product lines, technologies, and platforms), and prioritize them. Then, define new product goals for the business: what percentage of sales or profit or growth new products will contribute.

Next, develop spending splits across key dimensions (for example, these might be markets, product lines, or project types; or pick dimensions that represent strategic thrusts to you). Define Strategic Buckets or Target Spending Levels across dimensions, much like Agro did in Exhibit 6.5. Finally define attack plans for each arena: how you plan to win on each battlefield or in each arena.

Using the Strategy-Process Matrix to Decide the Portfolio Approach

Which PMP is right for your company and BU? Consider the matrix in Exhibit 6.4, which is bounded by the two dimensions of *strategy* and *process*.

Quadrant IV: The Business Unit Has Both a Well-Defined New Product Strategy and a Systematic New Product Process, Complete with Gates

Quadrant IV in Exhibit 6.4 is a mixed blessing. It is by far the best quadrant to be in from a performance standpoint.* Recall that our major benchmarking study revealed that the two strongest drivers of new product performance at the business unit level are having a high-quality, systematic new product process and also having a well-defined new product strategy for the business.[3] That's the good news.

The bad news is that this quadrant presents the greatest challenges—both conceptual and operational—to effective portfolio management. It is by far the most complex in that *several potentially competing decision processes* are in play. Having both a strategy and a new product or Stage-Gate process means that the Portfolio Management Process must be synchronized with both the strategy and the gating process. Here's how:

In quadrant IV, *the BU's strategy drives the portfolio decision process*. The *Portfolio Review* and models driven by strategy are the foundation for portfolio decisions. These strategically driven reviews and decisions should occur quarterly or semiannually.** At the same time, a *strong Stage-Gate process* is also in place, and therefore the gates must help decide the projects. The gating process is where the decisions are made on individual projects on an ongoing basis. Note that the gating process is continuous, occurring throughout the year. The two decision processes are, thus, the Portfolio Review and the Stage-Gate process. One is periodic; one is real-time. Both decision processes must be fully integrated and closely linked to the BU's strategy. This integrated Portfolio Management Process is shown conceptually in Exhibit 6.6. Note how each decision process feeds the other.

Since the recommended Portfolio Management Process for quadrant IV is the most complex of the four quadrants, we outline it in much more depth in the next chapter. But first, let's take a quick look at the three other quadrants. Note that the recommended methods in each are abbreviated versions of the full-fledged PMP for quadrant IV outlined in Chapter 7.

---

*An analysis of our benchmarking data reveals that BUs with explicit new product strategies and also effective new product processes with gates—quadrant IV businesses—fare the best in terms of numerous performance metrics (for example, percentage of sales by new products; success rates; meeting sales and profit objectives; and so on). Businesses in quadrants II and III fare moderately well, consistently across all metrics. By contrast, quadrant I business perform consistently and significantly more poorly across all performance measures.

**Some firms stretch the timing and only have annual Portfolio Reviews. Experience suggests that the world moves too quickly for these annual course adjustments, and that semiannual or even quarterly Portfolio Reviews are preferable.

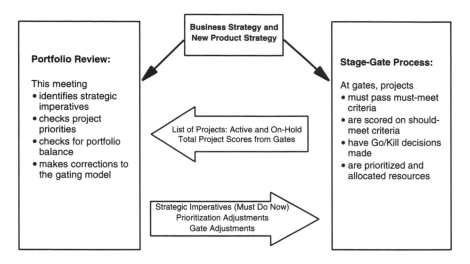

Exhibit 6.6   An Overview of the Portfolio Management Process

Note: The Portfolio Review feeds the Stage-Gate model, and the Stage-Gate model feeds the Portfolio Review. Both approaches are synchronized and both are driven by strategy.

Quadrant II: The BU Has a Well-Defined Business and New Product Strategy, But No New Product Process with Gates in Place

As in quadrant IV, the portfolio must also be driven by the BU's strategy. However, the portfolio of projects—project selection—must occur at the periodic Portfolio Review. Indeed, lacking a new product process and with no real gates, the Portfolio Review must *serve double duty:* making project selection decisions on individual projects and overseeing the total portfolio!

In effect, *only half the decision-making processes* are at work here, and according to our benchmarking studies, the results are inferior.[4] Recall that some progressive firms view the Portfolio Review as just that—a chance to oversee the entire portfolio—but not to become immersed in the details of project selection. But with no gates in place, the Portfolio Review soon becomes the only project selection forum—not an ideal situation.

There are many problems with this quadrant II approach. First, project selection decisions made at the Portfolio Review are made in calender time (often with long lead times); and thus the method fails to respond to changing circumstances and new opportunities, which tend to occur in real time. Next, the Portfolio Review must deal with many projects at one meeting and so cuts short the informed, in-depth decision-making that occurs at gates, where the focus is only on one or a few projects. Finally, lacking tough Go/Kill gates, once a project is "approved" at a Portfolio Review, it tends never again to receive a serious Go/Kill review. Once "in the portfolio," it takes on a life of its own!

The Portfolio Management Process for quadrant II is an abbreviated version of the PMP found in quadrant IV (the left side of Exhibit 6.6). Project selection occurs at the Portfolio Review meetings held semiannually or quarterly (lacking tough gates, the portfolio reviews are really the *only place* where Go/Kill and resource allocation decisions are made on specific projects). At Portfolio Reviews, projects are reviewed much like in quadrant IV, and resource allocations are made (described later).

Although there is no gating system in place, projects nonetheless should be reviewed periodically. But the quadrant II project review is more a check that projects are on time, on budget, and not in trouble—in effect, it is a project status and information session. These real-time project reviews are not resource allocation or decision meetings.

If your business fits in quadrant II—a defined BU strategy but no new product process—we have two recommendations:

- *Short term:* use half of the PMP method outlined for quadrant IV (the left side in Exhibit 6.6), namely, the Portfolio Review to make sharper project selection decisions.
- *Longer term:* design and implement a Stage-Gate process with tough gates and move to quadrant IV (see Appendix A).

Quadrant III: The BU Has a Systematic Stage-Gate Process, But Has No Defined Business or New Product Strategy (or the One That Exists Is Vaguely Defined)

This situation is the opposite of quadrant II. The PMP cannot be driven by the BU's business strategy because there is none (or it is so loosely defined that it provides no real direction). Lacking a well-defined strategy, Portfolio Reviews are ineffective. How can one debate portfolio balance and the right split in resources if there is no strategy to guide this? So, the *gates must be where all the project selection and all portfolio decisions are made.* That is, the gates in the new product process drive the PMP. Once again, we have half the decision processes at work, this time the right side of Exhibit 6.6.

As might be predicted, the results are inferior to those found in quadrant IV. While gate decisions may be very astute—each project is a sound one from a financial and business standpoint—taken together, these gate decisions may be wrong. There is no attempt to stand back and look at the totality of projects and there is no real direction to the portfolio of projects simply because there is no BU strategy to guide the Portfolio Review. The end result might be a portfolio of solid projects, each considered on its own, but a portfolio that lacks balance, has no direction, and does not support the business's strategy.

The approach here is that, once again, an abbreviated version of the full quadrant IV PMP be employed. Strong, effective gates are key to success here. Gates must be rigorous and employ defined criteria for making resource allocations.

These Go/Kill criteria are outlined in Chapter 7, but include reward, probabilities of success, and other criteria that are proxies for reward and success likelihood. You may also have periodic portfolio meetings, but lacking strategy, these meetings are likely to be impotent updates of gate decisions already made.

If your business fits in quadrant III—a new product process with gates, but no well-defined BU strategy—we have two recommendations:

- *Short term:* use half of the PMP method outlined for quadrant IV (the right side in Exhibit 6.6). Employ the gates in your new product process to make sound project selection decisions. At least you'll have solid projects in the portfolio!
- *Longer term:* move to quadrant IV. Work on sharpening your business and new product strategy (see section entitled "What Is New Product Strategy?" earlier in this chapter).

Quadrant I: The BU Has Neither a Business Nor a New Product Strategy—Nor Does It Have a New Product Process with Gates

Quadrant I is the simplest of four situations. In quadrant I, there exists no new product process and there are no tough Go/Kill gates to yield sound project selection decisions. Further, there is no new product strategy to provide direction. Lacking a strategy and a Stage-Gate or new product process, "portfolio management" amounts to a simple annual budgeting exercise, where projects are rated and ranked largely on straightforward financial criteria: Which project has the highest return, the highest NPV, and the greatest chances of commercial success? Project reviews, when held, are not decision points; rather, they are information sessions. It's a simple game in quadrant I. The trouble is that there is no strategic direction to the portfolio, and Go/Kill decisions on specific projects are lacking. Quadrant I may not yield great results, but the decision process is straightforward!

Our recommendation:

- Move toward quadrant IV. Start thinking about a business and new product strategy for your BU, and consider installing a Stage-Gate new product process with tough Go/Kill gates (see Appendix A).

    Example: The corporation, in which Agro is a BU, had installed a five-stage, five-gate new product process several years previously. Indeed, it was the use of this Stage-Gate process that alerted management to the fact that most of the BUs really did not have a very clearly defined new product strategy for their businesses; hence, the effort to define a strategy. Thus, Agro fits into the preferred quadrant IV: both a Stage-Gate process, as well as a business and new product strategy, are in place.

Now, it is time to revisit the most complex, yet most effective, situation in Exhibit 6.4—quadrant IV. The next chapter outlines in detail the Portfolio Management Process for firms in quadrant IV. Note that the other quadrants are essentially abbreviations of what you will see in Chapter 7.

POINTS FOR MANAGEMENT TO PONDER

In which of the four quadrants is your business? If you're in quadrants II or III, you have at least some of the decision processes in place to provide effective portfolio management. However, consider installing the missing pieces and act on the recommendations outlined above. If you're in quadrant I, you have much work to do, but at least you have the advantage of beginning with a clean slate! If you're in the desirable quadrant, quadrant IV, you are well positioned; but there may be much left to do before your Portfolio Management Process is up and running effectively. The next chapter provides the road ahead!

Making Portfolio Management Work for You: A Closer Look at the Portfolio Management Process

The Portfolio Management Process for Quadrant IV

Consider the business unit in quadrant IV in the strategy-process matrix of the previous chapter (Exhibit 6.4). Here the BU has both a business and new product strategy, as well as a Stage-Gate process in place. Recall that this quadrant is the best one from a performance standpoint; it is also the most complex in terms of the portfolio management process, simply because of the various but valid decision processes that must be in harmony. In this chapter we describe the PMP in quadrant IV in considerable detail. (Note that firms in quadrants II and III can employ parts of the quadrant IV PMP as noted in the previous chapter.)

The key components of the Portfolio Management Process are outlined in Exhibit 7.1 and form the major sections in this chapter. Recall that there are three important decision processes at work in quadrant IV: the development of the BU's business and new product strategy; the new product process or Stage-Gate process; and the Portfolio Review. In this chapter:

- we begin in the shaded box at the top of Exhibit 7.1 with the role of new product strategy, how it must drive the portfolio, and how this is done in practice.
- we move to the right side of Exhibit 7.1, where we focus on the gates in the new product process and how the portfolio management process is operationalized at the gate decisions.
- we next move to the left side of Exhibit 7.1 and outline the Portfolio Review and models, how the portfolio is adjusted, and how the Portfolio Review provides corrections to the gating model in the new product process.
- we bring all three decision processes together to form an integrated decision system.

151

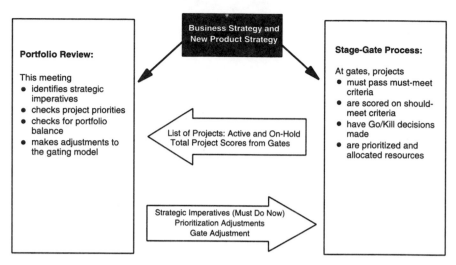

Exhibit 7.1   Strategy Drives the Portfolio Management Process

Strategy Drives the Portfolio

The Portfolio Management Process is driven by strategy (see the shaded box at the top of Exhibit 7.1). Why? Because strategy begins when you start spending money. Up to that point, strategy is just words on paper. Since portfolio choice is about allocating resources and making Go/Kill decisions on projects—in short, where you spend your money—then the *portfolio choice must begin with strategy.*

After all, strategy guides and directs a business. It defines what is in or out of bounds; and it defines arenas of focus as well as their relative emphasis. The *manifestation of strategy* is decisions about where you will spend your money—the portfolio decisions.

Strategy Is Vital to the PMP

In the PMP, strategy provides direction in three ways:

1. *Strategic Fit and Importance:* The BU's business and new product strategy is used as a criterion to ensure that all projects are on-strategy; that is, all projects are within a product, market, or technology area defined as *an arena of strategic focus,* and to ensure that selected projects are indeed the *strategically important* ones.
2. *Breakdown of Spending:* Strategy should also be used to define spending breakdowns across markets, product types, technologies, and even project types (extensions versus new products, long-term versus short-term, and so on). In the section on strategy in the previous chapter, we saw how a defined new product strategy for the BU should not only define what is on-

---

Key Strategic Selection Criteria

Strategy defines the key criteria—strategic fit and strategic importance—in the gate and portfolio models. These criteria are used in a checklist or a scoring model to rate and rank projects. Sample criteria that are driven by strategy and might be used at a gate (or at a Portfolio Review meeting) are:

Must-Meet (Checklist):

Does the project fit our strategy? That is, is it within a product, market, or technology arena that we have defined in our business strategy?

Yes ___ No ___

Here, a "No" kills the project—culls it out of the project pipeline.

Should-Meet (Scoring Model) (these are scored 1–5 or 0–10):

* To what degree is the project on-strategy (fits our strategy)? (0 = not at all; 10 = perfectly fits strategy)
* What is the strategic importance of the project—how important is this project to the business? (0 = not at all; 10 = essential from a strategic viewpoint)

---

strategy but should go as far as defining desired spending splits along key dimensions. For example, strategy should define spending priorities and splits in terms of:

▶ strategic arenas of focus (product types, markets, or technology areas)
▶ project types (platform projects, new products, modifications, and product maintenance projects).

In this way, Strategic Buckets of funds—envelopes of money—or Target Spending Levels are preestablished (desired levels of spending in different areas), which should mirror the business's new product strategy.

Recall from Chapter 4 that these first two points—strategic fit and importance, and breakdown of spending reflecting strategic priorities—are subtly different. For example, a portfolio can have every project consistent with the business's strategy, yet the breakdown of the spending is skewed too much toward one market or product line. When all projects fit the BU's strategy, and when the spending breakdown across project types reflects the BU's strategic priorities, then we have *strategic alignment.*

3. *Strategic Imperatives:* Strategy may also define some "must do" projects right away (that is, unless there exist some other killer variables, let's give these projects a "Go" and top priority). These "must do" projects are called *strategic imperatives.* For example, if the business's strategy were to expand aggressively in one key market, and one new product project was identified as pivotal to this expansion, the decision here might be an immediate "Go." Alternately, if another market were defined as a strategic priority, and a key product improvement was needed just to defend share in that market, once again a "strategic decision" might be made: an immediate "Go"!

POINTS FOR MANAGEMENT TO PONDER

The business's new product strategy must drive the portfolio. It does so in three ways:

- ▶ by providing the key "strategic fit" and "strategic importance criteria" used to rate and rank projects via checklists and scoring models (at either gate meetings or portfolio reviews)
- ▶ by providing guides to spending breakdowns—either Strategic Buckets or Target Spending Levels—so that spending mirrors the business's strategic priorities
- ▶ by identifying strategic imperatives—"must do now" projects.

If your business lacks a new product strategy, then you are missing a key element in the PMP. Revisit Chapters 4 and 6 for some guidance.

The New Product Process—Gating Is Also Key for the PMP

The second vital decision-making system in the PMP is the new product Stage-Gate process, specifically the gates (the shaded box on the right side of Exhibit 7.2). In an effective new product process, gates are the quality control checkpoints. Gates are where senior management puts their blessing on projects; and gates are where the resources are allocated on a day-to-day basis throughout the year. Thus, the PMP is operationalized at gate meetings on individual projects. Note that these individual decisions on specific projects must be integrated into a greater whole, the portfolio. View the individual projects as fingers, the portfolio of projects as the fist!

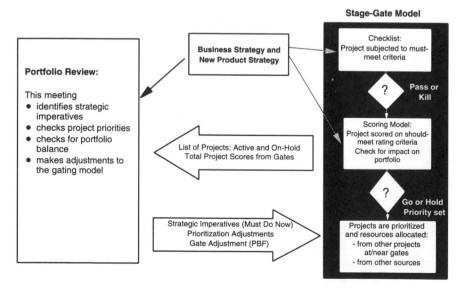

Exhibit 7.2 An Important Facet of PMP: The Gates in the Stage-Gate Process

Note: The gates in the Stage-Gate process (right side) are where day-to-day Go/Kill decisions are made, and are an important facet of the total Portfolio Management Process.

Getting the gates right is a difficult challenge, so we devote a major section of this chapter to gates. Here is a road map of this critical section:

1. First, we introduce the concept of a *Stage-Gate process* and provide a brief outline.
2. Next, we propose a scoring model and checklist method to *achieve the three goals* of effective portfolio management: value maximization, balance, and strategic alignment.
3. *Gate criteria*—the items you can use to score, rate, and rank projects—are outlined, with samples provided.
4. How gates indeed *achieve the three goals* is summarized next.
5. How gates consider *balance* and *strategic alignment* is outlined, a difficult but important issue.
6. Next, we discuss *correcting the balance* at the gate decision points, and outline the details of correcting mechanisms so that gate decisions move the portfolio toward the ideal.
7. *Prioritizing projects and resource allocation* is the next topic. Here we view the gates as a two-part decision process.
8. A final and controversial issue dealt with in this section is just *how firm resource commitments* made to projects are.

This road map for this section on gates is sketched in Exhibit 7.3.

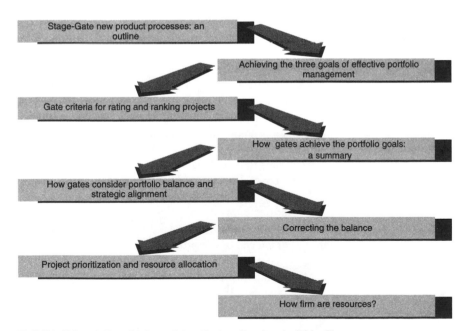

Exhibit 7.3 A Road Map of the Gating Section in This Chapter

Stage-Gate Processes

A Stage-Gate process is a road map to drive new product projects from idea through to launch.[1] A typical Stage-Gate process is shown in Exhibit 7.4 and described in more detail in Appendix A. The process illustrated in the exhibit has five stages, including familiar ones such as development, validation, and launch. Preceding each stage is a gate—a Go/Kill decision point, where management meets to decide on the merits of the project and whether it should receive funding or resources for the next stage. These decision-makers or gatekeepers are usually the senior managers in the BU, especially at gate 3 on, where resource commitments increase.

Numerous companies have adopted Stage-Gate and similar new product processes, including Exxon Chemical, P&G, GTE, Hoechst, SC Johnsons Wax, Polaroid, Corning, Dow Chemicals, Reckitt & Colman, International Paper, Union Camp, Lego, Rohm and Haas, St. Gobain, Carlsberg, Pillsbury, American Express, Royal Bank of Canada, and many others.

Stage-Gate New Product Processes: An Outline

A Stage-Gate Process is the game plan to drive projects from the idea stage through to launch (see box entitled "Stage-Gate Processes" and Appendix A). Embedded within the process are *gate decision points,* where the day-to-day Go/Kill decisions are made on projects.

Example: Recall that Agro's new product process is a five-stage, five-gate model, very similar to the one in Exhibit 7.4. The gates were working effectively, according to management, culling out the poor projects. But an overall Portfolio Management Process that took a more holistic and integrated view of all projects was missing.

At some gate in the Stage-Gate Process, resource commitments become sufficiently large that prioritization must take place. Prior to this gate, projects are reasonably small and ill-defined so that putting them into the PMP—subjecting them to a formal portfolio prioritization—does not make much sense. Either the data on each project are very uncertain (for example, financial projections, and estimates of future resource requirements, timing and success likelihoods), the resource commitments are too small, or both (see box, "When Does the PMP Kick In?").

Assume that the Portfolio Management Process kicks in at the pivotal "Go to Development" decision point, or gate 3 in the model in Exhibit 7.4.* This means:

- Projects are prioritized starting at this gate.
- From this gate onward, resource commitments are firm either until the next gate or possibly through to the end of the project.

From this gate onward, one rule might be that the project continues to receive resources as long as it doesn't shoot itself. If the project meets all deliverables, stays

---

*This "kick-in" point may vary by company. For example, some firms spend considerable resources in stage 2, the stage before development, so that gate 2 is the point at which the portfolio model kicks in and project prioritization begins.

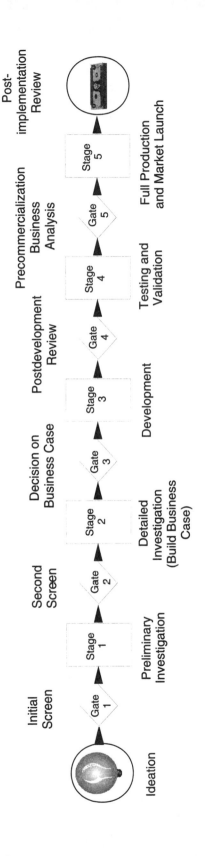

Exhibit 7.4 An Overview of a Generic Stage-Gate Process

Note: There are five stages plus the idea stage. Each stage is preceded by a Go/Kill decision point or "gate."

Source: Adapted from *Winning at New Products* by Robert G. Cooper. Stage-Gate is a trademark of R. G. Cooper and Associates Inc.

When Does the PMP Kick In?

This is a tricky issue. One does not want to ignore early-stage projects; yet most of these are ill-defined and lack the data needed for inclusion in a formal portfolio model. Recall the discussion in Chapter 5 on the topic (issue 2). Our suggestion:

▶ Design your formal PMP to begin at a gate in your Stage-Gate process where the project is sufficiently de-

fined and estimates of data needed to do portfolio analysis are available.

▶ In addition, design an *early-stage portfolio* of projects: a separate bucket of "seed corn money" for early-stage projects, which are too ill-defined to subject to a formal Portfolio Review; monitor this portfolio separately and informally (that is, less rigorously, less quantitatively).

---

on its time line, and continues to meet all successive gate criteria, it remains a "Go" and the resource commitments remain in place.

Note that different businesses employ *different rules* regarding the firmness of resource commitments. Later in this chapter, we will see some sample rules in the box entitled "How Firm Are Resource Commitments?" We recommend one of two rules:

- the one just cited above: once past a certain gate, resource commitments are firm, as long as the project remains a good one and continues to meet all criteria at successive gates.
- an alternate rule: resources are firm between gates (unless a project turns sour); but reprioritization occurs at every gate.

Achieving the Three Goals of Effective Portfolio Management

The gate decision criteria must be deliberately constructed to achieve three portfolio goals. Recall from Chapters 2, 3, and 4 what these goals were:

▶ *Maximization of value* to the business (here, value is measured in many ways—see Chapter 2)
▶ *Proper balance* of projects; for example, between high-risk and low-risk, between high payoff and more modest projects (see Chapter 3)
▶ *Strategic alignment,* where projects and spending breakdowns are consistent with the business's strategy (see Chapter 4).

How can these three potentially *conflicting goals* be realized in the same decision model? And how can projects be quantitatively rank-ordered from best to worst? Scoring models are a preferred tool here. When multiple goals exist, scoring models are particularly suited to *rating projects* as well as *ranking them* in order to yield a prioritized list. Recall that financial models are particularly limited in dealing with multiple goals.

In practice, we recommend that the gates should first use a checklist method (yes/no) to provide an initial culling, followed by a scoring model to deal with the multiple portfolio goals defined above:

- The checklist is used to weed out obvious misfit projects; for example, those that are way off-strategy or nonstarters for other reasons.
- The scoring model is then used to rate and rank projects against the multiple goals noted above.

Gate Criteria for Rating and Ranking Projects

The checklist and scoring model should consider specific criteria in several broad areas:

- Strategic (both strategic fit and strategic importance—highlighted in the box "Key Strategic Selection Criteria")
- Reward (What is the size of the prize [for example, NPV] if successful?)[*]
- Probability of success (commercial or technical)
- Balance (Does this project move us closer to the ideal portfolio in terms of balance across markets, technologies, product types, project types, and, most important, spending breakdowns that are consistent with strategy?).

In practice, a much longer list of factors is built into the scoring model and check-list—factors such as product advantage, market attractiveness, and synergies. These are simply proxies for reward or probability of success, hence, the long list of items used in the typical gate scoring model.

An excellent checklist and scoring model is shown in Exhibit 7.5. This is similar to the Hoechst model presented in Chapter 2, but has the advantage of being validated across more companies; further, many of the questions or criteria have been empirically shown to be strongly tied to new product profitability and success. Exhibit 7.5 provides an overview of the criteria: a set of must-meet and should-meet criteria for the "Go to Development" decision point. This is the gate where the portfolio model may kick in and serious project prioritization begins (gate 3 in Exhibit 7.4). The details of the model—how the scales are operationalized—are provided in Appendix B.

Example: Agro uses a combination checklist and scoring model at the various gates in its Stage-Gate process. Gate 3 is a vital decision point, where the project becomes a full-fledged development project. The gate 3 gatekeepers are senior management, and the meeting is chaired by the general manager of the business. The checklist and scoring models used at gate 3 are quite similar to the samples shown in Exhibit 7.5.

Consider a real project of Agro's at the gate 3 decision point, *Bio-55*. The project has had a small, two-person team working on it for the past four months.

---

[*]There exists debate about whether reward should be considered after or before probabilities of success have been factored in. Some firms use "most likely" but single-point estimates to determine the NPV; others use a probability model (for example, a decision tree) with various possible outcomes and probabilities of occurring; still others use a Monte Carlo simulation model that yields an expected NPV as well as a probability distribution around it; finally, some companies simply use a "risk-adjusted" NPV," obtained by using a higher discount rate in the case of riskier projects. See Chapter 3.

Market studies have been completed; some preliminary technical (laboratory) work has been undertaken, enough to establish a reasonable likelihood of technical feasibility. And the business case has been built. The product has been defined (target market, product benefits, price point, technical requirements, and high-level specs); the project justified (the financial analysis and business rationale); and the project plan or action plan mapped out for the next stages of the project.

At gate 3, senior management reviews the *Bio-55* project against a set of must-meet criteria (as in Exhibit 7.5). *Bio-55* passes all of them: there are no negative votes here. Next, the project is scored on the should-meet items. Here a 0–10 scoring model is used, and scores are averaged in an unweighted fashion to yield factors; factors are added to yield a total project score. In Agro's method, all factors must clear a minimum hurdle, and so must the total project score. Exhibit 7.5 shows the scoring model results accorded *Bio-55*. Out of a possible 60 points, the project scores 45.5, for a total project score of 76%. The *Bio-55* project scores very well and clears all the gate 3 hurdles, including the 60% hurdle on the total project score. It looks like a "Go"—or is it?

How Gates Achieve the Portfolio Goals: A Summary

Here's how the gates achieve the desired goals of maximum value, balance, and strategic alignment via a checklist and a scoring model:

Should Gate Criteria Change from Gate to Gate?

The dilemma is this: one wants to compare projects against each other that are at different stages of the development process. After all, they compete for the same pool of resources. Logically, then, all projects should be rated and ranked on the *same set of criteria*, regardless of the gate. The trouble is that the quality and nature of information available change as one moves through the process. Additionally, some of the issues may change at different stages of the project. So how can one use the same criteria for making Go/Kill and prioritization decisions from gate to gate?

Our suggestion: For the first few gates, the project is likely not in the formal Portfolio Management Process (see box, "When Does the PMP Kick In?"). Thus, these early gates need not have criteria identical to those of later ones.

Suppose the PMP kicks in at gate 3 in Exhibit 7.4. From gate 3 on, then, one should use the *same criteria* for Go/Kill and prioritization decisions (see sample list in Exhibit 7.5). The wording of the questions may change somewhat, as the rigor of the questioning increases; and the certainty of information also increases from gate to gate, hence allowing more definite decisions. However, the main criteria should remain the same.

To accommodate the fact that there are special issues that arise at later gates, some firms just add a blanket question at the beginning of the list of must-meet criteria: "Are all deliverables requested on the table; and are they of satisfactory quality?"

One more point: although the early gates can have their own criteria for Go/Kill decisions, for purposes of continuity, you should try to use a subset of the gate 3, 4, and 5 criteria even at these early gates. For example, gate 1 may just use the must-meet items in Exhibit 7.5, while gate 2 uses the must-meet and perhaps the six main factors in the should-meet list (scored).

Must-Meet Criteria (must yield "Yes" answers):	

- Strategic Alignment (fits BU's strategy)
- Existence of Market Need (sufficient size)
- Reasonable Likelihood of Technical Feasibility
- Product Advantages (unique customer benefits; value for money)
- Meets SHEL (safety, health, environmental, legal) Policies of Company
- Positive Return versus Risk
- No Showstoppers (absence of killer variables)

Bio-55 passes all must-meet items

Should-Meet Criteria (scored 0–10):

Strategic	**Bio-55 *Scores* out of 10**	
• degree to which project aligns with BU's strategy	8	
• strategic importance	7	Strategic = 7.5
Product/Competitive Advantage:		
• unique customer benefits	9	
• meets customer needs better	8	
• good value for money	7	Product Average = 8.0
Market Attractiveness:		
• market size	9	
• margins in this market	7	
• market growth	7	Market
• competitive situation	5	Attractiveness = 7.0
Synergies (Leverages Core Competencies):		
• marketing synergies	6	
• technological synergies	8	
• manufacturing/processing synergies	7	Synergies = 7.0
Technical Feasibility:		
• technical gap	9	
• technical complexity	6	Technical
• technical uncertainty	9	Feasibility = 8.0
Financial Reward:		
• expected profitability (magnitude; for example, NPV)	9	
• return (for example, IRR %)	9	
• payback period	9	
• certainty of return/profit estimates	7	Financial
• low cost and fast to do	6	Reward = 8.0

These should-meet items above are scored (for example, 1–5 or 0–10) and added (in a weighted or unweighted fashion) to yield factor scores. The factor scores must clear hurdles. They are also added (weighted or unweighted) to yield the total project score. In this example, scales are 0–10; items and factors are added in an unweighted fashion.

Total project score for *Bio-55* = 45.5 out of a possible 60 points, which is 76%.

Exhibit 7.5 Sample Gate 3 Criteria and Scores for *Bio-55* Project

- Goal 1. Maximization of the portfolio value:
  Many criteria in the checklist and scoring model deal with the value of the project to the corporation. In sample criteria shown in Exhibit 7.5, these "value to the corporation" items include criteria dealing with strategic importance, product/competitive advantage, market attractiveness, reward (including financial payoff), and probability of success. Projects that score high on these criteria tend to achieve high overall total project scores via the scoring model, and most likely pass the gate hurdles easily.
- Goals 2–3. Properly balanced and strategically aligned portfolio:
  This is an important concept, often missed by the firms we studied:

  ▶ *Strategically aligned* means all projects are on-strategy and the spending breakdown across projects is consistent with the business's priorities and strategies.
  ▶ *Properly balanced* means that we have the appropriate breakdown in spending (or numbers of projects) across markets, product types, technologies, and project types.

These two goals (2 and 3) go hand in hand.

How Gates Consider Portfolio Balance and Strategic Alignment

Balance and strategic alignment are achieved at gates in four ways:

1. First, as part of the BU's business and new product strategy, Strategic Buckets should have been defined (see box entitled "Strategic Buckets"). At minimum, we recommend an a priori split in terms of project types:
   - platform projects (and fundamental research[*])
   - genuine new and improved products (significantly visible to the customer)
   - product fixes and maintenance
   - process improvements and cost reductions.

   Within each bucket, similar projects can be rated, ranked, and prioritized against each other. The Strategic Buckets approach ensures that the balance of spending on projects more or less mirrors spending priorities as dictated by the BU's strategy. The end result is three or four lists of prioritized projects, each within a bucket. Alternately, Target Spending Levels can be defined on some of the dimensions.
2. The *strategic criteria* in the checklist and scoring model are designed to deliberately favor *strategically important* and *high strategic fit* projects. As noted above, these strategic criteria might be either must-meet or should-meet criteria (or both[**]).

---

[*]Fundamental research is sometimes lumped into platform projects, or it may be split out as a separate category, depending on the nature of your business.

[**]For example, strategic fit could be a Yes/No criterion; it could also be a scaled question as a should-meet item, as shown in Exhibit 7.5.

The use of a checklist and a scoring model at gates based on the sample criteria in Exhibit 7.5 means that all off-strategy projects will be culled out; the remaining projects in the portfolio will be strongly weighted toward very high strategic fit and strategically important ones. So strategy is built into the gates via the must-meet and should-meet criteria.

3. At gate meetings, the portfolio lists and maps are reviewed. The question is posed: How does a "Go" decision on this project impact the total portfolio? The approach here is to discuss the portfolio of projects—the list of active projects, prioritized; and the various maps or charts that display the portfolio—with and without the new proposed project. Note that discussion should focus *only on the impact* that the addition of this one project at the gate will have on the portfolio. This is *not the venue to address the total portfolio of projects.* Opening up this discussion at every gate meeting would lead to chaos!

Strategic Buckets

The Strategic Buckets approach forces spending breakdowns to mirror strategic priorities. In developing your BU business and new product strategy, recall from the "Strategy" section that decisions should be made about desired spending levels or splits in terms of some or all of the following (see Agro example in Exhibit 6.4):

- split by strategic arena (for example, market, product types or lines, or technology arenas)
- types of projects (for example, new products versus minor changes)
- project newness (across the cells in the newness matrix).

These desired splits, derived from strategic priorities, can be used as a point of comparison at Portfolio Review meetings. For example, how does your actual spending breakdown compare with the desired split? If there are gaps, then course corrections can be made.

These splits can be used *more aggressively* as well via a Strategic Buckets approach (see Chapter 4). These desired splits are translated into buckets of money for different types of projects. The result is three or four prioritized lists of projects— one for each bucket.

Example: Agro's management developed desired splits of spending across arenas, such as markets and product types (see the pie charts in Exhibit 6.4). But they chose not to force these spending splits by establishing strategic buckets; they merely elected Target Spending Levels across product lines and markets. One dimension was of vital concern, however: types of projects. So Strategic Buckets were developed here: five Strategic Buckets (different project types) with assigned resources to each:

- genuine new products
- product improvements
- product fixes, maintenance, and product necessity work
- cost reductions and process improvements
- fundamental "knowledge build" research.

Projects within each of these five categories compete against each other; but there is no competition among projects between buckets, so that the overall split of spending is dictated by the Strategic Buckets.

---

4. The final way the gates yield a *strategically aligned* and *properly balanced portfolio* is via building a *correction factor* or *adjustment* into the gate decision model. This can be done in one of several ways:
   - by adding a few more gate criteria
   - by adjusting the scoring model score
   - by adjusting the minimum acceptable gate hurdles.

These maneuvers are all designed to favor certain types of projects; namely, projects that bring the portfolio closer to the ideal balance and to the desired spending breakdown. More on this in the next section.

Correcting the Balance

One key role of the Portfolio Review (left side of Exhibit 7.2) is to signal needed corrections or adjustments in balance or mix of projects. Note that individual decisions on projects are made at gates; thus, the corrections to the portfolio balance must also be made at gates. How is this done? Easy: the gates are adjusted to allow underrepresented projects to pass through more easily (give these higher priority) and to decrease the flow of overrepresented projects in the pipeline. In this way, underrepresented projects are favored, and over time, the portfolio comes back into balance.

In practice, these adjustments to the gates are done via a "correction factor," and are operationalized in one of three ways, all variations on the same theme:

- *Adjust the hurdles:* The hurdles on some must-meet criteria, or the total project score hurdle, can be shifted, as Reckitt & Colman does (see Exhibit 5.2). For example, the financial or scoring model hurdles can be relaxed for projects that are highly desired in the portfolio,[*] and increased for project types that are overrepresented. The end result is that gate decisions will be tilted slightly in favor of desired projects, and over time the portfolio imbalance will be corrected. We don't recommend this route: while the method makes it easier for underrepresented projects to pass the gates, it is difficult to compare projects against each other.
- *Add criteria:* Another way to build in a correction factor is to add some balance criteria to the scoring model that ask the question: *Does this project move us closer to the ideal portfolio in terms of spending across project types, markets, product lines, and the like?* Projects that are desired score more points, obtain a higher total project score, and hence, have a higher likelihood of passing the gate. This is a simple method, easy to understand, and one we recommend. You can place more or less weight on these add-on questions or balance criteria depending on how much you are prepared to trade off in order to achieve the right portfolio balance. For example, if port-

---

[*]For example, by decreasing the financial hurdle rate from, say, 25% ROI to 20% for certain desired types of projects.

folio balance is essential (top priority), then you should place more weight on these balance criteria in computing the total project score. The box entitled "Adding Balance Criteria" outlines some sample questions.

- *Adjust the score:* This is another method that we recommend for its operational simplicity, and is much like adding additional questions. Moreover, it's simple and it works! Adjust the scores in the scoring model by multiplying them by a Portfolio Balance Factor (PBF)—a "fudge factor" or correction factor. The Portfolio Balance Factor is determined from the answer to the question: *Does this project move us closer to the ideal portfolio?* If the portfolio is in total balance (that is, the right mix of projects), the PBF is always 1.0, regardless of project types. But when out of balance, the PBF might be increased to 1.1 for underrepresented projects (ones you want more of) and 0.90 for overrepresented projects (ones you have too many of). The PBF is simply multiplied by the total project score to tilt the scales in favor of desired projects.[*]

Example: Agro elected the PBF approach to adjust their scoring model scores for portfolio balance and strategic alignment; they could just as easily have added extra questions to the scoring model in the form of balance criteria. Both methods work!

In Agro's scoring model at gate 3, the minimum hurdle is normally 60 points out of a possible 100. If the portfolio were totally in balance and strategically aligned, the PBF would be 1.0. However, suppose it was already decided by management that there are too many projects aimed at market C and not enough aimed at market B. The PBF works this way: for market B projects—which are very much needed—the PBF is increased to 1.1 and the resulting total project score multiplied by 1.1. For market C projects—

Adding Balance Criteria

The goal is to score project types that are underrepresented in the portfolio more points. Typical questions that are added to the scoring model (Exhibit 7.5) to induce a better balance might include:

1. Does this project fit into a high-priority market (that is, the market is a strategic priority and is underrepresented in the current portfolio)?
2. Does this project fit into a high-priority product line (that is, a strategic line, but underrepresented in the portfolio)?
3. Is this project type a high-priority one (that is, a gap between current and target spending)?

Each question is scored (1–5 or 0–10) to capture the "desirability" of having this project in the portfolio from a balance standpoint.

---

[*]The use of this multiplicative PBF is almost the same as *adjusting the hurdles to favor certain projects,* but a little easier to use when ranking projects; and it is similar to *adding a few criteria* to the scoring model, except that it is multiplicative rather than additive.

there are too many of these in the portfolio already—the PBF drops to, say 0.9. In effect, the method favors market B projects and penalizes market C projects. This means that unless market C projects are really good ones, they fail the gate.

As it turned out, the *Bio-55* project was in a market area, market B, deemed vital to Agro—a high-priority market. Recall that management had developed a desired split in R&D spending across markets via its strategic exercise (see Exhibit 6.5). It was thought that market B should receive about 40% of spending. Currently market B only accounts for about 28% of spending, so that a *considerable gap* exists. Thus the PBF for projects aimed at market B (such as *Bio-55*) was set at 1.1. Multiplying *Bio-55*'s total project score of 76% by 1.1 now makes *Bio-55* an even more attractive project, with a total project score of 84%, simply because *Bio-55* drives the portfolio closer to achieving strategic alignment.

But where and how does one decide that there are too many market C projects and not enough market B projects? Surely not at each and every gate meeting—that would be too cumbersome. Defining gaps and establishing PBF values (or establishing the weights to place on balance criteria or extra questions in the scoring model) is one role of the Portfolio Review in the next major section of this chapter.

Project Prioritization and Resource Allocation

The outcome of the checklist and scoring model exercise at the gate is a decision: the project is either a "kill" (it fails the criteria and hurdles) or a "pass." Merely being a "pass" does not guarantee that the project will be immediately resourced, however. There is still the question of finding the resources for the project.

The gate meeting is conceptually a two-part decision process (see Exhibit 7.6). The first part rates and scores the project, leading to a "Kill" or "Pass" decision. The second facet of the gate meeting deals with prioritization and the decision to allocate resources to the "Go" projects.

Assume that the project at the gate review passes the must-meet criteria, and its total project score clears the hurdles for the should-meet criteria. Will it be resourced? And where will the resources come from? These are the questions for the second part of the gate meeting (the second diamond in Exhibit 7.6).

The gatekeepers face two choices here: either they resource the project (it becomes or continues as an active or "Go" project) or they place it on hold. Projects in the hold tank are good projects; it's just that resources are scarce and other projects are better.

At this point, the project under review must be compared to other projects—both active projects already underway as well as projects in the hold tank. If the project under consideration rates better than projects in the hold tank, and is equal to active projects, then it should be resourced. The total project score from the scoring model should be used to make this comparison. Recall that this total project score captures the value of the project to the business (strategic importance and fit, reward, and probability of success) as well as how well the project

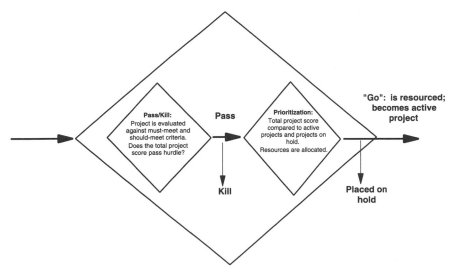

Exhibit 7.6   The Two-Step Decision Process at Gates

fits into the total portfolio. A useful chart to assist this discussion is the prioritized scored list (see example in Exhibit 7.7), which portrays the rank-ordered list of active and on-hold projects, together with their total project scores.

If the decision is to resource the project, then the gatekeepers must find the resources. Usually these are not just lying around waiting to be allocated: people invariably are very busy on other worthwhile projects and tasks! And many companies have a rule that other projects cannot be deprioritized between gates just to fund a relative newcomer. Nonetheless, resources must be found. The potential sources of resources that gatekeepers must investigate include:

- resources already assigned to the project under review, which would have been spun off had this project been stopped (normally, there are some people already working on the project, who are available to continue this work)
- resources available in the very near future from projects completing certain phases, where certain project people are no longer required on that team
- resources from projects in trouble, which should be shut down or curtailed (this could entail an "unscheduled" or emergency gate meeting in order to kill a project in trouble)
- resources from projects soon to be facing a gate meeting (note that one rule is that although resources are firm between gates, at gates, each project is reviewed and may indeed be killed, thereby freeing resources for other projects)
- new resources (for example, new hires, transfers, people between assignments)
- outside sources (for example, other divisions, corporate labs, strategic partners, universities, outside labs, consultants, or contract people).

Project Name	Rank (Priority Level)	Total Project Score	Portfolio Balance Factor	Adjusted Total Project Score
Soya-44	1	80	1.10	88
Encapsulated	2	82	1.00	82
Legume N-2	3	70	1.10	77
Spread-Ease	4	75	1.00	75
Charcoal-Base	5	80	0.90	72
Projects on Hold				
N2-Fix	1	80	1.00	80
Slow-Release	2	70	1.10	77
Multi-Purpose	3	75	0.90	68
.	.	.	.	.

Exhibit 7.7   Agro's Prioritized Scored List of Active and On-Hold Projects (New Products Bucket Only)

Note: The adjusted total project score is the total project score multiplied by the correction factor, the Portfolio Balance Factor (PBF).

If the resources cannot be found, then the project is placed in the hold tank. This should happen only after every effort has been found to support this worthwhile, high-scoring project.

Example: Agro's *Bio-55* achieved a very positive adjusted score of 84% at gate 3. Recall that its original score of 76% was adjusted upward, simply because *Bio-55* helped balance the portfolio. This score of 84% placed *Bio-55* above other projects in the hold tank, and indeed among the better projects on the active list (see Exhibit 7.7).

So the decision was "Go." Indeed, the decision was a strong "Go," and maximum resources were allocated. Resources were acquired from several sources. First, the two-person team already on the project was assigned to continue as key team players. Other technology players were added from another project, soon to be entering the launch phase, where their services would not be required full-time. Finally, a project with several people assigned was approaching a gate 4 meeting, and might be cancelled, potentially freeing up a few more people for *Bio-55*. They were also tentatively ear-marked for *Bio-55*.

How Firm Are Resources?

A thorny question is this: How firm are the resources, once they are committed to a project (see issue 3 in Chapter 5)? Our recommendation is that each business develop its own rule on resource commitment. At one extreme is the "resources are infinitely flexible" paradigm. This means that resource commitments are certainly not firm and that senior management can move resources from one project

How Firm Are Resource Commitments?

Different firms employ different rules of thumb. Here are some samples:

1. Resources committed at gates are infinitely flexible. In short, if a better project comes along, resources can be readily stripped from projects already underway. There is no such thing as a "firm resource commitment"!

2. Resources are only firm between one gate and the next. At every gate, the project is "up for grabs" and can be reprioritized, or even put on hold, if it does not score as high as other projects in the pipeline or those in the hold tank. If a project gets into trouble between gates—shoots itself—an immediate gate review is called and the resources may be taken away from the project (for example, it is killed). Exxon Chemical employs this rule.

3. Resources are firm, starting at a certain gate. That is, as long as the project continues as a good one—meets time lines, budgets, and all successive gate criteria—then the project leader and team can expect continued funding. Even if a newer and better project comes along, top management will resist the temptation to strip resources from the al-ready approved project. As in rule 2, if the project gets into trouble between gates, an immediate gate review is called and the resources may be taken away from the project. The NSD division of GTE employs this rule.

4. Resources are firm, starting at a certain gate. The project is expected to pass all successive gates; thus, these gate reviews are largely perfunctory. That is, once the project is commissioned, the expectation is that it will reach the marketplace.

We recommend either rule 2 or rule 3. Rule 1—infinitely flexible resources—may be great in economic theory (efficient allocation of resources), but plays havoc with project teams and morale. Moreover, newcomer projects always look better than ones that are three-quarters complete; hence, resources tend to be stripped from the latter. Taken to an extreme, no project ever gets completed! Rule 4 is seen far too often. It is the express-train approach, where gates become "project reviews" but there's never any intention or will to stop a mediocre project. This rule results in many poor projects reaching the marketplace, and misallocation of scarce and valuable resources.

---

to the next at will. At the other extreme is the "resource commitments are kept" paradigm, which is equally problematic: this is a good way to throw a lot of money at projects in trouble. Between these extremes, there are a number of commonsense rules. See the box entitled "How Firm Are Resource Commitments" for some examples.

Example: In *Bio-55*'s case, resources were committed at gate 3. These allocations were firm, provided the project remained a good one. Thus the project leader could plan confidently. She was well aware, however, that the project could fail at gate 4 and be cancelled or deprioritized.

So much for gates and decisions on individual projects—the fingers. Now let's turn to the fist—the portfolio of all projects considered together.

Here are the key points from this section:

1. You must have an effective gating process in place—the right side of the PMP. Do not expect your Portfolio Reviews to correct the problems created by a broken gating process! For more information on designing and implementing a Stage-Gate process, see Appendix A.

2. Gates should have clearly defined, consistent, prespecified, and visible criteria for making Go/Kill and prioritization decisions.

3. Consider using a set of must-meet questions to weed out the bad projects, followed by a set of should-meet questions to be scored via a scoring model (see Exhibit 7.5 and Appendix B for excellent examples).

4. Note that gates achieve portfolio balance and strategic alignment in four ways:

   • via Strategic Buckets or Target Spending Levels
   • by building strategic criteria into the scoring model used at the gate
   • by utilizing the prioritized scored list and various bubble diagrams and charts at gate meetings (maps and lists that show other projects in the portfolio, and where the current project would fit in)
   • by using an adjustment or correction factor to the project score.

5. This correction factor is applied either by using the Portfolio Balance Factor or by adding balance criteria to the scoring model.

The Portfolio Review

The Portfolio Review is a holistic review of all projects in the portfolio, and is held periodically. This review takes the inputs and decisions made at gates and makes needed adjustments both to the portfolio of projects and to the gating decision process (this Portfolio Review is the shaded box on the left side of Exhibit 7.8).

Ideally, the Portfolio Review should be merely a *course correction*. If the gating process and gate criteria are well-designed and effectively applied, the portfolio meeting should not result in a major adjustment to the portfolio. That is, Portfolio Reviews should not witness multiple cancellations of projects and numerous approvals of others: this is *not* a project selection meeting! The hope here is that the gates are working well and doing a good job of selecting and prioritizing projects throughout the year. Thus, instead of massive reallocations of resources occurring at the Portfolio Review—a 90 degree turn in direction—the desire is to have minor corrections to the portfolio of projects—a 5 degree change. Recall that maximizing the value, strategic fit and importance, and portfolio balance are very much the key criteria at the gates. Hence, projects selected at gates should be fairly good ones.

Steps in the Portfolio Review

This Portfolio Review or course correction, which ideally takes place semiannually, perhaps even quarterly, involves the following steps (see Exhibit 7.8):

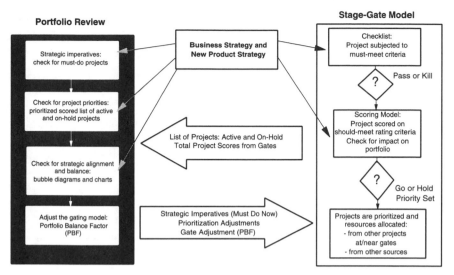

Exhibit 7.8 The Portfolio Review

Note: The Portfolio Review (left side) provides a holistic view of the portfolio of all projects considered together, and is a key part of the total portfolio management process.

1. *Identify Strategic Imperatives:* First, there is a review of the BU's strategy and an identification of any strategic imperatives, that is, projects that are absolutely essential to achieving the strategy.

   Example: Agro management has a Portfolio Review meeting twice a year. At the December Portfolio Review, each of the key strategic thrusts and arenas was discussed. One question focused on the need to move ahead right now with any projects essential to the BU's strategy. At this meeting no such "Go" decisions were made. There were no strategically vital projects currently on hold.

   Note: If you find that much of the Portfolio Review is taken up discussing and approving "must do" projects, then something is wrong with your gating process. The Portfolio Review is not a substitute for effective gates!

2. *Check Project Priorities—The Prioritized Scored List:* Next, there is a check that projects are ranked and prioritized appropriately: that the projects scoring highest on the key criteria—those with the greatest value to the corporation—are indeed being given top priority and maximum resources. If too many projects in the hold tank score higher than active projects, something is amiss!

   The key criteria at the Portfolio Review *are the same as those at the gate* (reward, probabilities, strategic fit, and importance). Indeed, the *same scoring model* should be used, but this time across all projects together. The scores or ratings given to projects at their most recent gate meetings are used at the Portfolio Review. For some projects, these scores are updated in the event of new information acquired since the gate meeting.

The total project score for each project becomes the ranking criterion for use in a prioritized scored list. This prioritized scored list is simply a rank-ordered list of active and on-hold projects (see Exhibit 7.7).

Example: Agro's list of active and funded new product projects past gate 3—the prioritized scored list—was reviewed (see Exhibit 7.7). In Agro's case, recall that a priori, management had split resources into five strategic buckets. One of these buckets was for genuine new products. (Exhibit 7.7 shows these projects; a similar rank-ordered list—not shown—was prepared for product modifications and improvements.) The exhibit also shows projects in the hold tank; these are shown below the line. The projects are rank-ordered on this prioritized scored list according to the total project score. Note that these scores have been adjusted by the PBF in order to push projects that bring the portfolio closer to strategic alignment and proper balance toward the top. For example, the project *Legume N-2,* with an initial score of 70, might not have made the active list, except for the adjustment via the PBF, which drives its score up to a respectable 77.

Management now checks to ensure that projects at the top of the list are indeed receiving the right priorities in terms of resource allocation and that the active projects have higher scores than projects on hold. Several projects on hold have excellent scores, namely, *N2-Fix* and *Slow-Release.* Indeed, they both have better adjusted scores than some active and funded projects, specifically *Spread-Ease* and *Charcoal-Base.* But both *Spread-Ease* and *Charcoal-Base* are well on their way through testing and moving toward launch. Both still have good scores and continue to clear the gate hurdles. So the decision is to continue with *Spread-Ease* and *Charcoal-Base,* and to seek resources for the two top-rated on-hold projects, *N-2 Fix* and *Slow-Release,* resourcing these as soon as people become available.

3. *Check for Balance and Alignment:* Here the key question is: When all the active or "Go" projects are considered together, is the resulting portfolio strategically aligned and properly balanced? Recall from above that:

    ▶ strategically aligned means all projects are on-strategy, and the spending breakdown across projects is consistent with the business's priorities and strategies
    ▶ properly balanced means that there exists the appropriate breakdown in spending (or numbers of projects) across markets, product types, technologies, and project types.

Various visual displays are recommended to portray the existing portfolio of active projects and to check for balance. Our study of portfolio methods in use revealed that visual displays were best suited to portray balance in the portfolio (see Chapter 3). Here are the more useful charts:

- *Bubble diagrams:* A reward versus risk chart. Here the vertical axis is the probability of technical success; the horizontal axis is the reward measured via NPV (already adjusted for commercial risks); and the size of the circles denotes the magnitude of spending on that project (Exhibit 7.9; see also Exhibit 3.1 for an interpretation of risk–reward bubble diagrams).

If there is a fear of overemphasis on financial measures (such as NPV), instead of using NPV, try a risk–reward diagram where reward is qualitatively assessed (such as in Exhibit 3.4). A more creative yet rigorous approach is to utilize the scores derived from the gate scoring model. Such a risk–reward bubble diagram is shown in Exhibit 7.10, whose axes are simply the weighted combinations of scoring model factors scores from Exhibit 7.5:

▶ Reward is the horizontal axis, and is comprised of a weighted addition of market attractiveness, financial reward, and strategic.
▶ Probability of success is the vertical axis, and is made up of the weighted addition of product/competitive advantage, synergies (leverages core competencies), and probability of technical success.

This risk–reward diagram (Exhibit 7.10) thus combines methods outlined in Chapter 3: the ease-and-attractiveness scored axes used by Reckitt & Colman

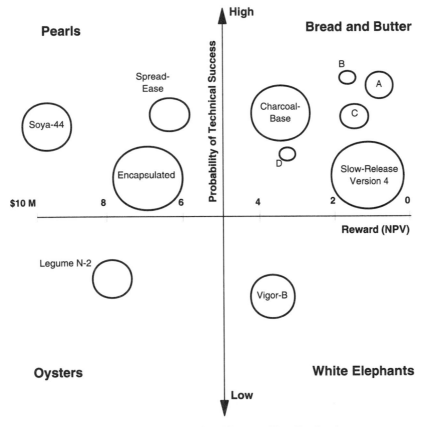

Exhibit 7.9 Agro's Risk–Return Bubble Diagram (Two Buckets)

Note: Circle sizes = resources (annual) per project.

Source: Adapted from Strategic Decisions Group method.

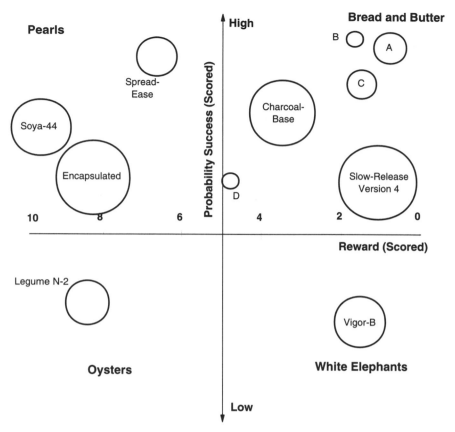

Exhibit 7.10   Alternate Version of Agro's Risk–Return Diagram

Note: Reward = 0.3Str + 0.3MA + 0.4FR; Probability = 0.4PC + 0.25Syn + 0.35Pts. Factors are from scoring model. See Exhibit 7.5.

Source: Adapted from Specialty Minerals.

(Exhibits 3.7 and 3.8); Specialty Minerals' scored axes based on their gate scoring model (Exhibit 3.6); and ADL's nonfinancial approach to estimating reward (Exhibit 3.4).

An alternative version of this bubble diagram is to adapt the 3M approach, depicting certainty of estimates via the size of the circles (small circles denote very certain estimates; large circles or ellipses portray widely varying and hence uncertain estimates—see Exhibit 7.11).

Example: The bubble diagrams for Agro in Exhibits 7.9, 7.10, and 7.11 portray the risk–reward snapshots of the portfolio. Note that these exhibits show two types of projects from two strategic buckets, both new product projects as well as product improvements and modifications. Agro has three clear Pearls—high-reward, high-probability projects. Not surprisingly, they were also at the top of the prioritized scored list of new product projects in Exhibit 7.7. One new product project is a longshot, or

Oyster, namely, *Legume N-2.* Bread and Butter projects are numerous, and include one low-risk major new product with a modest reward *(Charcoal-Base)* and one major product *(Slow-Release-4),* a product improvement on an existing Agro product. Smaller projects in this Bread and Butter quadrant are A, B, C, and D. All are product improvements. There is one White Elephant, *Vigor-B,* a product improvement that has run into trouble. This project began life with a higher likelihood of success, but technical problems arose and the project had drifted into the White Elephant quadrant.

Overall, management's assessment of the distribution of projects in the bubble diagram of Exhibit 7.9 was positive. The risk–reward pattern showed no obvious patterns for concern. For example, one longshot Oyster project was deemed about right. The one White Elephant was discussed, and the decision was to call for an immediate gate meeting for an imminent Go/Kill decision. Within weeks, *Vigor-B* was killed.

The bubble diagrams in Exhibits 7.10 and 7.11 show essentially the same information as Exhibit 7.9. In Exhibit 7.10, reward is portrayed in nonfinancial terms

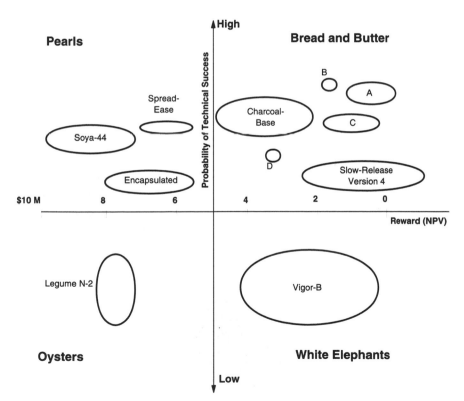

Exhibit 7.11 Agro's Ellipse Bubble Diagram

Note: Ellipse size denotes uncertainties in projects (adapted from 3M).

with both axes derived from the scoring model results; Exhibit 7.11 shows uncertainties around estimates, illustrated by the sizes and shapes of the ellipses.

- *Pie charts:* These charts show splits in resources being spent, or numbers of projects, across key dimensions, compared against the ideal or desired spending pattern. These charts provide a check for *strategic alignment.* Spending displays can be broken down by:

  ▶ product type, product category, or product line (see left pie chart, Exhibit 7.12)
  ▶ market or segment (right pie chart, Exhibit 7.12)
  ▶ types of projects: genuine new products, modifications and improvement, customer request projects, and product maintenance projects or fixes (bottom pie chart, Exhibit 7.12)
  ▶ project newness via the "newness" matrix (not shown; see Exhibits 4.1 or 4.3 for an example).

  Example: Agro's project spending breakdowns in Exhibit 7.12 reveal *gaps between actual spending and desired spending splits.* Recall that management had specified desired spending splits as part of the strategic planning exercise (see Exhibit 6.5 for desired breakdowns for both new product projects as well as product improvements).

- *Product line split:* Exhibit 7.12 reveals that projects for product line X accounted for about 67% of spending (versus a desired 75%). This 8% gap was relatively small as a percent, so no corrective actions were taken.

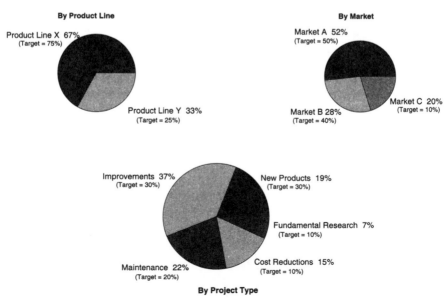

By Product Line

Product Line X 67%
(Target = 75%)

Product Line Y 33%
(Target = 25%)

By Market

Market A 52%
(Target = 50%)

Market C 20%
(Target = 10%)

Market B 28%
(Target = 40%)

Improvements 37%
(Target = 30%)

New Products 19%
(Target = 30%)

Fundamental Research 7%
(Target = 10%)

Maintenance 22%
(Target = 20%)

Cost Reductions 15%
(Target = 10%)

By Project Type

Exhibit 7.12   Agro's Spending Breakdowns

Note: Numbers in parentheses denote desired spending splits (see Exhibit 6.5).

- *Market split:* Projects targeted at market B accounted for 28% of the spending; this is far short of the goal of 40%. Further, projects for market C accounted for far more than the goal (20% versus a target of 10%). Corrections were agreed to here via a portfolio balance factor. Market B's PBF was set at 1.1 to encourage more projects, while market C's PBF was set at 0.9. Recall from Exhibit 7.7 the application of these PBFs in the calculation of Agro's adjusted total project scores, which then were used to prioritize projects.
- *Project type:* Strategic Buckets were established a priori for the six project types. Only two types are considered in Exhibits 7.9–7.12. They are new products and product improvements (goal: 30% spending on each, or a 50–50 split). As shown in Exhibit 7.12, the desired spending levels were not achieved. Too much was going to product improvements and not enough to genuine new products. Sadly for Agro, it was simply a matter of not enough really good new product concepts in the pipe and far too many proposed product improvements. Management decided to remain with these desired splits, and took action to stimulate the conception of more high-quality new product projects for the next year.

Corrections and Adjustments

The Portfolio Review and discussion results in corrections to the mix of projects (that is, corrects gate decisions already made) and in adjustments to the gating model itself (that is, creates a shift in the mix of projects for the upcoming time period):

- *"Kill" decisions:* Some projects might be killed outright (for example, those with low scores or voted not strategically important). In effect, the portfolio meeting overrides (or takes the place of) a gate meeting. The hope is that "Kill" decisions here are rare. They should have been made at gate meetings! In other companies, the rule is that Portfolio Reviews should not be used to make "Kill" decisions; but they might signal the need for an immediate gate review on some projects in trouble or in doubt.
- *Immediate "Go" decisions:* Some projects are designated as strategic imperatives and elevated to "Go's" or top priority (maximum spend). Once again, resist the temptation to use the Portfolio Review meeting to make the most of your "Go" decisions; that's the role of gate meetings!
- *Adjustments to the gating model:* A final result of the Portfolio Review is consensus on the need to adjust the balance of projects during the next period to better reflect both the desired balance and strategic priorities. For example, the decision might be that there are too many projects aimed at market C and not enough at market B. Next steps would aim to correct this imbalance over the next time period. This can be done by:

  —adding some questions to the scoring model in the form of balance criteria (recall from earlier in this chapter that the scoring model results can be adjusted by adding a few extra questions—see box entitled "Adding Balance Criteria")

—the use of a Portfolio Balance Factor—a multiplicative correction factor.

Note that the PBFs or weights on the balance criteria for different types of projects are decided here.

Example: Agro's adjustment and correction decisions:

▶ There were no strategic imperatives.

▶ Nor were any projects on the hold list moved to active projects.

▶ A decision was made to seek resources for the two top-rated hold projects, *N-2 Fix* and *Slow-Release.*

▶ *Vigor-B* was identified as problematic (a White Elephant) and killed off at a subsequent gate meeting.

▶ It was agreed that market B projects were underrepresented in the portfolio, and that market C projects were overrepresented. Hence, the PBF was set at 1.1 for market B and 0.9 for market C to provide needed adjustments to gate decisions.

The magnitude of the PBF is decided from experience. In the Agro example above, a 10% correction factor was used (PBF = 1.1 for underrepresented projects; and PBF = 0.90 for overrepresented ones). In effect, management is declaring that they are prepared to trade off 10% of the value of the portfolio in order to achieve the right portfolio balance and strategic alignment. Similarly, if you decide to use balance criteria instead of a PBF, the weights on these questions are also decided from experience, and again are based on how much you are prepared to trade off balance and alignment for value.

Portfolio Balance Factors

Recall that Portfolio Balance Factors or extra scoring model questions—balance criteria—can be established for one or more of several project dimensions:

* *Market type:* Note the example above with PBFs for market B projects versus market C projects.
* *Product type:* This is similar, but in order to tilt the scales for or against more projects in given product lines, balance factors are used.
* *Project types:* The conclusion at the portfolio meeting might be that there are too many minor projects—tweaks and modifications—and not enough major or genuine product developments. Portfolio Balance Factors or balance criteria can be agreed to, such that the scoring model used at gates would start to favor the major projects.
* *Risk and reward:* The bubble diagram may reveal too many small reward projects or perhaps not enough high-risk projects. Portfolio Balance Factors or balance criteria, again, can be constructed to tilt the scales at the gates.
* *Project newness:* The conclusion might be that there are too many projects toward the lower left of the newness matrix (Exhibits 4.1 or 4.3), and that we need more product and business development projects and fewer share maintenance projects.

The point to note is that the Portfolio Review scans the list of projects, ensures that the ranking and prioritization are correct, and then adjusts for balance. Corrections are made to the list of active and on-hold projects. Adjustments are also made via the Portfolio Balance Factors (or balance criteria) to be used at gate meetings throughout the successive year.

POINTS FOR MANAGEMENT TO PONDER

Here are the key points from this section:

1. In addition to a sound new product process with effective gates, you must also have periodic Portfolio Reviews (left side of Exhibit 7.8). Recall that gates look at individual projects (the fingers), whereas Portfolio Reviews look at all projects together and in aggregate (the fist).

2. Here are the important steps in the Portfolio Review:
   - Check for strategic imperatives—"must do now" projects.
   - Check project priorities: use the prioritized scored list and spot inconsistencies.
   - Check for balance and alignment: use various bubble diagrams, charts, and maps.
   - Define adjustments needed to the gating process (either via PBFs or by adding balance criteria).

3. Charts and maps to use at Portfolio Reviews might include:
   - the risk–reward bubble diagram (NPV versus probability; nonfinancial reward versus success probabilities; or scored axes)
   - pie charts showing splits in resources (versus Strategic Buckets or Target Spending Levels).

In Conclusion: An Integrated Decision System

The Portfolio Management Process ideally is an integrated decision system (see the full model in Exhibit 7.13).

At the top center is the strategy for the BU. This is the driver, because strategy starts when you start spending money. So the *choice of new product projects is the operationalization of strategy*. Recall that *strategy* in our context includes the BU's business and its new product strategy. The latter specifies the new product goals for the BU, the arenas of focus (for example, markets, product types, and technologies), and the desired spending splits across these, or in terms of project types.

Next, there is the new product process or Stage-Gate model (to the right in Exhibit 7.13). Its focus is on individual projects: the "fingers." The gates in the new product process must be working well in order that the total Portfolio Management Process performs. Note that the gates are where most of the ongoing Go/Kill decisions are made on projects, and where resources are allocated throughout the year. Gates can be constructed around a set of must-meet or culling (knockout) criteria, and also a set of should-meet items, which are scored and added via a

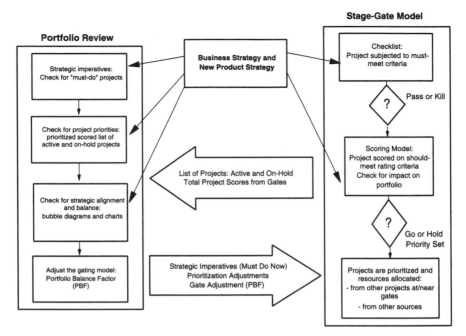

Exhibit 7.13   The Total Portfolio Management Process

Note: The Portfolio Review feeds the Stage-Gate model; and the Stage-Gate model feeds the Portfolio Review. Both models are in sync and driven by strategy.

scoring model. Criteria here include items that capture strategic fit and importance, value of the project to the BU, and likelihood of success. The total project score becomes the key input to the Go/Kill decision at the gate, and also a key ranking criterion for use in prioritizing projects.

Then there is the Portfolio Review (left side of Exhibit 7.13). If the gates consider the "fingers," then the Portfolio Review looks at the "fist." It is holistic in nature and enables management to stand back and consider all projects—those that are active versus those on hold—together. Strategic imperatives may be identified: "must do now" projects. The prioritized scored list derived from gate decisions and the gate scoring model enable projects to be ranked against each other. Decisions may be made to deprioritize some and to elevate others. The balance of the portfolio is also reviewed using various bubble diagrams and pie charts. The risk–reward breakdown and spending breakdowns by project types, markets, products, technologies, project newness, and so on are topics of discussion here. Again, decisions may be made to reprioritize certain projects. Finally, adjustments are made to the gating process via choice of Portfolio Balance Factors or additional scoring model questions, balance criteria. These are *correction factors* to be applied to project scores at the gates to tilt the scales in favor of certain desired types of projects.

If all three elements of the process exist—strategy, the Stage-Gate process, and the Portfolio Review (with its various models and tools)—then a harmonized system should yield excellent portfolio choices: projects that deliver economic pay-offs, mirror the business's strategy, and achieve the BU's goals for new products. But if any piece of the PMP in Exhibit 7.13 is not working—for example, if there is no clearly defined strategy or if the new product gating process is broken—the results are less than satisfactory.

In the next chapter, we turn to the vital question: Now that you understand the elements and ingredients of a robust Portfolio Management Process, how does one proceed? In short, how do you move ahead with the design and implementation of an PMP in your business? That's the topic of Chapter 8.

Designing and Implementing the Portfolio Management Process: Some Thoughts and Tips before You Charge In

Before You Charge In

The development of new products is one of the most important endeavors of the modern corporation. It is also the most difficult task to do successfully! Likewise, designing and implementing a Portfolio Management Process is also one of the most difficult tasks in the corporation—both conceptually and operationally.

So think before you act. This is not the flavor of the month, nor will it take only a few weeks. Rather, designing and implementing an effective PMP is a major undertaking that will require the help and input of many people in your organization, including executive sponsorship and leadership, and may take several years before it is up and running successfully. So don't underestimate the costs and time required to do it right. Take care before you proceed, but do proceed. The stakes are too high and the payoffs too great to postpone taking action.

The design and implementation of a PMP is much like rolling out a new product. The difference is that you are developing a *new management process* rather than a new product and that the "customers" are internal ones—inside your own company—rather than external. Nonetheless, you can borrow many of the principles of product development when you design a new PMP. The first of these is that the design process is a stage-wise one, not unlike the five-stage, five-gate new product process outlined in Exhibit 7.4. Here, we propose a three-stage, three-gate method for the design and implementation of a PMP:

▶ Step 1: understanding the problem and defining the requirements for an effective PMP.

▶ Step 2: designing the PMP on paper, starting with a skeleton process and then fleshing out the details.

▶ Step 3: implementing the process in the business: getting projects into the process, running Portfolio Reviews, making the gates work; developing an IT support system; and so on.

Step 1: Defining the Requirements

Step 1 entails defining the requirements for an effective PMP in your business. This is a first and necessary stage, and one that is often skipped over by portfolio task forces* with very negative results. Remember: understanding the problem is the first step to a solution! Too often we witness well-intentioned portfolio task forces that meet in private, arrive at a solution, and then charge out with solution in hand, determined to change the way the company operates. When their initiative is greeted with less than the enthusiastic response they expected, doom sets in. Task force members become frustrated, and before long, it's another worthwhile initiative that went nowhere. Very often, the roots of disaster can be found right at the beginning: failure to do the up-front homework and to understand the needs and problems that the PMP must address.

The purpose of this definitional step is twofold:

* to gain an understanding of the problems and issues faced in the business regarding portfolio management and project selection: in short, to identify what needs fixing
* to map out the "specs" and requirements for the PMP—what the process must be and do; how it must function; and what its requirements should be.

Example: In a major international brewery, an in-depth audit of product development and project selection revealed several critical fail points. First, too many projects were reaching the prelaunch decision point, only to have senior management pull the rug out from under the project team, usually for strategic reasons: there simply were too many "eleventh-hour kills," often after several years of work, and many dollars, had gone into the project. Second, it wasn't evident that the senior management had a clear or unified notion of their business's new product strategy: arenas were not prioritized, nor had spending splits across arenas been defined (perhaps this fuzziness helped explain why so many projects went so far in the process before being killed). Finally, while there was indeed a new product process in place, it lacked specificity (for example, no clearly defined gate criteria for making

---

*We assume here that you're not trying single-handedly to implement a PMP—that you've put together a portfolio management task force.

Go/Kill decisions), nor was the process being adhered to (due to a lack of agreement as to what projects went through the process).

Based on these problems, the requirements for the new PMP for this business became clear:

1. The PMP must involve senior management earlier in the life of a project: they should be involved in the predevelopment decision points. Portfolio reviews of active projects in the pipeline must be also involve senior people, so there are no eleventh-hour surprises.
2. Senior management must lead: they are the generals and their obligation to the business is to develop strategy. (In our first session with the executive group, they committed to moving ahead to fleshing out their business strategy and moving toward a new product strategy for the business: defined arenas, priorities on these, and target spending levels by arena and project type).
3. The new product process must be revamped and fixed where needed; for example, gates must have visible criteria; there must be agreement on what projects are in the process; and so on.

Here are some of the key tasks to be undertaken in step 1:

1. *Assemble a task force:* The design of a company PMP is beyond the capabilities of one or a few people. This is not an easy task, and assigning it to one person to handle will lead to:

   • a fairly narrow view of the problem (note that different perspectives are required to fully understand the role and implications of portfolio management in the business)
   • a lack of buy-in by those who must use the process

   We recommend that you assemble a portfolio task force charged with executing the steps outlined below, leading to the design and implementation of your PMP. Carefully select the task force members: thought-leaders in the company with experience in new products (although not necessarily senior management); representative of different functions and businesses in the corporation, and if necessary, from different geographies; and with time available to do the work. The task force should have strong senior executive sponsorship (with a designated executive sponsor) and a respected, strong task force leader with passion for and commitment to the task at hand.
2. *Define and seek concurrence on the mandate:* The task force together with the executive sponsor (or sponsoring group) should develop its mandate: what the task force is charged with doing, what it should not do, and what deliverables are expected by the sponsoring group. The sponsoring group (for example, leadership team of the business) should sign off on this mandate and also agree on their own role and availability to the task force.
3. *Hold a kickoff session:* Consider inaugurating the task with a kickoff seminar/workshop—a one- to two-day event. The session might be billed

as a "best practices in product development" seminar, but focuses on project selection, portfolio management, and best-practice techniques (see Chapters 2–4 of this book). Invite a fairly large group, essentially those in your business who will become the "users" of the new process: project team members, project leaders, their immediate bosses, and so on. Senior management should also be brought into the loop, either at this kickoff event or in a session tailored for them. This kickoff session helps for three reasons:

▶ First, it creates awareness of the need for improvement. Observing best practices in other firms is an excellent start. Further, the seminar is the venue where the executive sponsors reiterate the business's new product goals and strategy; usually this points to the need for a change in direction. Additionally, the executive sponsors announce the PMP initiative at the seminar and introduce the task force members.

▶ Second, such a seminar/workshop helps identify the problems in project selection and prioritization faced in the business. For example, build a "problem detection" team exercise into the seminar. Thus the seminar/ workshop can double as a "town hall meeting," enabling a wide audience to air their views, concerns, and suggestions.

▶ Finally, a kickoff seminar helps generate organizational buy-in. Remember: obtaining organizational buy-in to new methods and practices is a formidable task; and organizational buy-in must begin in the first few days of this initiative. Use this kickoff event to begin the buy-in process. For example, build in a "what's the path forward" team exercise toward the end of the kickoff event, so that participants can provide direction to the task force as to the next steps and what's needed. Note that the task force members are the hosts at this kickoff session, and must use it to full advantage to seek input and agreement as to the road ahead.

4. *Do a literature review:* The task force should conduct a thorough literature review, and find out what others have said and done. There's no sense reinventing the wheel. Authors and pundits have been writing about portfolio management, project selection, and new product resource allocation since the 60s. As is often the case, many of the earlier works offer the best insights; but there have been new insights in recent years, so look into these articles and books, too. In Chapter 1, a quick review and many of the references you might wish to look at were provided. Require that the task force immerse itself in the writings.

5. *Benchmark other firms:* This we suggest, but with some caution. First, thorough benchmarking takes a lot of time. Second, some better-practice firms have been benchmarked so often that they're now resisting such overtures (or acquiescing but not providing full support). Finally, task force members are amateurs at business research, and hence are likely to do a mediocre job of benchmarking. Task force members often set out to benchmark others with great zeal, but lose their enthusiasm when they quickly realize it's not so easy and they're not learning all that much. We offer two suggestions:

‣ Seek some professional help, especially in the design of your benchmarking methodology. Numerous suppliers exist who are experienced and capable at benchmarking exercises: use them!

‣ Turn to the literature. Chapters 2–5 of this book provide results of a fairly comprehensive benchmarking of industry best practices.[1] Your literature search may also turn up other reports of firms' practices in portfolio management.

6. *Conduct an internal audit of current practices:* Undertake a study of current practices and deficiencies in your own business and company. This poses fewer problems than external benchmarking and should be an easier task. Surprisingly, many task forces skip this, largely because they think they know the answers. Wrong! In every internal 3-P study we have been involved with—internal investigations into new product *practices, performance,* and *problems*—there have been *major revelations;* that is, the findings of the study went far beyond the knowledge and understanding possessed by the task force; and there were definitely new learnings that the task force had to deal with. Don't skip this task. Here are some suggestions for how to proceed:

‣ Undertake a *3-P study:* We call this a 3-P study because it focuses on just that—*practices, performance,* and *problems.* We've even coined a term to capture the effort: *ProBE* or *Pro*duct *B*enchmarking and *E*valuation.[2] Our *ProBE* methodology is a questionnaire-based internal audit of a business's new product practices, performance, and problems, and in part looks at portfolio management practices and related issues. *ProBE* then compares a company's practices and performance against those of the average business, and against the top 20%; the method and database are based on our benchmarking study of a large sample of businesses. Alternately, you can develop your own benchmarking questionnaire and via individual interviews, e-mail surveys, or focus groups within your business, try to uncover current project selection, prioritization, and resource allocation practices and deficiencies—what needs fixing and what seems to be working.

‣ Another approach is to *focus on individual new product projects.* Dissecting a reasonable sample of past projects—both winners and losers—provides valuable insights into current practices and deficiencies, particularly in terms of the Go/Kill and prioritization decisions—the gating process—found on the right side of the PMP (Exhibit 7.13). More specifically, require that project teams of already completed projects undertake a *retrospective analysis* of their projects. That is, dissect each project, focusing first on mapping out just what happened from beginning to end, from idea to launch. Then lower the microscope on each of the key decision points in the process—how the Go/Kill decisions were made, who made them, what information was available (or should have been available), and what criteria were used. Assess the "goodness" of the decision points and resource allocation decisions, especially in the case of projects that should have been killed, yet were allowed to proceed.[3]

7. *Review your own portfolio of projects:* One revealing task is to undertake a review of the current portfolio of active projects. Begin with characterizing the portfolio along key dimensions. That is, undertake a breakdown of either projects or project spending across important dimensions: by market segment, product lines, project types, technologies, and so on. You can also develop breakdowns—both numbers of projects and spending—on other dimensions introduced in Chapter 3:

   - fit with business or corporate strategy (low, medium, high)
   - inventive merit and strategic importance to the business (low, medium, high)
   - durability of the competitive advantage (short-, medium-, long-term)
   - reward based on financial expectations (modest to excellent; or dollar categories)
   - competitive impact of technologies (base, key, pacing, and embryonic technologies)
   - probabilities of success (technical success and commercial success as percentages)
   - R&D costs to completion (dollar categories)
   - time to completion (years)
   - capital and marketing investment required to exploit (dollar categories).

   You might even try developing a bubble diagram or two to display the current portfolio (assuming that some of the bubble diagram data are available). An additional benefit of this portfolio review is that you're already piloting or testing some of the portfolio models and displays that you might eventually elect as portfolio models in your PMP.

   Assessing the *value of the portfolio* ought to be part of this task. That is, try to place a dollar amount on the current portfolio of projects using one of the financial methods outlined in Chapter 2. If the total value of the portfolio is less than what you've spent on it, then something clearly is amiss!

8. *Write up the specs and requirements of the process and define the work plan for step 2:* Integrate your many findings and conclusions from step 1 into a set of specs and requirements for the PMP. For example, Hallmark's task force came up with a detailed list of goals or specs for its new product process or gating system (the right side of the PMP in Exhibit 7.13). Some sample items included:
   "Our new product process must . . .

   - Encourage the inception of creative ideas and aid in getting innovative and creative products to market.
   - Foster the amplification or plusing of ideas—making ideas bigger.
   - Promote objective Go/Kill decision-making, using common criteria, based on facts, and yielding consistency and continuity in decision-making.
   - Improve resource allocation—better focus, sharper prioritization, and the right people on projects."

This final step should now map out a detailed work plan for the next phase of the effort, namely the design of the various elements of the PMP. For example, if your business lacks an effective gating process, then its development becomes a major part of the work plan.

9. *Seek concurrence from sponsors and selected users:* The specs of the PMP and the proposed work plan are now presented to senior management for their concurrence and sign-off. This "gate" marks the end of the homework or audit phase and the entry into step 2. Selected and knowledgeable people who will be the eventual users of the PMP can also act as sounding boards here. While you might be tempted to hold a "town hall meeting" and get everyone who attended the initial kickoff event to review your specs and work plan, unfortunately you really have very little of interest to show people at this point. When you have the first draft of the PMP in step 2 is when you begin your iterations with users.

The tasks outlined above are not easy, nor can they be done overnight. However, they provide an excellent foundation to the design and implementation work that lies ahead.

POINTS FOR MANAGEMENT TO PONDER

Before you charge ahead, be sure to spend time defining the requirements of your Portfolio Management Process. Remember: understanding the problem is the first step to a solution. So take a little extra time here and lay the foundation carefully. Tasks you might consider in this step 1 definitional phase include:

1. assembling a task force for the job
2. defining the mandate and seeking concurrence from the sponsor or sponsoring group
3. holding a kickoff session—this builds buy-in and also solicits useful input
4. undertaking a thorough literature review (don't reinvent the wheel)
5. benchmarking other firms (with caution)
6. undertaking a thorough internal audit of current portfolio management and project selection practices in your business
7. reviewing and evaluating your current portfolio of projects
8. defining the specs and requirements for your PMP—what needs fixing
9. gaining the sponsor's concurrence regarding your PMP's specs and the proposed action plan.

Step 2: Designing the Portfolio Management Process— Key Actions

The homework has been done; the problems are identified; and the specs or requirements for the ideal PMP for your business have been defined—what your PMP must be and do. Now it's time to begin designing the process in earnest.

Design your Portfolio Management Process module by module. Begin with an overview or skeleton process, using Exhibit 7.13 as a guide. Map out the key components and decide roughly how the gating process, the Portfolio Review process, and the new product strategy should be developed and linked.

Recall that there are three components to the PMP, all of which might have to be designed, modified, or developed: strategy, gating process, and Portfolio Review. Your own company situation determines where and how you begin; indeed, you may wish to tackle all three components simultaneously. What follows is a quick look at some of the typical "design tasks" inherent in each of the three components of a PMP.

1. New Product Strategy

First, begin with the business's overall strategy.* Reconfirm the goals, arenas of strategic thrust, and strategies of the business. Work with senior management if needed to seek clarification and additional input. Move toward developing a *new product strategy* for the business. Recall from Chapters 4 and 6 that this entails the following actions:

1. Define arenas, much like the Modified Plastics example in Chapter 4. Arenas could be markets, segments, product categories or types, technologies, platforms, or some combination of these. Recall Telenor's product/market matrix in Chapter 1, which defined that firm's arenas.
2. Assess each arena. Undertake a SWOT analysis and perform a market assessment; you might also use the Porter Five Forces model as a template to assess each arena: market/customers, suppliers, competitors (rivals), substitutes, and barriers to entry to others.[4]
3. Select the arenas—the ones that your new products will focus on. Use a scoring model with defined business criteria to assist here: see box entitled "Key Business Arena Criteria."

   Each arena can be scored on these or similar criteria, and scores added to yield market attractiveness, business position, and strategic scores. Some businesses even use bubble diagrams to represent the relative positions of the various arenas.
4. Prioritize these arenas and decide spending splits across them. The "scores" on each arena from item 3 above based on the business criteria (see box insert) help in this prioritization. Also, be sure to refer back to the Strategic Buckets approach and the top-down, bottom-up approach, both outlined in Chapter 4.
5. Develop plans on how to attack each arena.

Further details of how to develop a new product strategy are beyond the scope of this book. This is an important facet of the PMP, however. So seek guidance here.[5]

---

*We assume here that a business strategy is already in place for your business, but not necessarily a new product strategy for the business.

Key Business Arena Criteria

▸ Market attractiveness of this arena:

- size of market
- market growth
- long-term potential
- margins in market
- competitive situation
- opportunities for new products in this market.

▸ Your business position in this arena:

- your business's core competencies and relative strengths versus competition in areas of
  - technological (R&D, technology, and engineering design)
  - production or operations and delivery
  - marketing, sales, distribution, and channels.
- your business's position in this arena: market share, reputation, and presence

- your business's ability to leverage its strengths to develop products with real competitive advantage
- financial: your business's current profitability in this arena.

▸ Strategic aspects of focusing on this arena:

- the arena's fit with the strategy of your business
- the strategic importance of the arena to your business
- strategic leverage: opportunity to develop new windows of opportunity
- platform potential: degree to which the arena is a platform opportunity (versus a "one off" opportunity)
- synergy with other businesses in the corporation.

2. New Product Process

This is the right side of Exhibit 7.13, namely, the gating process. An effective Stage-Gate process must be in place for a PMP to be effective, so you must tackle this task fairly early. If you already have a new product process in place, your audit may have identified weaknesses and things that need fixing (for example, gates that lack criteria or stages with unclear deliverables). So design the fixes here. Designing a new product process involves much more than merely sketching out a Stage-Gate diagram; here are some of the elements:

1. First, map the process—a flow diagram similar to Exhibit 7.4, with your stages and gates identified. Label each stage and gate with a name that connotes what the stage or gate does or stands for. Briefly characterize each stage and gate.

2. Define the purpose, spirit, or flavor of each stage and gate.

   Example: Stage 2 amounts to a quick and inexpensive set of activities to gain a better understanding of the idea: that is, to identify which are the best ideas; to assess market potential and technical feasibility; to identify possible showstoppers; and to determine the need for further work. The spirit here is to make professional assessments and "best educated guesses"—a first cut—often with very limited data and in a very short time period. Detailed assessments and studies are *not* expected in stage 2. The stage 2 work effort *varies by project,* but the order of magnitude is *typically about 10 to 25 person-days of work,* with elapsed time about *one calendar month.*

3. For each stage, define the key tasks, actions, or activities, and also the resulting deliverables from these actions. Try to build in best practices here: sharp, early product definition; a strong market and customer orientation; the quest for product superiority; solid up-front homework; and so on.* For problematic actions and deliverables, or for unfamiliar ones, you may wish to develop guides, templates, or examples for users. Some firms also define accountability for each stage, that is, who is accountable for seeing that these tasks are completed.

4. For each gate, define the gatekeepers, the Go/Kill and prioritization criteria, and the gate outputs—what happens next. Exhibit 7.5 provides a good starting point for both must-meet and should-meet (scored) criteria for gate 3. Early gates conveniently use a subset of these. For example, gate 1 may use only the must-meet items as criteria for weeding out inappropriate ideas; gate 2 may use the must-meet and a handful of should-meet or scored items (for example, the six main factors in Exhibit 7.5). Gates 3–5 can use the full list of criteria in Exhibit 7.5.

5. Capture the behavioral and organizational issues: team structure and leadership; the gatekeepers' role, responsibilities, and rules of the game; how gate reviews are to be conducted; rewards and recognition; the need for and job description of a process manager or *gate meister.*

6. Define other peripheral but vital elements: what projects are "in the process"; flexibility and fast-tracking projects; designing an IT support system (to track projects and keep vital stats on each); improving idea generation and solicitation; developing an "open" idea vault and a convenient idea-handling system; integrating the process with other company processes (for example, the capital expenditure process; or the release-to-plant process); and so on.

7. Deal with and decide on some of the issues and challenges raised in Chapter 5 (Exhibit 5.1): for example:

   • How firm are resource commitments made at gate meetings?
   • How should you overcome the problem of imaginary precision?
   • At what gate should the portfolio management process kick in?
   • How should you correctly incorporate financial analysis methods into the gate and gate criteria?
   • How does one spot projects in trouble (use red flags)? (list found in Chapter 5).

3. Portfolio Review

Designing the portfolio review process is a little more complex than it first seems. After all, what's involved in designing a review meeting to be held four times per year? Plenty! Here are some portfolio review issues and challenges:

---

*For a guide to the Stage-Gate process, see Appendix A or *Winning at New Products.*[6]

1. Determine who the portfolio reviewers will be. Often this is controversial. In some firms, they are simply the leadership team of the business or the gate 2 or gate 3 gatekeepers (often these are the same people).
2. Define what portfolio models will be used at this review. In Chapter 6, we offered some suggestions:

   - a prioritized scored list of active and on-hold projects (recall that this list is developed from the gate scores).
   - a risk–reward bubble diagram (either with financial and probability axes; or with scored axes).
   - various pie charts: breakdown of spending by project type (the Mercedes star), by market, by product line, and so on.

   These are our suggestions, but every business and culture is different. You should review the various models and methods outlined in Chapters 2–4 and select or modify these accordingly to suit your own decision styles, culture, and needs.

3. Outline the structure and procedure of the meeting. For example, what materials will attendees receive ahead of time? How will the meeting be conducted? Will you use computers at the meeting to assist in the decision-making and review process? Will there be a facilitator? How often will the Portfolio Review be conducted—quarterly, semiannually?
4. Decide how the Portfolio Review will enable corrective action to be taken on the portfolio of projects. For example, in the event of an unbalanced portfolio or one that lacks strategic alignment, what happens? Do you start killing projects at the Portfolio Review and approving others? Or does the Portfolio Review merely send a signal to the gatekeepers to tighten up the criteria for certain overrepresented types of projects? In short, what is the outcome of the Portfolio Review?
5. Develop the mechanism for adjusting gates to favor certain types of projects and for blocking others. We suggested using a Portfolio Balance Factor or adding some balance criteria to the gate scoring model in Chapter 7. One company had gone as far as linking the Portfolio Review to the gate meeting electronically (via IT): recall Reckitt & Colman's IT-based portfolio model which "signaled" the gate scoring model to increase or decrease the gate hurdles! (See Exhibit 5.2).
6. Define the information flow into and from this Portfolio Review (for example, where and how are data obtained to generate the various bubble diagrams or pie charts?).
7. Define the IT support system required to store the vital data on each project and to provide the various displays. For example, if you plan on using bubble diagrams, note that these are not usually available on standard graphics packages, such as PowerPoint, Freelance, or Harvard Graphics, and hence might require some specialized or add-on software.
8. Deal with the remaining challenges and issues outlined in Exhibit 5.1. For example:

   - Will your Portfolio Reviews be monitoring reviews or project selection meetings?

- What should be done with too many on-hold projects?
- Why have a prioritized or rank-ordered list at all?
- Should your portfolio models provide information displays or be decision models?
- How should needed information on projects be acquired?
- How should gate decisions and portfolio decisions be best integrated?
- What types of projects should be considered in the PMP? (All projects that compete for resources? Or only some?)
- How do you avoid information overload in the PMP?

An Iterative Process

To carry out this difficult design phase—step 2—we recommend that your task force set aside blocks of time and meet in two-day sessions, roughly two to four weeks apart. Meeting an hour here and two hours there usually results in a lack of dedicated effort and too many people missing too many meetings. Block out time blocks months ahead, and get off premises! The two- to four-week intervals are prescribed simply because that's approximately how long it takes to pull together the conclusions from each two-day session, disseminate this to team members, share it with others in the organization, and obtain the necessary feedback. Additionally, there are other "off-line" activities underway by some task force members—subgroups of the task force—that often take a few weeks.

A word of warning: the toughest job by far is not the design of an effective PMP on paper; it's getting it implemented! So implementation must be a primary concern all the way through this step 2 design phase. A fundamental truth is that people who have not had a hand in crafting something will invariably resist its implementation. Thus the goal here is to involve as many of the potential users of the PMP as possible in its design. Clearly, a committee of 100 makes no sense, but feed-forward and feedback sessions are one method to solicit organizational buy-in long before formal implementation begins.

Making Task Forces Work: Checklist

√ Executive sponsorship secured
√ Membership carefully selected
√ Strong, respected leader with passion for the task
√ Mandate developed and signed-off by sponsors
√ Homework done (audit: step 1)

√ Goals for PMP defined and a work plan signed-off
√ Meet off premises
√ Calendars cleared (blocks of time set aside)
√ Outside facilitator or expert in place
√ Iterations with users (feedback sought)

Example: When GTE designed its Stage-Gate and project selection method, a series of two-day meetings were scheduled by the task force, about two to three weeks apart. There was both a facilitator and an outside expert at each session.

Each two-day session had very specific goals and an agenda. After each meeting, one person pulled together the material and provided a write-up of each successive draft of the process. This write-up was available within days, and then e-mailed or faxed to each task force member for critical review. Additionally, a PowerPoint presentation was developed and e-mailed to all members, so that they in turn could make oral and visual presentations of the process to their colleagues, subordinates, and superiors. Feedback from the presentations and the written document was solicited, and sent to all members one week before the next meeting. The agenda was prepared and goals for the next meeting established. With military-like discipline, the task force moved from one draft version to the next—each one better than the last. But most important, by the time the process was rolled out to the user community, *they had each seen it several times* and had been given ample opportunity to critique it and suggest improvements. The end result was a much better process (than if the task force had designed it in isolation), and critical buy-in had already begun!

Note that the process in step 2 is very iterative. A task force meeting is held; the outcomes are written up; this is fed forward to potential users and senior management; feedback is sought; and the task force meets again to integrate the feedback and move ahead on the design of the PMP.

Top Management Is Part of Step 2

Top management involvement is critical throughout this entire design phase. The executive sponsor should stay very close to the task force and show up at many of their meetings (not for the full two days!); the sponsor needs to closely review the outcome of each session with the task force leader. Top management is involved more than simply as the sponsoring group, however. They must also take an active role in the design of the process:

- ▶ The development of a new product strategy for the business is one area where senior management's inputs, views, decisions, and approvals must be sought. Ideally they should lead the charge here.
- ▶ Another top management input is the development of criteria for use at the Portfolio Review and the gates they attend.
- ▶ Similarly, the development of rules of the game at Portfolio Reviews or gates should either be led by top management or at least their concurrence should be sought.

Off-Line Activities

Much work also goes on in the two- to three-week interval between the two-day task force sessions. This "off-line" work is undertaken by task force members working alone or perhaps in small groups on specific tasks defined by the task force. Some larger task forces define subgroups with leaders to accomplish certain tasks. Examples include:

- a subgroup to investigate and define IT needs
- a subgroup to start designing appropriate documentation
- a subgroup to handle communications and "press releases" to other parts of the company
- a subgroup to liaise regularly with the executive sponsors
- a subgroup to work with the finance department to define the appropriate financial models, calculations, and spreadsheets.

The point is that there is much work to be done, and not all can be accomplished in a set of two-day meetings. Organize to undertake some work off-line.

An Implementation Plan

The final action in step 2 is the design of an implementation plan for the PMP. Such a plan deals with challenges like:

- communicating the process to users and seeking buy-in at all levels (documentation, events, in-company media)
- providing training to teams, gatekeepers, portfolio reviewers, and resource providers
- piloting some projects, some gates, and a Portfolio Review
- bringing projects into the process
- gathering data on all existing projects to kick-start the Portfolio Review
- developing an IT support system for the gating process and the Portfolio Review
- putting in place a process manager
- defining metrics: measures of new product performance (how well are we doing at new products?) and measures of the performance of various components of the PMP (for example, are gates working? Are projects prioritized correctly?).

More on implementation in the next major section.

Results of Step 2

The deliverables at the conclusion of step 2 include two items:

- a Portfolio Management Process "on paper" that has been reviewed by both users and management, and meets their needs and demands: buy-in has already begun!
- a detailed implementation plan.

These two items are presented to the sponsoring group for final approval (and approval of needed resources for implementation). Assuming concurrence is obtained, then it's on to step 3: implementation!

POINTS FOR MANAGEMENT TO PONDER

Step 2 involves designing your Portfolio Management Process. There are three major components that may need work or improvement in your business. Your step 1 should indicate what needs attention:

- ◗ the new product strategy for your business—this may need development from scratch or just sharpening
- ◗ the Stage-Gate new product process—stages and gates must be defined, complete with deliverables to gates, gate criteria, and gatekeepers
- ◗ the Portfolio Review—the role of the review; who the reviewers are; what models to use; how information will be collected; and the output of the review.

You might wish to review the section above to recall just how to proceed to attack each of these three components of a PMP.

Consider structuring your task force so that it meets in a two-day session off premises, roughly two to four weeks apart. Between sessions, there is much off-line work to be done, including sharing the evolving process with users and sponsors and seeking their feedback and suggestions. Buy-in has already begun. And remember: there is an important role for senior people to play in this design phase too.

The result is a Portfolio Management Process on paper—one that has been reviewed a number of times by users groups and senior management, and where each has had considerable input. Also, an implementation plan is a deliverable from step 2.

Step 3: Implementation

Implementation of the PMP is perhaps the most challenging phase, but unfortunately is often underestimated by companies.

Here is a sample of the key tasks:

1. *Install a process manager:* No process, however excellent its design and concept, ever implemented itself. And committees or task forces, again well-intentioned, have a history of being poor at implementation. They may do an excellent job on the design of the process, but once that task is finished, task force members seem to drift off to other work and fail to see the implementation through. One person must be charged with making the PMP happen: the process manager or process keeper (other names include: *gate meister,* portfolio manager, and key master). Ideally this person is selected from the task force members and is designated before implementation begins. His or her job is to ensure that the PMP is implemented; that is, that the steps laid out below are indeed executed.

2. *Secure senior management buy-in:* The PMP is doomed to failure unless senior management buy in and *commit totally* to it. In spite of the fact that senior management has sponsored the PMP initiative, and in spite of their

apparent sign-off of the process on paper (step 2), in almost every organization we've worked with, there is still some hesitancy around total buy-in to the principles and methods of the PMP: they *talk the talk,* but they're not quite ready to *walk the talk.* The dilemma is that intellectually senior management agrees with the concept of a PMP—a gating process with discipline and tough gates, and a Portfolio Review process based on facts, all driven by a new product strategy. What they don't realize is that the biggest change in behavior occurs at the top. Effective gate meetings demand quite different behavior on the part of senior people than they are used to; the gatekeeper rules of the game bring a certain discipline that is foreign to some senior groups; and Portfolio Reviews mean that all projects are subjected to the same scrutiny, so that even the general manager's pet projects are under the microscope.

Here are some ways we ensure senior management buy-in:

▶ First, involve senior management in the design of the process. For example, during step 2, ensure that a senior management session is built in where they help design the Portfolio Reviews or gates (for example, design the prioritization criteria or design the rules of the game).

▶ Early in the implementation phase, run some pilots (for example, run a mock Portfolio Review with senior management as participants).

▶ Provide a gatekeeper training session, where senior people can not only learn about the PMP, but also can be briefed on expected behaviors and their rules of the game.

Example: When English China Clay introduced their gating process in the United States, the first group to take a training course was the executives, including the president of the company. This one-day training session laid out the details of the process, defined the gate criteria (which they had helped craft), and outlined the gatekeepers' rules (which they had already accepted). Then a mock gate meeting took place, using a real company case. Here the company president and some senior VPs played the role of the project leader and team, while the more junior executives were the gatekeepers—a complete role reversal. The results were both humorous and instructive.

Example: At Reckitt & Colman, every executive right up to the CEO's office attended a two-day training program when their gating process was rolled out worldwide. The difference here was that the training session featured attendees from different levels in the company, so that managing directors sat on the same teams as entry-level product managers. This approach proved very instructive, especially to senior people who lacked the insights on the problems faced at the project team level.

3. *Develop user-friendly documentation:* Most documentation in support of new management processes is not very user-friendly: it's heavy reading, too long, and not very inviting. So most such manuals are never read! Too bad, because no doubt a lot of thought and hard work went into their prepa-

ration by some well-intentioned task forces. We recommend that you take a look at some of the manuals and guide books that have been developed for computer software programs in recent years. They certainly are a far cry from the deadly ones of the mid-80s. Learn from their experience. We're not suggesting that you develop a guide that reads like "Portfolio Management for Dummies," but maybe a few ideas from this style of guide might be appropriate.

One way to handle the documentation is to develop several pieces or booklets with different levels of detail. Here are three we often use:

- *Brochure:* This is a four- to six-page glossy four-color brochure that outlines the concept and purpose of the PMP. It looks much like a product sales brochure, and that's exactly what it is. First impressions count! Additionally, some companies use such a brochure as a selling tool with their customers and customer-partners, outlining how their new product process and portfolio management approach works.
- *Guide:* This is typically a 10- to 25-page guide book. It provides a fairly in-depth description of the process: for example, the prioritization criteria; the various bubble diagrams and charts to be used at the Portfolio Review; an outline of the stages and gates in the new product process; and so on. But not much detail is available.
- *Manual:* The manual can be much longer, and has much operational detail (for example, the guide might list the prioritization criteria, much like Exhibit 7.5, while the manual provides operational definitions of the criteria, as in Appendix B). The manual also contains examples, illustrations, and templates. The manual is what a project leader of a new product project would refer to as she or he provides input for a Portfolio Review or prepares for a gate review.

Some firms provide limited circulation copies of their PMP guides and manuals (numbered copies, much in the tradition of ISO 9000). Other companies have no hard copy of their manuals and guides at all: the entire PMP is on the LAN or PC. A PC-based manual or guide has the advantage of easy, timely updates and also the use of hypertext (that is, there is a drill-down capability built right into the guide).

4. *Undertake internal marketing:* Earlier in this chapter, we noted that rolling out a PMP is a bit like developing and launching a new product. So don't forget the marketing and selling! Here are some common marketing and promotional approaches:

- Have an "announcement event" to roll out the PM process. This might coincide with some other company event. The goal is to have the sponsor or executive group place their blessing on the new PMP and announce that "effective March 1, this process is in place." Next the task force presents some of the details of the PMP, and outlines what will happen as rollout proceeds (for example, training, bringing existing projects in, and so on).

- Use in-company communications, for example, your company newsletter or magazine or even e-mail. It is excellent practice to keep the rest of the company informed of your task force progress all the way through step 2. Sometimes there is a long pause between the initial kickoff event and eventual rollout of the PMP, so you should be considering "news releases" or "press releases" and news articles all the way along, and not just as rollout begins. Someone on the task force can be appointed as "communications manager."

5. *Provide training on the PM process:* Most companies underestimate the need for training when they roll out a new product process, a gating method, or a PMP. The assumption seems to be that "all this stage-gate and bubble diagram stuff is obvious, and anyone ought to be able to handle it by reading the manual." Wrong! First, many people don't read. Second, learning via reading is not everyone's forte. Third, this "stage-gate and bubble diagram stuff" is considerably more complex than you might expect. Finally, recall that buy-in is a critical goal. People will not use something new if they either fear it or don't understand it, no matter how loud the boss screams. So take every precaution to ensure that people appreciate the benefits of the new process (no fear!) and that they fully understand how it works. Training is essential for organizational buy-in.

    You might consider different levels and types of training for different groups of people. For example:

    - For project teams and leaders: Typically a two- to three-day course is developed for about 25 to 30 attendees per session. The seminar involves lectures or "show and tell" sessions revealing how the PMP works, as well as experiential work—teams working their way through stage 2 of a real company case or attending a mock Portfolio Review.
    - For gatekeepers, portfolio reviewers, and senior people: They require the most training, because their behavior must change the most. Unfortunately, life at the top is rushed, so one day is typically allotted. Here the two- to three-day program is compressed into a single day.
    - For peripheral players and resource providers (people who are not on project teams, but nonetheless are associated with new product projects; for example, someone in finance, legal, or regulatory affairs): for these individuals usually a shorter version of the program—enough to outline the essence of the PMP—suffices.

6. *Bring existing projects into the PM process:* First, assemble a list of the projects to be included (this should be available from step 1, where you already undertook a total review of the existing portfolio). Then obtain and update the data on each—data needed to characterize and describe each project (name, leader, project type, market, and so on) as well as data needed for the various portfolio models (probability of success, NPV, expenditures, and so on).

Hold gate reviews soon! Note that some of the required data might be of doubtful validity; additionally, some data needed in certain portfolio models are not yet available (for example, project scores from gate reviews). Thus the next challenge is ensuring that all projects pass through a gate review. This should be done as early as possible for two reasons:

- First, the sooner all projects are "in" the Stage-Gate process, the better. At least the right side of the PMP in Exhibit 7.13 will be up and running.
- Second, the gate reviews provide or validate much of the data needed for the portfolio models and Portfolio Review. For example, gates are where the gatekeepers accept the NPV values as valid; and gates are where project scores on key criteria are determined, scores that become inputs to bubble diagrams (scored axes) or to the prioritized scored list (rank-ordered list of active projects).

An effective approach here is to have a series of "welcome gates" to ensure that all projects pass through at least one gate within the first months of rollout. These welcome gates are somewhat gentler than real gates, and require that project leaders declare in advance where they are in the process (what stage) and what they will deliver to the welcome gate. It is understood by gatekeepers that likely not all the desired deliverables will be available for the welcome gate. One output of the welcome gate is a decision as to what and when the next "real" gate will be, and what deliverables will be available then. Another outcome of the welcome gate is the data—the NPVs, the approved expenditures, the project scores on key factors, probability estimates, and the like—needed for the portfolio database and model.

Another approach is to begin with some pilot projects. This can start in step 2 once a skeleton process is in place. That is, pick a handful of projects whose project leaders are willing (ideally their leaders might even be on the task force). These should be typical projects and perhaps at different stages. Then start running these projects through the gating process to test the process, and in particular, to test the gate criteria and gate procedures. With a limited number of projects, you can also start to pilot the portfolio IT system and database and some of the portfolio models. Note that in step 2, when you undertook a review of the existing portfolio and generated various charts and diagrams, you were in effect piloting the various portfolio models.

7. *Develop or acquire an IT support system:* There are several facets of an IT system you may wish to consider to support your PMP. While off-the-shelf software can be used as the shell, usually there is some original, custom programming or setup required. Here are the types of IT support firms use:

- Database software, where all the vital stats and characteristics of projects can be stored. This information is important for tracking projects, for providing input data for the portfolio models, and for gauging new product performance. These data are usually generated and collected at gate reviews.

▶ Software to display portfolio charts, such as pie charts, histograms, and especially bubble diagrams.

▶ The use of software or IT to provide easy access to documentation of the gating process or entire PMP (for example, a LAN-based PMP manual complete with hypertext).

▶ Tools that are software-based. These include:

- screening and diagnostic tools such as NewProd
- project management tools (time lines and Gantt charts), such as Microsoft Project
- financial analysis tools such as spreadsheets, Monte Carlo simulation packages, and so on. (Many finance departments provide the task force with a compiled, preformatted spreadsheet with the appropriate columns and rows for project financial analysis.)
- information exchange software (such as Lotus notes) so that team members can share information; or two remote parties can work on a common document; or people outside the project can review its progress
- software to facilitate idea dissemination and feedback
- IT to support gates and Portfolio Reviews (for example, wireless voting machines; PC-based meetings facilitation software).

POINTS FOR MANAGEMENT TO PONDER

The toughest phase by far is step 3, implementing the PMP. Don't underestimate the challenge here. Some tasks you should consider building into your implementation, and that will help pave the way for smoother adoption of the PMP, include:

1. putting a portfolio manager or process manager in place—someone who is charged with implementing the PMP on a day-to-day basis
2. seeking senior management buy-in (ensuring they walk the talk)
3. developing user-friendly documentation: brochure, guide, and manual
4. doing some internal marketing—don't forget, you're introducing a new concept here and need to market it!
5. developing and providing training for project team members and leaders, senior people, and resource providers
6. getting projects into the PMP quickly—don't let projects linger here
7. developing an IT system to support the PMP
8. defining metrics to measure how well the PMP and new products are doing.

One more suggestion: read the "Ten Ways to Fail" in Exhibit 8.1.

The task of designing and implementing a systematic PMP is not an easy one. On the other hand, new products are the future of your business. How you invest your R&D and new product resources will dictate how well your business does in the years ahead. So make the extra effort that's needed here.

---

8. *Develop metrics:* You cannot manage what you haven't measured! Metrics or performance measures are required in order that the PMP be effectively managed. Consider two types of metrics:

   ▶ *In-process metrics* capture how well the PMP process is functioning. These are metrics that are measured inside the process, before a project is launched. For example, are Portfolio Reviews working? Are projects hitting the gates on time? And do we have the right number of projects for the resources available?

   ▶ *Post-process metrics* measure the longer-term performance of your entire product development effort, and are gauged some time after launch. Examples: Are you achieving your new product sales or profit goals (for example, percentage of sales from new products)? What proportion of development projects are commercial successes? And what is the profitability of the total new product effort?

Metrics should be designed in step 2 and be part of the implementation plan.

---

1. Design the portfolio management process on your own, in your own office, and in a vacuum. You know best—task forces are a waste of time!

2. Don't do any homework or auditing (step 1). You already know what the problem is in your company, so jump immediately to a solution.

3. Don't bother looking at other companies' methods—their approaches, models, charts, criteria and scoring models, and so on. You have nothing to learn from them.

4. If you do assemble a task force, meet over several months in private. Then present "your grand design" and assume everyone in the company will applaud, even though they have not been involved.

5. Don't seek outside help: just read the book and design your process based on the generic one. If you do seek help, hire a reengineering consultant who knows nothing about new product management or portfolio management.

6. Don't waste time testing and seeking feedback from others in the company as your task force designs the process. After all, you're the task force. What do these "outsiders" know? Your "process design" is likely to be nearly perfect!

7. When others do have questions or criticisms, treat these people as "cynics" and "negative thinkers." Refuse to deal with these objections, and never, never modify the process. It's yours, and it's cast in marble.

8. Don't provide training—most of this "portfolio management stuff" is obvious. Anyone ought to be able to do it just by reading the manual.

9. Speaking of manuals: make sure the PMP guide is thick and full of checklists and forms. If in doubt, overwhelm the reader and user.

10. Don't bother installing a process or portfolio manager—the process is so good, it will be automatically implemented.

Exhibit 8.1   Ten Ways to Fail at Portfolio Management Design and Implementation

Note: Based on real companies' experiences.

There is much work involved in the implementation of a PMP. If parts of the process are already in place—for example, you already have a new product strategy, or you already have a perfectly fine Stage-Gate process—then the task is certainly lighter. There are also many pitfalls along the way: see Exhibit 8.1 entitled "Ten Ways to Fail," our tongue-in-cheek reminder list of don'ts. We could continue with the warnings and cautions, but we think you get the point. Before you proceed, think through the design and implementation of a PMP carefully, and be prepared to make a major commitment here. But at all costs, do proceed! The costs of doing nothing are just too high.

Winning at New Products

There are two ways to win big at new products: doing the right projects and doing projects right. This book is about doing the right projects. If you pick the right projects, then you're halfway to winning. You end up with an enviable portfolio of high-value projects; a portfolio that is properly balanced; and, most important, a portfolio that supports your business's strategy. Picking the right number of projects for the resources available—making sure that you don't overload your process and end up with pipeline gridlock—also has an added payoff in terms of doing projects right: better portfolio management should impact positively the quality of execution of projects, the end result being higher success rates and shorter cycle times.

New products are the leading edge of your business strategy. The product choices you make today determine what your business's product offerings and market position will be in the future. Making the right choices today is critical. Portfolio management and new product project selection is fundamental to business success. How you invest your R&D and new product resources will shape the future of your business. Indeed, business history is littered with the remains of companies that failed at this task—failed to make the right strategic choices about what new products, developments, platforms, and technologies they wished to focus on. Over the next decade, some companies will win at new products, and others will lose. The winners will be the next generation of Microsofts, 3Ms, Mercks, and P&Gs. You won't hear too much about the losers as they fade away into obscurity. So take the needed steps to ensure that your business is on the winning side. Make sure that you have the tools you need to make these right choices—an effective Portfolio Management Process—in your business!

Overhauling the New Product Process: Stage-Gate Methods— A Synopsis[1]

Goals of a New Product Process

Numerous companies have undertaken internal audits only to conclude that their new product process isn't working: projects take too long; key activities and tasks are missing; and Go/Kill decisions are problematic. As a result, they have *overhauled their new product process* using a Stage-Gate approach. Numerous benchmarking studies and investigations into winners versus losers have pointed to the following goals for a successful new product process.

Goal 1: Quality of Execution

A quality-of-execution crisis exists in the product innovation process. This deficiency is evident in many benchmarking studies, including our own: key activities are poorly done or not done at all; too many projects omit too many vital actions; and both quality of execution and thoroughness of the process are lacking. There is also clear evidence that the activities of the new product process—the quality of execution and whether these activities are carried out at all—have a dramatic impact on performance.

This quality-of-execution crisis provides strong evidence in support of the need for a more *systematic and quality approach* to the way firms conceive, develop, and launch new products. The way to deal with the quality problem is to visualize product innovation as a process, and to apply *process management* and *quality management techniques* to this process. Note that any process in business can be managed with a view to quality. Get the details of your processes right, and the result will be a high-quality output.

Quality of execution is the goal of the new product process. More specifically, the ideal game plan should:

1. *focus on completeness:* ensure that the key activities that are central to the success of a new product project are indeed carried out—no gaps, no omissions, a "complete" process.
2. *focus on quality:* ensure that the execution of these activities is proficient— that is, treat innovation as a process, emphasize DIRTFooT (doing it right the first time), and build in quality controls and checks.
3. *focus on the important:* devote attention and resources to the pivotal and particularly weak steps in the new product process, notably the up-front and market-oriented activities.

The new product process or Stage-Gate system is simply a *process management tool.* One builds into this process *quality of execution* in much the same way that quality programs have been successfully implemented on the factory floor.

Goal 2: Sharper Focus, Better Project Prioritization

Most firms' new product efforts suffer from a lack of focus: too many projects and not enough resources. Adequate resources has been identified as a principal driver of firms' new product performance, but a lack of resources plagues too many firms' development efforts. Sometimes this lack is simply because management has not devoted the needed people and money to the firm's new product effort. Often, this resource problem stems from a lack of focus, the result of inadequate project evaluations: the failure to set priorities and make tough Go/Kill decisions. In short, the "gates" are weak.

The need is for a *new product funnel,* not *tunnel.* A new product funnel builds in tough Go/Kill decision points (or bail-out points throughout the process); the poor projects are weeded out; scarce resources are directed toward the truly meritorious projects; and more focus is the result. One funneling method is to build the new product process or game plan around a set of gates or Go/Kill decision points. These gates are the bail-out points where we ask, "Are we still in the game?" They are the *quality-control checkpoints* in the new product process, and focus on the quality, merit, and progress of the project.

Goal 3: A Strong Market Orientation

A market orientation is the missing ingredient in most new product projects. A lack of a market orientation and inadequate market assessment are consistently cited as reasons for new product failure. Moreover, the market-related activities tend to be the weakest in the new product process, yet are strongly linked to success. While many managers profess a market orientation, the evidence—where the time and money are spent on projects—proves otherwise.

If positive new product performance is the goal, then a market orientation— executing the key marketing activities in a quality fashion—must be built into the new product process as a matter of routine rather than by exception. Marketing inputs must play a decisive role from beginning to end of the project. The following actions are *integral and mandatory plays* in the new product game plan (but they rarely are):

- *Preliminary market assessment:* a relatively inexpensive step very early in the life of a project, designed to assess market attractiveness and to test market acceptance of the proposed new product.
- *Market research to determine user needs and wants:* in-depth surveys or face-to-face interviews with customers to determine customer needs, wants, preferences, likes, dislikes, buying criteria, and so on as an input to the design of the new product.
- *Competitive analysis:* an assessment of competitors—their products and product deficiencies, prices, costs, technologies, production capacities, and marketing strategies.
- *Concept testing:* testing the proposed product in concept form to determine likely market acceptance. Note that the product is not yet developed, but a model or representation of the product is displayed to prospective users to gauge reaction and purchase intent.
- *Customer reaction during development:* continuing concept and product testing throughout the development phase, using rapid prototypes, models, and partially completed products to gauge customer reaction and seek feedback.
- *User tests:* field trials using the finished product (or prototype) with users to verify the performance of the product under customer conditions, and to confirm purchase intent and market acceptance.
- *Test market or trial sell:* a minilaunch of the product in a limited geographic area or single sales territory. This is a test of all elements of the marketing mix, including the product itself.
- *Market launch:* a proficient launch, based on a solid marketing plan and backed by sufficient resources.

Goal 4: Better Up-Front Homework and Sharp, Early Product Definition

New product success or failure is largely decided in the first few plays of the game—in those crucial steps and tasks that precede the actual development of the product. Solid up-front homework and sharp early product definition are key ingredients in a successful new product process (according to the benchmarking study) and result in higher success rates and profitability. The up-front homework helps define the product and build the business case for development. Ironically, most of the money and time spent on projects is devoted to the middle and back-end stages of the process, while the up-front actions suffer from errors of omission, poor quality of execution, and underresourcing.

The ideal new product process ensures that these early stages are carried out and that the product is fully defined before the project is allowed to proceed—before the project is allowed to become a full-fledged development project.

Goal 5: A True Cross-Functional Team Approach

The new product process is multifunctional: it requires the input and active participation of players from many different functions in the organization. The multifunctional nature of innovation coupled with the desire for parallel processing means that a *cross-functional team approach* is mandatory. Essential characteristics of this team are as follows:

- The team is cross-functional, with committed team players from the various functions and departments—marketing, engineering, R&D, manufacturing. Release time for the project is provided to team members.
- Every significant project team has a clearly defined team captain or leader. This leader is dedicated to the project (not spread across numerous other duties or projects) and is accountable from beginning to end of the project—not just for one phase.
- The leader has formal authority: this means co-opting authority from the functional heads. When senior management approves the team's action plan at gate meetings, they also commit the resources—money, people, and release time—to the project leader and team; at the same time, senior management *transfers decision-making power* to the team. Expectations and the scope of this authority are made very clear to the team at the gate.
- The team structure is fluid, with new members joining the team (or leaving it) as work requirements demand. But a *small core group of responsible, committed, and accountable team players should be present from beginning to end of the project.*

Goal 6: Delivery of Products with Competitive Advantage— Differentiated Products, Unique Benefits, Superior Value for the Customer

Don't forget to build in product superiority at every opportunity. This is one key to new product success, yet all too often, when redesigning their new product processes, firms fall into the trap of repeating current, often faulty, practices: there's no attempt to seek truly superior products. And so the results are predicable: more ho-hum, tired products. Here's how to drive the quest for product advantage:

- Ensure that at least some of the criteria at every gate focus on product superiority. Questions such as "Does the product have at least one element of competitive advantage?", "Does it offer the user new or different benefits?", "Is it excellent value for money for the user?" become vital to rating and ranking would-be projects. (See criteria in Exhibit 7.5, for example.)
- Require that certain key actions designed to deliver product superiority be included in each stage of the process. Some of these have been mentioned above (goal 3) and include customer-focused ideation; user needs-and-wants market research studies; competitive product analysis; concept and protocept tests, preference tests, and trial sells; and constant iterations with customers during development via rapid-prototype-and-tests.
- Demand that project teams deliver evidence of product superiority to project Go/Kill reviews: make product superiority an important deliverable and issue at such meetings (rather than dwelling on the financial calculations).

Goal 7: A Fast-Paced and Flexible Process

The new product process must be built for speed. This means eliminating all the time-wasters and work that add no value in your current new product process. It also means designing a flexible process, one that accommodates the risks and nature of different projects. Some firms are moving toward a *third-generation process,*[2] which features three Fs:

- *Flexible:* the process is not a straitjacket or hard-and-fast set of rules; rather, each project can be routed through the process according to its risk level and needs; stages can be omitted and gates combined, provided the decision is made consciously, at gates, and with a full understanding of the risks involved.
- *Fuzzy gates:* "Go" decisions can be conditional; the decision can be made in the absence of perfect information, conditional on positive results delivered later.
- *Fluidity:* the process is fluid and adaptable. For example, stages can be overlapped—a project can be in two stages at the same time; and activities are done concurrently within stages, much like a rugby approach (rather than a series or relay race scheme).

The Structure of the Stage-Gate™ Process

Fashion these seven key goals into a Stage-Gate new product game plan—a *conceptual and operational model* for moving a new product project from idea to launch. This Stage-Gate system is a blueprint for managing the new product process to improve effectiveness and efficiency.

Stage-Gate systems break the innovation process down into a predetermined set of stages, each stage consisting of a set of prescribed, cross-functional, and parallel activities (see Exhibit 7.4). The entrance to each stage is a gate: these gates control the process and serve as the quality-control and Go/Kill checkpoints.

The Stages

The Stage-Gate system breaks the new product project down into discrete and identifiable stages, typically four, five, or six in number. Each stage is designed to gather information needed to move the project forward to the next gate or decision point. Each stage is multi- or cross-functional: There is no "R&D stage" or "marketing stage." Rather, each stage consists of a set of parallel activities undertaken by people from different functional areas within the firm, but working together as a team led by a project team leader.

In order to manage risk via a Stage-Gate scheme, the parallel activities within a stage must be designed to gather vital information (technical, market, financial, and so on) in order to drive down technical and business uncertainties. Each stage costs more than the preceding one, so that the game plan is an incremental commitment one. As uncertainties decrease, expenditures are allowed to mount.

Finally, flexibility is built in to promote acceleration of projects. In order to speed products to market, stages can overlap each other; long lead-time activities can be brought forward from one stage to an earlier one; projects can proceed into the next stage, even though the previous stage has not been totally completed; and stages can be collapsed and combined.

The general flow of the typical or a *generic* Stage-Gate process is shown pictorially in Exhibit 7.4. Here the five key and overlapping stages are as follows:

Stage 1. Preliminary Investigation: a quick investigation and scoping of the project. Typically, this stage is undertaken by a very small core team of technical and marketing people; it includes the first-cut homework, such as preliminary market assessment, preliminary technical assessment, and preliminary business assessment.

Stage 2. Detailed Investigation: the detailed homework leading to a *business case.* Stage 2 includes market research (a user needs and wants study to identify requirements for the ideal product; competitive analysis; and a concept test to confirm purchase intent); detailed technical and manufacturing assessment; and a detailed financial and business analysis. This stage should be undertaken by a core team of marketing, technical, and manufacturing people—the beginnings of the ultimate project team in stage 3. The deliverables from stage 2 include a defined product (on paper: target market, product concept and benefits, and product requirements); a business justification (economic and business rationale), and a detailed plan of action for the next stages (including resource requirements and timing).

Stage 3. Development: the actual design and development of the new product. Here the development plan is implemented; a prototype or sample product is developed; and the product undergoes in-house testing along with limited customer testing (for example, rapid-prototype-and-tests with potential users). Additionally, the manufacturing process and requirements are mapped out; the marketing launch plan is developed; and the test plans for the next stage are defined. Stage 3 sees the project gain momentum, with a marked increase in resource commitment: here the full cross-functional project team—marketing, technical, manufacturing, and perhaps quality assurance, purchasing, sales, and finance people—is in place.

Stage 4. Testing and Validation: the verification and validation of the proposed new product, its marketing, and its production. This stage witnesses extensive in-house product testing; customer field trials or trials in the marketplace; pilot or preproduction trials in the plant; and even test marketing or a trial sell. The deliverable is a fully tested product and production process, ready for commercialization. The project team and leader from stage 3 remain accountable for actions and deliverables in stage 4.

Stage 5. Full Production and Market Launch: full commercialization of the product. Stage 5 marks the beginning of full production and commercial selling.

This stage sees the implementation of the marketing launch plan, the production plan, and the postlaunch activities, including monitoring and adjustment. While new members may be added to this "commercialization team" (for example, from the sales force and from operations), the core project team from stages 4 and 5 remains in place and accountable for commercialization and beyond. There are no handoffs in this game!

Note that there are two homework stages in this process: stage 1, a quick homework phase done on a number of projects; and stage 2, which provides for a more detailed investigation, but on fewer projects. The result is superb up-front homework and sharp, early product definition (goal 4). Additionally, constant customer contact and a market orientation are evident throughout all five stages: the actions outlined in goal 3 are heavily featured in the process. These actions heighten the odds of delivering a superior product with real value to the customer (goal 6). Finally, a cross-functional team approach is mandatory in order to successfully execute each stage (goal 5).

The Gates

Preceding each stage is an entry gate or a Go/Kill decision point, shown as diamonds in Exhibit 7.4. Effective gates are central to the success of a fast-paced new product process:

▶ Gates serve as quality-control checkpoints, where quality of execution is the focus: Is this project being executed in a quality fashion (goal 1)?
▶ Gates also serve as Go/Kill and prioritization decision points (goal 2). Gates provide for the funneling of projects, in which mediocre projects are culled out at each successive gate.
▶ Finally, gates are the points where the path forward for the next play or stage of the process is decided, along with resource commitments. Once again, quality of execution becomes a central issue.

Gate meetings are usually staffed by senior managers from different functions, who own the resources required by the project leader and team for the next stage. Gates have a common format:

• *Inputs:* these are the *deliverables* to a gate review—what the project leader and team deliver to the meeting; they are the results of the actions of the previous stage, and are based on a standard menu of deliverables for each gate.
• *Criteria:* these are questions or metrics on which the project is judged in order to make the Go/Kill and prioritization decision. They include both qualitative (for example, strategic fit; product superiority; market attractiveness) and quantitative criteria (financial return; risk via sensitivity analysis), and can include must-meet (mandatory) as well as should-meet (desirable) criteria—see Exhibit 7.5 or Appendix B.
• *Outputs:* these are the results of the gate review—a decision (Go/Kill/ Hold/Recycle); a prioritization level; resource commitments and action plan approved; and date and deliverables for next gate agreed on.

In the fastest Stage-Gate processes, gate decisions are made with incomplete information: this means that the project team is given a "Go" decision, conditional on positive results occurring early in the next stage. In this way, the project is not held up, awaiting the completion of one or two tasks from the previous stage.

Understanding the critical success factors—what separates high-performing business units and winning new products from the rest—is the first step toward improving one's own performance. Overhauling your new product process, and incorporating these success factors into this *Stage-Gate process,* is the way many companies are now *winning at new products.*

Sample Gate 3 Screening Criteria (Scored)

Key Criteria	Rating Scale				Rating
	1	**4**	**7**	**10**	
Strategic					
1. Degree to which project aligns with BU's strategy	Slight fit with BU's strategy	Modest fit; not a key element	Good fit; matches some of the key elements	Strong, clear fit with BU's strategy	
2. Strategic importance	Minor; no noticeable harm if project dropped	Modest; competi- tive, finan- cial impact	Significant; difficult to recover if project un- successful or dropped	Very high; business unit future depends on this project	

	Rating Scale				
Key Criteria	**1**	**4**	**7**	**10**	**Rating**
Product/ Competitive Advantage					
1. Product has unique customer benefits	No unique benefits provided	Minor; unique benefits provided	Some unique benefits provided (at least one major benefit)	Clearly provides unique and important customer benefits	
2. Meets customer needs better than competition	No competitive advantage	Minor advantages over competition	Provides some advantages over competition	Clearly meets customer needs better than competition	
3. Provides good value for money	Poor; no advantage over existing products	Modest; some additional value provided	Good; provides consider-able value for money	High; clearly better value for money than competition	

	Rating Scale				
Key Criteria	**1**	**4**	**7**	**10**	**Rating**
Synergies (Leverages Core Competencies)					
1. Degree of marketing synergies	Low; need to acquire or hire/build	Modest; matches some, but need new skills/ resources	Moderate; available, but must tailor	High; can successfully leverage existing skills/ resources	
2. Degree of technological synergies	Technology new to the company; (almost) no skills	Some R&D experience, but probably insufficient	Selectively practiced in company	Widely practiced in company	
3. Degree of manufacturing/ processing synergies	Low; new to us; need to acquire or build	Modest; do-able, but means major modifications	Good; do-able with minor modifications only	High; can be done with existing people and facilities	

	Rating Scale				
Key Criteria	**1**	**4**	**7**	**10**	**Rating**
Technical Feasibility					
1. Magnitude of technical gap	Large gap between current and desired technology; high risk	Major changes needed, but should be able to achieve	Some minor changes needed, but do-able	Low; incremental in nature	
2. Degree of technical complexity	Very high; many hurdles	High; many hurdles,but definable	Challenging but do-able	Straight-forward	
3. Degree of technical uncertainty	High	Moderately high	Moderately low	Low	

	Rating Scale				
Key Criteria	**1**	**4**	**7**	**10**	**Rating**
Financial Reward*					
1. Expected profitability (for example, NPV)	Low; < $1MM	Modest; $2–4MM	Good; $6–8MM	High; > $10MM	
2. Financial return (for example, IRR%)	Low; < 7%	Modest; 8–10%	Good; 12%	High; > 15%	
3. Payback period	> 5 years	3 years	2 years	< 1 year	
4. Certainty of return/profit estimates	Low; pure guess < 20% probability	40% probability	70% probability	Highly certain < 90% probability	

*Will vary by business unit, company, and industry.

Reference Notes

Chapter 1

1. Archer, N.P., and Ghasemzadeh, F., "Project Portfolio Selection Techniques: A Review and a Suggested Integrated Approach," Innovation Research Centre Working Paper No. 46, McMaster University, 1996.

2. Baker, N.R., "R&D Project Selection Models: An Assessment," *IEEE Transactions on Engineering Management,* EM-21(4):165–170, 1974.

3. Baker, N.R., and Pound, W.H., "R&D Project Selection: Where We Stand," *IEEE Transactions on Engineering Management,* EM-11(4):124–134, 1964.

4. Bard, J.F., Balachandra, R., and Kaufmann, P.E., "An Interactive Approach to R&D Project Selection and Termination," *IEEE Transactions on Engineering Management,* 35(3):139–146, 1988.

5. Belton, V., "Project Planning and Prioritization in the Social Services—An OR Contribution," *Journal of the Operational Research Society,* 44(2):115–124, 1993.

6. Cooley, S.C., Hehmeyer, J., and Sweeney, P.J., "Modelling R&D Resource Allocation," *Research Management,* 29(1):40–49, 1986.

7. Cooper, R.G., *Winning at New Products,* 2nd edition, Addison-Wesley, Reading, Mass., 1993.

8. Cooper, R.G., "Third-Generation New Product Processes," *Journal of Product Innovation Management,* 11:3–14, 1994.

9. Cooper, R.G., and Kleinschmidt, E.J., "Benchmarking Firm's New Product Performance and Practices," *Engineering Management Review,* 23(3):112–120, 1995.

10. Cooper, R.G., and Kleinschmidt, E.J., "Winning Businesses in Product Development: Critical Success Factors," *Research Technology Management,* 39(4):18–29, 1996.

11. Czinkota, M., and Kotabe, M., "Product Development the Japanese Way," *The Journal of Business Strategy,* November–December: 31–36, 1990.

12. Danila, N., "Strategic Evaluation and Selection of R&D Projects," *R&D Management,* 19(1):47–62, 1989.

13. De Maio, A., Verganti, R., and Corso, M., "A Multi-Project Management Framework for New Product Development," *European Journal of Operational Research,* 78(2):178–191, 1994.

14. Erickson, T.J., "Worldwide R&D Management: Concepts and Applications," *Columbia Journal of World Business,* 25(4):8–13, 1990.

15. Griffin, A., and Page, A.L., "An Interim Report on Measuring Product Development Success and Failure," *Journal of Product Innovation Management,* 9(1): 291–308, 1993.

16. Hall, D.L., and Naudia, A., "An Interactive Approach for Selecting IR&D Projects," *IEEE Transactions on Engineering Management,* 37(2):126–133, 1990.

17. Jackson, B., "Decision Methods for Selecting a Portfolio of R&D Projects," *Research Management,* September–October:21–26, 1983.

18. Khorramshahgol, R., and Gousty, Y., "Delphic Goal Programming (DGP): A Multi-Objective Cost/Benefit Approach to R&D Portfolio Analysis," *IEEE Transactions on Engineering Management,* EM-33(3):172–175, 1986.

19. Liberatore, M.J., "An Extension of the Analytic Hierarchy Process for Industrial R&D Project Selection and Resource Allocation," *IEEE Transactions on Engineering Management,* EM-34(1):12–18, 1987.

20. Liberatore, M.J., "A Decision Support System Linking Research and Development Project Selection with Business Strategy," *Project Management Journal,* 19(5):14–21, 1988.

21. Lilien, G.L., and Kotler, P., *Marketing Decision Making: A Model-Building Approach,* Harper & Row, New York, 1983.

22. Parts of this are taken from Matheson, J.E., Menke, M.M., and Derby, S.L., "Improving the Quality of R&D Decision: A Synopsis of the SDG Approach," *Journal of Science Policy and Research Management* (in Japanese), 4(4), 1989. See also reference no. 2 in Chapter 3.

23. Morris, P.A., Teisberg, E.O., and Kolbe, A.L., "When Choosing R&D Projects, Go with the Long Shots," *Research Technology Management,* 34:35–49, 1991.

24. Page, A.L., "Assessing New Product Development Practices and Performance: Establishing Crucial Norms," *Journal of Product Innovation Management,* 10(4): 273–290, 1993.

25. Adapted from *Third Generation R&D, Managing the Link to Corporate Strategy,* by Roussel, P., Saad, K., and Erickson, T., Harvard Business School Press and Arthur D. Little Inc., Boston, Mass., 1991, p. 93.

26. Schmidt, R.L., "A Model for R&D Project Selection with Combined Benefit, Outcome and Resource Interactions," *IEEE Transactions on Engineering Management,* 40(4):403–410, 1993.

27. Souder, W.E., and Mandakovic, T., "R&D Project Selection Models," *Research Management,* 29(4):36–42, 1986.

28. Taggart, J H., and Blaxter, T.J., "Strategy in Pharmaceutical R&D: A Portfolio Risk Matrix," *R&D Management,* 22(3):241–254, 1992.

29. Weber, R., Werners, B., and Zimmermann, H.J., "Planning Models for Research and Development," *European Journal of Operational Research,* 48(2): 175–188, 1990.

30. Wheelwright, S.C., and Clark, K.B., "Creating Project Plans to Focus Product Development," *Harvard Business Review,* 70(2):70–82, 1992.

31. Wind, Y., and Mahajan, V., "New Product Development Process: A Perspective for Reexamination," *Journal of Product Innovation Management,* 5(4):304–310, 1988.

32. Yorke, D.A., and Droussiotis, G., "The Use of Customer Portfolio Theory: An Empirical Survey," *Journal of Business & Industrial Marketing,* 9(3):6–18, 1994.

33. Zahedi, F., "The Analytic Hierarchy Process—A Survey of the Method and Its Applications," *Interfaces,* 16(4):96–108, 1986.

34. For the pharmaceutical industry, see Henderson, R., "Managing Innovation in the Information Age," *Harvard Business Review,* January–February:100–105, 1994.

Chapter 2

1. Cooper, R.G., *Winning at New Products,* 2nd ed., Addison-Wesley, Reading, Mass., 1993.

2. Cooper, R.G. "Third-Generation New Product Processes," *Journal of Product Innovation Management,* 11:3–14, 1994.

3. See reference, Chapter 3, no. 2.

4. More, R., and Little, B., "The Application of Discriminant Analysis to the Prediction of Sales Forecast Uncertainty in New Product Situations," *Journal of Operations Research Society,* 31:71–77, 1980.

5. Haley, G., and Goldberg, S., "Net Present Value Techniques and Their Effects on New Product Research," *Industrial Marketing Management,* 24:177–190, 1995.

6. Taken from a presentation by H. Korotkin, Controller—*New Product Process, Polaroid Corporation,* Portfolio Planning and Management for New Product Development Conference, by Institute of International Research and Product Development Management Association, December 1996.

7. See Cooper, R.G., and Kleinschmidt, E.J., "Benchmarking Firm's New Product Performance and Practices," *Engineering Management Review,* 23(3):112–120, 1995; also Cooper, R.G., and Kleinschmidt, E.J., "Winning Businesses in Product Development: Critical Success Factors," *Research Technology Management,* 39(4): 18–29, 1996. For the service sector refer to Cooper, R.G., and Edgett, S.J., "Critical Success Factors for New Financial Services," *Marketing Management,* 5(3): 26–37, 1996.

8. For more information on NewProd, see Cooper, R.G., "The NewProd System: The Industry Experience," *Journal of Product Innovation Management,* 9:113–127, 1992; or Cooper, R.G., *Winning at New Products,* 2nd ed., Addison-Wesley, Reading, Mass., 1993. For additional information, contact the authors or see Web page www.prod-dev.com.

9. Davis, R.E., "The Role of Market Research in the Development of New Consumer Products," *Journal of Product Innovation Management,* 10(4):309–317, 1993.

10. Bronnrenberg, J., and van Englelen, L., "A Dutch Test with the NewProd-Model," *R&D Management,* 18(4):321–332, 1988.

11. Souder, W.E., "A Scoring Methodology for Assessing the Suitability of Management Science Models," *Management Science,* 18:B526–543, 1972.

12. For more information on this issue and options pricing in general, refer to Deaves, R., and Krinsky, I., "New Tools for Investment Decision-making: Real Options Analysis," McMaster University Working Paper, April 1997; Faulkner, T., "Applying 'Options Thinking' to R&D Valuation," *Research-Technology Management,* (May–June):50–57, 1996; Luehrman, T., "What's It Worth? A General Manager's Guide to Valuation," *Harvard Business Review;* May–June:132, 142, 1997.

13. Faulkner, T., "Applying 'Options Thinking' to R&D Valuation," *Research-Technology Management,* May–June:50–57, 1996.

Chapter 3

1. Roussel, P., Saad, K., and Erickson, T., *Third Generation R&D, Managing the Link to Corporate Strategy,* Harvard Business School Press and Arthur D. Little Inc., Boston, Mass., 1991.

2. Taken from the Strategic Decisions Group (SDG). For more information, refer to Matheson, D., Matheson, J.E., and Menke, M.M., "Making Excellent R&D Decisions," *Research Technology Management,* November–December: 21–24, 1994; and Evans, P., "Streamlining Formal Portfolio Management," *Scrip Magazine,* February, 1996.

3. Taken from internal 3M documents: Dr. Gary L. Tritle, "New Product Investment Portfolio."

4. Source: discussions with Tom Chorman, Corporate New Ventures Group, Procter & Gamble.

Chapter 4

1. Adapted from Roberts, E., and Berry, C., "Entering New Businesses: Selecting Strategies for Success," *Sloan Management Review,* Spring: 3–17, 1983. *New Products Management for the 1980s* (New York: Booz, Allen & Hamilton, 1982).

Chapter 5

1. Source: Exxon Chemical, Product Innovation Process (company brochure).

2. See, for example, Cooper, R.G., and Kleinschmidt, E.J., "Benchmarking Firm's New Product Performance and Practices," *Engineering Management Review,* 23(3):112–120, 1995; Cooper, R.G., and Kleinschmidt, E.J., "Winning Businesses in Product Development: Critical Success Factors," *Research Technology Management,* 39(4):18–29, 1996; Edgett, S.J., "The Development of New Financial Services: Identifying Determinants of Success and Failure," *International Journal of Service Industry Management,* 5(4):24–38, 1994; Cooper, R.G., and Edgett, S.J., "Critical Success Factors for New Financial Services," *Marketing Management,* 5(3):26–37, 1996; Montoya-Weiss, M.M., and Calantone, R., "Determinants of New Product Performance: A Review and Meta-Analysis," *Journal of Product Innovation Management,* 11(5):397–417, 1994.

Chapter 6

1. See above, Chapter 5, no. 2.

2. For more information on the Boston Consulting Group's growth-share matrix, refer to Heldey, B., "Strategy and the Business Portfolio," *Long Range Planning,*

1977; for more information on the General Electric approach, refer to Day, G., *Analysis for Strategic Marketing Decisions,* West Publishing, St. Paul, Minn., and Hosner, L., *Strategic Management,* Prentice-Hall, Englewood Cliffs, N.J., 1984.

3. See Cooper, R. G., and Kleinschmidt, E.J., "Benchmarking Firm's New Product Performance and Practices," *Engineering Management Review,* 23(3), 1995.

4. See Cooper, R.G., and Kleinschmidt, E.J., "Benchmarking Firm's New Product Performance and Practices," *Engineering Management Review,* 23(3):112–120, 1995; also Cooper, R.G., and Kleinschmidt, E.J., "Winning Businesses in Product Development: Critical Success Factors," *Research Technology Management,* 39(4): 18–29, 1996.

Chapter 7

1. For more information on Stage-Gate and the new product development process, see Cooper, R.G., *Winning at New Products,* 2nd ed., Addison-Wesley, Reading, Mass., 1993.

2. For more information on ProBE and how it can help your organization benchmark the new product development process, contact the authors or see Web page www.prod-dev.com.

Chapter 8

1. At the time of writing this book the authors were continuing their benchmarking study of firms' practices in portfolio management via a joint study with the Industrial Research Institute (IRI), in part funded by Exxon/Esso Chemical Canada and the Innovation Research Centre at McMaster University. For additional information, contact the authors directly.

2. ProBE is a software product developed by Robert Cooper, Scott Edgett, and Jens Arleth. For more information, contact the authors or U-3 Consultants in Denmark directly or see Web page www.prod-dev.com.

3. A useful list of questions to use as the audit questionnaire can be found in Appendix A of *Winning at New Products* by Cooper, R.G., 2nd ed., Addison-Wesley, Reading, Mass., 1993.

4. Porter, M., *Competitive Strategy: Techniques for Analyzing Industries and Competitors,* New York, The Free Press, 1980.

5. Some useful references include: *Winning at New Products,* chapter 11, by Cooper, R.G., 2nd ed., Addison-Wesley, Reading, Mass., 1993; *New Products Management,* 5th ed., by Crawford, M.C., Irwin, Chicago, 1997; *Design and Marketing of New Products,* 2nd ed., by Urban, G.L., and Hauser, J.R., Prentice-Hall: Englewood Cliffs, N.J., 1993; *The PDMA Handbook of New Product Development,* ed. by M.D. Rosenau Jr., A. Griffin, G.A. Castellion, and N.F. Anschuetz, John Wiley & Sons, Inc., New York, 1996.

6. Cooper, R.G., *Winning at New Products,* 2nd ed., Addison-Wesley, Reading, Mass., 1993.

Appendix A

1. Much of this appendix has been adapted from *Winning at New Products,* by Cooper, R.G., 2nd ed., Addison-Wesley, Reading, Mass., 1993, and Cooper, R.G., "Overhauling the New Product Process," *Industrial Marketing Management,* 25: 465–482, 1996.

2. Cooper, R.G., "Third-Generation New Product Processes," *Journal of Product Innovation Management,* 11:3–14, 1994.

Index

An "n" after a page number indicates a note.

A

Allied Signal, 88–89, 95, 117
Arthur D. Little Inc., 57, 63, 74
"At Risk" model, 61, 73
attrition curve, 17
audit, internal, 187–88. *See also*
    ProBE methodology; 3-P study

B

balance, 3, 19, 110, 111, 158, 172
    critique of, 80–81
    See also bar charts; bubble dia-
        grams; histograms; pie charts;
        portfolio maps; risk–reward bub-
        ble diagrams
balance criteria, 165, 177–79
bar charts, 76–77
benchmarking, 186–87
Boston Consulting Group (BCG)
    model, 7, 9, 55, 104, 136
"Bread and Butter," 58
breakdowns, 80. *See also* spending,
    breakdowns
bubble diagrams, 55–56, 74–76, 111,
    172–76
    "plots," 56
business position, 56, 191
business strategy, 3, 15, 22, 107–8,
    111, 140, 190
business unit (BU), 22
    and suboptimization, 135
    See also strategic business unit
        (SBU)

buy-in
    in multinational corporations, 11–12
    organizational, 186, 195, 196, 200
    of senior management, 197–98

C

cannibalization of products, 127
capacity utilization, 76–77
capital cost requirements, 127
cash flow, 77
checklists, 7, 52–53, 159
commercial attractiveness, 52
commercialization costs, 25
competitive advantage, 34, 35, 52
competitive parity, 104, 135
corporate strategy, 10–11
customer, building in voice of, 17,
    129, 138, 207

D

data
    acquisition of, 125–26
    areas of weakness, 116–17
    for scoring models, 44–48
decision framework, 11–12
decision model, 59, 80, 125
decision tree, 7, 24–28, 73–74
Delphi consensus, 7, 33–34
discounted cash flow (DCF) analysis,
    29, 127
    terminal value, 127
    See also net present value (NPV)

223

About the Authors

Dr. Robert G. Cooper is a world expert in the field of new product management and has been labeled "the quintessential scholar" in the field of new products in the U.S. publication, *Journal of Product Innovation Management*. He is a Professor of Marketing at Michael G. DeGroote School of Business, McMaster University, Ontario, Canada.

Bob is considered the father of the *Stage-Gate process,* now widely used by leading firms around the world to drive new products to market. His NewProd series of research—an extensive investigation over the past 20 years into the practices and pitfalls of product innovation in hundreds of companies and over 1,000 new product projects—has been widely cited. He has published more than 75 articles and four books on new products, including the popular *Winning at New Products: Accelerating the Process from Idea to Launch.*

Bob's dynamic talks have captivated thousands of businesspeople in North America, Europe, and the Pacific. He has consulted in the field of new product management for leading companies worldwide, including Bell-Canada, BF Goodrich, BP (U.K.), Carlsberg Breweries, Corning, Courtalds (U.K.), DuPont, Emerson Electric, Exxon Chemicals, Hallmark, Hoechst (U.S.), IBM, Kodak, Lego, Northern Telecom, Pfizer, Polaroid, Proctor & Gamble, Reckitt & Colman (U.K. and U.S.), Rohm and Haas, SC Johnsons Wax, Shell-Wavin (Netherlands), the Royal Bank of Canada, US West, and WR Grace. Many of these companies have implemented his Stage-Gate approach to accelerating new products to market.

Bob holds Bachelor's and Master's degrees in Chemical Engineering, an MBA, and a Ph.D. in Business.

Dr. Scott J. Edgett is an internationally recognized expert in the field of new product development and portfolio management. He is an Associate Professor of Marketing at the Michael G. DeGroote School of Business, McMaster University, Ontario, Canada, and a Director of the Product Development Institute.

Scott is a noted speaker and consultant, having conducted executive seminars and consulting projects in Canada, the United States, and England. Some of his recent clients include Amoco, Avery Dennison, CMHC, Dofasco, DowElanco, E.B. Eddy Paper, Hallmark, ISK Biosciences, Gennum, ICI, John Hancock Mutual Life, Manulife Financial, The Mutual Group, Nova Chemicals, NYNEX Information Resources, Reynolds Metals Company, Rohm and Haas, the Royal Bank of Canada, Xerox, and Zeneca Pharmaceutical.

He has considerable expertise as a researcher into the factors that make successful new products, and as a consultant to companies seeking to improve their new product processes or improve their approaches to portfolio management. He has published more than 40 articles and papers, including the "Best Practices" series.

Scott holds a bachelor of business administration in accounting, an MBA in marketing/finance, and a Ph.D. in Marketing (new product development).

Dr. Elko J. Kleinschmidt is a leading expert on the process of new product development and international factors that influence new product development outcomes. He is a Professor of Marketing and International Business and Director of the Engineering and Management Program at McMaster University.

He is a recognized researcher in the field of new product development, innovativeness, and the impact of the international dimension on new products. He has over 50 publications, including both articles and booklets.

Elko has international experience working in Europe, North America, and Africa. He has presented numerous seminars to companies in North America, Europe, Asia (China), and Australia, primarily in the area of new product development and marketing.

His consulting activities have included market forecasts, new product aspects, and developing new product processes for companies.

Elko holds a mechanical engineering degree, an MBA, and a Ph.D in business administration. His practical work experience includes engineering tasks, investment analysis for technical projects, and technical marketing.